# SCENERY

## DESIGN AND FABRICATION

# SCENERY

## DESIGN AND FABRICATION

by
W. Joseph Stell

**PLAYERS PRESS, Inc.**

P. O. Box 1132
Studio City, California 91614-0132
U.S.A.

**SCENERY - Design and Fabrication**
© Copyright 2001, by W. Joseph Stell and Players Press, Inc.
ISBN 0-88734-663-4

Editor: William-Alan Landes
Photo/Text Paste-Up: Chris Cordero
Catalogue: Wendy Landes

Simultaneously Published in
U.S.A., U.K., Canada and Australia

Printed in the U.S.A.

**Library of Congress Cataloging-in-Publication Data**

Stell, W. Joseph.
    Scenery : design and fabrication / W. Joseph Stell.
        p. cm.
    Includes bibliographical references and index.
    ISBN 0-88734-663-4 (alk. paper)
        1. Theaters--Stage-setting and scenery. I. Title.

    PN2091.S8 S73 2001
    792'.025--dc21

                                                        2001036371

## About the Author

W. JOSEPH STELL is Professor of Drama and Head of the Design Area at the University of Georgia Department of Drama. Prior to joining the faculty at the University of Georgia he was affiliated with the Richmond Professional Institute Department of Dramatic Art, Richmond, Virginia.

In addition to teaching in the areas of scenery and lighting design he has for 30 years been a free-lance designer of productions in such far-ranging venues as the Manitoba Theatre Centre, Winnipeg, Canada; Off-Broadway, New York City; and regional professional theatres such as the McCarter Theatre, Princeton, NJ, Walnut Street Theatre, Philadelphia, Baltimore Opera, Alliance Theatre, Atlanta, GA, and the Atlanta Ballet. He has designed scenery and/or lighting for over 200 productions, including dramas, musicals, children's plays, outdoor dramas, opera and ballet. His design for *Oliver!* at the Alliance Theatre was recognized by the *Atlanta Journal* as the best scenic design of the year.

Dr. Stell received a B.S. degree from East Carolina College (now University), Greenville, NC, an MA degree from New York University, and his Ph.D. degree from Bowling Green State University, Bowling Green, Ohio.

He has written articles on various aspects of theatrical design for *Theatre Design and Technology, Theatre Crafts, Southern Theatre,* and *Nineteenth Century Theatre*, and presented papers at many national and regional theatre conventions and conferences. He is a member of the U.S. Institute of Theatre Technology and founding member and Chair of the Southeast Section of USITT. For his creative activities he has received the University of Georgia Creative Research Medallion, the Christ-Janer Award for lifetime achievement in the arts, and the Athens/Clarke County Cultural Arts Award. His design work has been seen in the First USITT Scenographic Exposition, the 1987 Prague Quadrennial, and the 1987 Rosco Laboratories "Tech on Tour" presentations throughout the U.S. He is listed in *Who's Who in Entertainment* (1991), *Who's Who in the South and Southwest* (1986), and *International Who's Who in Education* (1980).

# ILLUSTRATIONS

# PREFACE

It is presumptuous to attempt to write a book on scenery that claims to be unique or completely original in every way, since many excellent books already are on the market dealing with both the art of designing scenery and the processes of stagecraft. Yet I suppose every designer-technician feels he has some ideas and processes, developed through his own experience, that might be unique, time-saving, or money-saving in some way. In this book, I have attempted to combine such time-savers and money-savers of my own with a simplified explanation of the more standard practices in designing and constructing scenery. My aim has been to produce a book that might be termed a primer on scenery—simple and clear enough to enable the high-school teacher, the weekend community theatre scene designer, or the bright student to grasp the essential requirements for a stage setting and produce scenery which is both serviceable and attractive. I have by no means attempted to write a comprehensive textbook on either the designing or the construction of scenery, although my own background and interests have caused me to place more emphasis on the design aspect than on stagecraft. Interested persons who desire to pursue further the study of scene designing or stagecraft should consult the Bibliography, which lists a number of more comprehensive and detailed books on the subject.

The first three sections of the book present some of the more standard ideas and methods of designing for the proscenium stage. Section IV, however, has tended to become a sort of summary of information on other types of theatres and some ideas on designing for each; simplified scenery; inexpensive substitutes for standard materials and methods; materials and methods produced by modern technology that might have application to the theatre; and some random thoughts regarding current trends and possibilities in staging and design. It may very well be that Chapter IX is, in some ways, the most valuable chapter for the beginning designer, since it may suggest short cuts and substitutes for more complicated processes, or it may, it is hoped, inspire some more creative approach.

I have tried to avoid using too technical language; however, theatre does have a very comprehensive jargon of its own, and it has been necessary to use some strictly theatrical terminology at times. Wherever possible, I have attempted to explain such terms at the time of their introduction; however, a more comprehensive glossary of commonly used stage terms will be found in Appendix A.

It seemed inconvenient within the organization of the text to include lengthy descriptions of tools and materials; in Appendix B, therefore, I have listed the principal tools, hardware, and materials with brief comments on each. I have also included a suggested list of the items most essential to a basic scenic shop, with suggested priorities for future expansion. Appendix C provides addresses of theatrical suppliers of such items as cannot be found in local stores.

Any volume such as this owes much to the contributions of many people other than the author. It is impossible to acknowledge all the persons who have contributed to what knowledge I have of the art and craft of theatre in general and scenery in particular, but I do wish to mention a few who have been particularly important to the successful completion and revision of this book. I am grateful to Paul Kozelka, Paul Camp, and William-Alan Landes for their generous assistance and advice on many matters. For the contribution of illustrations that are such a vital part of this book I wish to thank David Hays, Josef Svoboda, James Hull Miller, John Ross, Leonard Harmon, Tom Tutino, Eric Olson, Richard Mason,

Carl Lefko, The Goodman Theatre, The Guthrie Theatre, The Alley Theatre, and many others. Last, but certainly not least, I must acknowledge the one person without whose encouragement, advice, understanding, and unstinting help this book would not have been possible—the person who is, to quote a popular song, "the wind beneath my wings"—my wife Agnes.

W. Joseph Stell
Athens, Georgia

# CONTENTS

13

# SECTION I:
# AN INTRODUCTION TO DESIGNING SCENERY

# chapter I

# SCENERY: WHAT AND WHY?

Theatre is an art form that involves the combined creative efforts of a large number of people. During the dress-rehearsal period the products of their efforts—scenery, costumes, properties, lights, sound—are put together with the practiced motions and speeches of the actors, and the result is the theatre art. Not all art is good art, however; and theatre, perhaps more than any other art form, is susceptible to faults that mar the quality of the end product. In art forms such as painting, sculpture, poetry, or literature, in which the creation is the direct result of a single artist's effort, quality is conditional only upon the talent and skill of the artist. In theatre, in which a number of artists are involved, the quality of the production is based not only on the skill and talent of each individual artist, but on the integration of the separate elements into a singleness of purpose that should permeate the theatrical presentation.

The overall purpose of any dramatic performance is to furnish the clearest and most effective presentation of the meaning of the playscript as interpreted by the director. Scenery, like every other facet of the production, must serve this overall purpose. By virtue of its dominant position on stage, scenery that does not contribute to the action of the play detracts from the production. Good scenery is not intrusive. Bad scenery very often is. Scenery has its one moment of glory between the time the curtain is raised and the action of the play begins. Sometimes the audience applauds this moment, which is gratifying to the designer; but it would be more appropriate if the audience applauded the scenery at the end of the show, when it has proved its effectiveness. If, however, at the end of the performance, the audience, as I once heard it said, comes out "whistling the setting," then the designer had best hang his head and resolve henceforward to work for the greater glory of the production, rather than for his own greater glory as a set designer.

## THE PURPOSES OF SCENERY

In order to understand fully the purposes of scenery, other than concealing the back wall of the stage, we must examine briefly the elements of the play itself.

Within each play is a definite movement—not necessarily physical movement, but what "happens" in the play. Events occur that move a character, or group of characters, from one set of circumstances to another—either physically or mentally. Many plays are plays of ideas or emotions, and the movement of the play concerns the alteration of thoughts or feelings of the main characters. This movement is termed the *action* of the play.

The action is carried forward through the characters in the play as portrayed by the actors. As the prime moving forces in the play, the actors should usually be the center of attention during the performance; and all other elements of the production should aid the actors in their portrayal. Scenery has been described by Robert Edmond Jones as the "environment of the action." Environment is defined by Webster as "the aggregate of all the external conditions and influences affecting the life and development of an organism." Scenery, then, should visually present, as far as is possible, the conditions and influences that act upon or motivate the characters to perform the action of the play.

More specifically, scenery should help to establish: (1) place and time, (2) character, (3) style, (4) mood, and (5) composition.

### Place and Time

Perhaps the most obvious effect of scenery is the establishment of the specific place of the action. Even the worst scenery will usually go so far as to set the action indoors or outdoors, in a living room, a dining room, an office, an attic, a bedroom, a barroom, a stable, or one of the myriad other places called for by playwrights. Not only must the setting describe this

**17**

somewhat generalized place, but very often it must particularize the place in terms of a definite period of history or region of the world. This is accomplished by simulating the architecture, furniture, and decoration of that particular era or region. However, if the establishment of place and time were the only functions of scenery, then plays could and probably would be designed by interior decorators. Scenery also should give some indication of the personality of the individual characters in the play.

### Character

Rooms generally reflect the personalities of the people living in them. Our financial status, cultural and intellectual tastes, religion, hobbies, habits, and personality foibles are vividly displayed by our homes. We fill a room with objects that have meaning to us, and because of this they convey to someone else a great deal of information about us. Our choice of colors, draperies and furniture, rugs and wall decorations are dictated by our tastes and our pocketbooks, and very clearly tell others about these facets of our lives.

In like manner, a setting should be decorated to reflect the personalities of its inhabitants—the characters in the play. The settings for *A Streetcar Named Desire* and *The Glass Menagerie* are similar in terms of period, financial status, and, to a certain degree, place; but the characters in the two plays are totally different, and in reflecting the characters the settings present totally different appearances. The crude, primitive character of Stanley Kowalski in *Streetcar* should be obvious in the setting, which should evidence the brutally careless manner in which it is treated by its main character. The setting for *The Glass Menagerie*, on the other hand, should reflect the delicate, feminine personalities of Laura and Amanda Wingfield, the dominant characters in the play.

### Style

Style, the manner in which a play is presented, is determined by the manner in which the play is written and by the artistic decisions made by all the contributing artists—the director, designers and, frequently, the choreographer and musical director. Many contemporary plays are written and interpreted in a realistic style—a manner designed to

Plate 1. *REALISTIC INTERIOR: The careful attention to period detail in both the architecture of the room, as well as the selection of furniture and set dressing, produces a very realistic-seeming interior. Sketch of a setting for* Hay Fever *designed by Richard Durst for the University of Minnesota-Duluth.*

Plate 2. *REALISTIC EXTERIOR: Uneven weathered planking, realistic-looking foliage and other natural textures coupled with leaf patterns in the lighting enhance the naturalness of this setting for* The Night of The Iguana *at the Goodman Theatre, Chicago. Scenic design by Loy Arcenas. (Photo by Liz Lauren)*

make the characters and situations seem a "slice of life." The settings give a realistic illusion that they are actually a room or a particular portion of the outdoors. Note the settings in Plates 1 and 2. Realistic details such as architectural structures and trim, wallpaper, curtains, three-dimensional trees, simulated leaves, actual furniture and bric-a-brac convince us that we have been allowed to view, for a short time, the actual life of another person or group. The realistic style serves as the basis for comparison with other manners of presentation.

Movies and television can present "reality" much better than theatre. No theatrical setting should attempt to present the same degree of reality as a camera. Theatre can and should engage the imagination of the audience and entice them to join in creating the "reality" of the staged event. For this reason most theatrical settings take liberties with reality, that can enhance the visual composition, strengthen the mood and dramatic effect, take advantage of the contributions of stage lighting, or adjust to the limitations of time, space, or budget. Many settings provide full realism for those areas of the stage utilized by the actors—the lower walls, furniture and items of set dressing—but take liber-

ties with reality on the upper and outer portions of the setting. In the design shown in Plate 3 we can see such liberties taken while the acting area retains complete realistic detail. Simplified Realism may be found in settings which are basically realistic in concept but wherein the designer has eliminated all items not having a direct bearing on the action of the play. A portion of a wall and a grouping of furniture may suggest to the audience that the total room is present. These elements must be chosen with extreme care, as they must suggest the desired environment with a minimum of detail.

Settings which move further from the realm of reality have often been classified into a bewildering number of different "isms": Theatricalism, Expressionism, Symbolism, Constructivism, etc. For the sake of clarity, I prefer to categorize as Stylized any setting which departs from reality by exaggerating, distorting, or over-simplifying the component elements. The possible exception to this is the Formal setting which is usually considered to define a rather neutral form of setting composed primarily of steps, platforms, columns, and other architectural forms, used principally in the presentation of Shakespearean plays, as well as some romantic and classical dramas (see Plate 4). At other times, designers manipulate the elements of design (line, form, mass, texture, and color), exaggerating, diminishing, or eliminating the use of one or more elements in order to more strongly convey character, mood, and dramatic qualities to the audience. The overall effect of such plays as fantasies, musical comedies, romantic tragedies, expressionistic plays, farces, and even tragedies may be greatly enhanced by such designs, which maximize design elements to emphasize their inherent emotional and atmospheric extremes. Note, for

ing, we are thinking in terms of mood. When we try to be specific about the elements that contribute to the creation of this mood, however, we run into a great deal of difficulty. It is the interaction of all aspects of the production—acting, costumes, lighting, setting, sound—that produces an emotional response within the audience. In the setting, the contributing factors are color, line, shape, and texture. These elements in the setting in Plate 9 produce light, gay and romantic feelings. The designer must consider carefully all the effects which will be

Plate 3. *REALISTIC SETTING WITH STYLIZED AND FRAGMENTED BOUNDARIES: Architectural liberties have been taken in this setting where windows and doors project above the wall line, "gingerbread" ornament enlivens the upper space, and a projected image of trees fills in above the lowest wall unit. A rendering for* Crimes of the Heart *pro-duced at the University of Georgia. Designed by the author.*

example, the wide variety of moods and dramatic qualities which are expressed by the settings shown in Plates 5, 6, 7, 8, and 9. The only limits to a stylized setting are the designer's imagination and the demands of the play. The principal factor to keep in mind is that the style of the setting should be coordinated with the other elements of the production—the playscript, the acting, the costumes, and the lighting.

*Mood*

When we think of a play as being sad, happy, suspenseful, warm, cold, tragic, comic, gay, mysterious, threatening, depressing, or any similar feel-

produced by various combinations of line, color, mass, texture, and visual images. The somber, almost melancholy, effect achieved in the setting shown in plate 5 would be almost totally inappropriate for a comic production, while it becomes extremely difficult (although not impossible) to portray a serious drama in a setting that speaks visually in comic terms. Imagine to yourself the difficulty of producing a serious drama or tragedy in the settings shown in Plates 7, 8, and 9.

In a realistic setting, the expression of mood depends primarily on the use of color and the selection of realistic elements such as furniture, draperies, floor coverings and wall decorations that will con-

Plate 4.    *FORMALISM:  A permanent setting with a basic platform and stair arrangement enhanced by the use of period architectural shapes and strong textural effects.  A design for* Macbeth *by Tom Tutino for the University of Western Kentucky.*

Plate 5.    *STYLIZATION:   Platforms dappled with light add to the almost abstract combinations of textures and lights in this unusual interpretation of a modern American classic—a setting for* Death of a Salesman *designed by James Leonard Joy for The Guthrie Theatre.  (Photo by Michal Daniel)*

Plate 6. *STYLIZATION: Setting for* Boris Godunov *designed by Josef Svoboda for the State Opera, Hamburg, Germany. Projected details from a Medieval fresco painting surround an acting area defined only by a few simple levels and set pieces.*

Plate 7. *STYLIZATION: Isolated against black, this setting employs a few simple but elaborately detailed scenic elements to suggest the period and define the acting area. A setting for* Tartuffe *designed by Eric Olson for Samford University Theatre. (Photo by Eric Olson)*

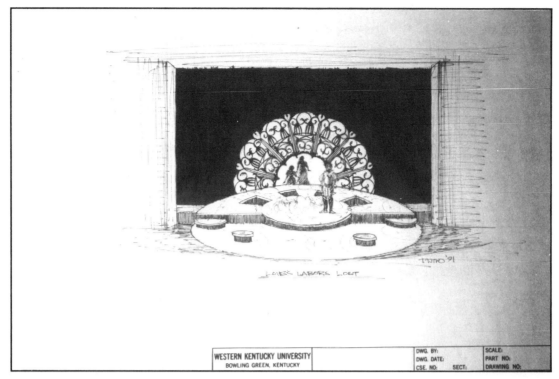

Plate 8. *STYLIZATION: An emphasis on semi-circular forms combined with curvilinear decorative patterns creates a very romantic permanent setting for* Love's Labors Lost. *A design by Tom Tutino for the University of Western Kentucky.*

Plate 9. *STYLIZATION: The emphasis on curvilinear shapes and lines found in the doorframes, roof unit, and floor arrangement provides a very light and romantic feeling to this setting for* Ring 'Round The Moon. *The cyc was cheesecloth flameproofed with sal ammoniac and borax which made it feel stiff, but look like china silk. Produced at the University of Alabama with designs by John Ross.*

vey the proper mood through their particular size, shape, or color. Stylized settings may exaggerate the appropriate colors, shapes, lines, and textures in order to achieve the desired effect. In fact, settings are very often designed in a stylized manner principally to enhance the particular mood necessary to the play.

*Composition*

The arrangement of the scenic elements on the stage establishes a definite pattern that the director and actors must use in presenting the action of the play. If the setting is well planned, this pattern will present a pleasing appearance to the audience. The total picture presented, composed of actors, scenic elements, costumes, and lighting, should at all times be attractive—pleasing to the eye. This does *not* mean the setting must always be "pretty." Many plays would die a quick death in a "pretty" setting. It does mean the setting should at all times adhere to the principles of good design—exhibiting visual balance, unity with variety, center of interest, and rhythm. Composition should never be sacrificed to the needs of actor or play—it should be merely adjusted to account for these needs. If the setting employs the principles of good design, the action taking place within the setting is allowed to flow in a pattern presenting a consistently pleasing composition to the audience.

## THE REQUIREMENTS OF SCENERY

If scenery is to serve the purposes just discussed, it must meet a number of demands placed upon it by the nature of the theatre art. Scenery must provide information to the audience concerning time and place, character, and mood; so it must be *expressive*. It must be *attractive* in order to establish a pleasing composition for the production. It must be constructed by a stage crew within definite limitations of time and budget, and it must be utilized by actors without fear of total collapse; therefore, it must be *practical*. Perhaps most important of all, it must be *integrated* in appearance, mood, and operation with all of the other theatrical elements in order to produce a unified production.

*Expressiveness*

We have already discussed at some length the information the scenery should convey to the audience, but a designer must take into consideration two factors before he can feel reasonably assured that the message is being received. First of all, the information should be presented in as simple and clear a manner as possible; secondly, the information should be presented strongly enough to project across the footlights to the audience. Perhaps the two key words in making a stage design expressive are *selectivity* and *emphasis*.

A designer must be extremely careful in choosing the elements of the design, selecting those that are most expressive of the idea he wishes to convey and discarding any that might confuse or clutter the stage. A single, carefully chosen detail can convey more to the audience than a multitude of poorly chosen, miscellaneous items. A stained-glass Gothic window can more clearly depict a church or cathedral than a multitude of columns and pews. Referring back to Plate 6, note the care with which the elements were chosen—only the most expressive objects and images were included in the setting.

Once selected, the elements must be strong enough to carry to the audience clearly. No designer dares forget that the majority of the audience is seated twenty or thirty feet from the stage—in some theatres as far away as forty to fifty feet. In order that scenic elements be clearly seen from such distances, they must be simplified and exaggerated. The designer must glean the essential features of the pattern or decorative device and then translate these into bold, simplified versions that will project the feeling of the original without every small, intricate detail. In Plate 9, note the simplified, exaggerated detail in the doors, the ceiling, the furniture, and the balustrade; Plate 10 shows a subtler simplification.

If scenic elements are carefully selected to convey the feeling of a specific region, period, or character information, and they are then exaggerated sufficiently to deliver this information clearly across the footlights, the setting as a whole cannot fail to be expressive.

*Attractiveness*

If the setting is to serve the purpose of establishing composition, it must be based upon the principles of good composition: *unity* with *variety, rhythm, center of interest,* and *balance.* These are the means by which the elements of composition—*line, mass, texture,* and *color* —are organized and utilized. These elements are, in fact, the tools and materials with which a designer works to create an attractive and expressive stage picture. Each of the elements has expressive qualities that, when properly

CRIMES OF THE HEART
DURST '84

Plate 10. *SIMPLIFICATION AND EXAGGERATION OF DETAIL: If you look closely at this sketch for an apparently realistic setting, you will note that the architectural detail has been simplified—reduced to the essentials—and the wallpaper pattern has been enlarged and exaggerated for clearer comprehension by a distant audience. Sketch by Richard Durst of a setting for* Crimes of the Heart *produced at the University of Minnesota-Duluth.*

handled, contribute to the total expressiveness of the setting.

The element of *line* is defined as being the outer description of a form or area, or the direction of indicated movement—the delineation of realistic forms or the direction the eye travels along a series of repeated shapes. Line may also be achieved by a series of varied objects that establish, in their relationship to one another, a straight or slightly curved eye movement. For instance, the wall decorations in a realistic setting, if carefully arranged, may establish a line—straight, diagonal, or curved. In Plate 9 the visual line created by the tops of the doorframes repeats the curved line of the floor arrangement and the suspended ceiling unit. For expressive purposes, line may be used to emphasize some quality of the realistic forms in order to evoke a particular mood, character, or feeling. Because of their association with certain realistic forms, lines of various types and character will convey an assortment of feelings and emotions

to an audience. Light, curvy lines give a happy, comic feeling; vertical lines create a sense of inspiration, majesty, and exalted emotion, as associated with Gothic cathedrals and tall trees; horizontal lines, as seen in low ceilings or heavy horizontal beams, give a feeling of stability or even oppression and hopelessness; diagonal and jagged lines convey energy, anger, violence, excitement, and distortion because of their association with lightning, movement, and falling objects. Plate 11 illustrates several of these effects.

This expressive use of line is limited by the degree of realism desired in the setting. The use of line in realistic settings is confined to the objects in the setting—the walls, doors, windows, furniture, wall hangings and decorations, and the decorative elements in the wallpaper, paneling, and set properties. In an unrealistic setting, of course, line usage is limited only by the style of setting, the demands of the director and script, and the imagination

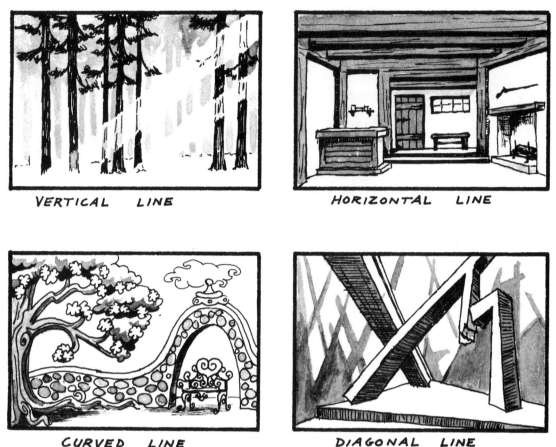

VERTICAL LINE

HORIZONTAL LINE

CURVED LINE

DIAGONAL LINE

Plate 11. *THE EXPRESSIVE QUALITIES OF LINE*

of the designer. Several pitfalls, however, should be avoided: (1) the use of too many varieties of line or too many extreme variations of one or two lines; (2) the use of only one kind of line, which would probably lack interest; (3) the use of equal amounts of two or more lines—pick one line as the predominant motif and let the other types provide contrast and interest; and (4) monotony produced in a realistic setting by lack of imagination in the choice of set dressing. Remember that the set dressing is the primary means of securing interest and variety in a realistic setting, which means choosing the dressing for its decorative and expressive qualities of line, mass, color, and texture. There are a number of very good books available which discuss the design, preparation and use of properties, including *Properties and Dressing the Stage* by Karl Bruder.

*Mass* may be roughly defined as the three-dimensionality of objects. The effect of mass is clearly seen in objects that present three or more sides to the audience, revealing the depth as well as the height and width of the object.

Because the outer boundaries of mass units are defined by lines, the expressive qualities of the two elements are closely related. Curved, horizontal, vertical, and diagonal masses all convey much the same feelings as indicated in the discussion of line. Beyond that, perhaps the most obvious quality of mass is the impression it gives of weight. The light or heavy appearance of furniture and other three-dimensional features of the setting can do much to express a particular quality or mood. In general, light elements work well in fantasies and comedies, and heavy ones are more conducive to the presentation of serious dramas and tragedies. These are only generalizations, however, and vary greatly with the particular demands of each script.

The opposite of mass is space—sometimes called negative mass. The stage itself is a hollowed-out space, defined by the walls, floor, and the proscenium opening. The size and shape of this area—whether used as is or altered for a particular setting—is capable of expressive use (see Plate 12). Vertically it

VERTICAL HEIGHT            VERTICAL DEPTH

HORIZONTAL EXPANSE

SPACIOUSNESS WITH INTIMACY

Plate 12. *THE EXPRESSIVE QUALITIES OF SPACE*

creates the feeling of exaltation—except when lighted exclusively from the top, which gives the impression of the actors' being in a pit. Emphasis of horizontal space creates the feeling of expansiveness, particularly when combined with undersized items such as small-scale furniture. An intimate feeling can be achieved when the area around an actor is enclosed by such devices as alcoves, bay windows, and fireplace nooks. These are particularly adaptable to love scenes, friendly conversations, and secrecy. Distance can be suggested by using overlapping masses—masses placed progressively farther from the front of the stage, each being low enough or open enough to allow the one behind it to be seen. A setting designed with a fence, beyond which can be seen low bushes, backed by a view of distant trees, over which can be seen far-off mountains, and backed with a lighted sky cloth, will do much to suggest extreme distance.

An element of composition that is often overlooked is *texture,* which may be thought of as the degree of roughness or smoothness of any surface. Every surface has a texture: a water-worn pebble, a piece of cloth, a brick wall, a sheet of glass—all display varying kinds and degrees of texture. We may derive sensual pleasure from texture: touching a fur coat or velvet material, stroking a soft kitten, fondling a smooth stone, or snuggling into a soft woolly blanket. In addition, textures have associative connotations for us and may, thereby, suggest definite personality or emotional qualities. For instance, with what type of person or place would you associate stone, wood, sand, satin, brocade, wool, cotton, fur, velvet, leather, or plastic? This expressive quality is extremely useful on stage, aiding the other design components in achieving the desired quality in the setting, as we will see in later chapters.

The use of texture on stage may be of two kinds: actual or simulated. Actual textures are achieved through the use of the actual material or by approximating the three-dimensional quality of the material by other stage means. Simulated texture is painted texture—using painting techniques to fool the audience into believing that a surface is textured. Actual texture, being three-dimensional, reacts much better under modern stage lighting than painted texture; but it is also more time-consuming and expensive and therefore not used quite as much as it might otherwise be.

The last design element, *color,* can do more than perhaps any other element to enhance the decorative and expressive qualities of a setting. Color theory and psychology, however, can became extremely complicated and confusing; so for the purposes of simplicity and clarity, this discussion will be limited to the bare essentials.

Every color has three variable qualities: *hue,* which describes whether the color is green, red, blue, yellow, orange, etc.—the "name" of the color; *value,* which refers to the range of the color between black and white; and *intensity,* or saturation, which refers to the quality of brilliance, varying from completely neutral gray to a color of greatest strength and purity. Hues are illustrated in the color wheel in Plate 13. Secondary hues are gained by mixture of the adjacent primary hues; tertiary hues are formed by mixing a primary with its neighboring secondary. The value of a color and the means of altering the value are illustrated in the value scale in Plate 13. White mixed with a color produces a lighter value of that color, which is called a *tint.* Black mixed with a color produces a darker value called a *shade.* The *intensity* of a color may be altered by mixing the color with gray or, preferably, by mixing the color with its complementary color —the color directly opposite it on the color wheel. As noted on the color wheel, mixing equal amounts of complementary colors produces a neutral gray.

The selection and control of combinations of colors is termed *color harmony.* Definitions of color harmonies are based on the color wheel. A *complementary* color scheme utilizes colors directly opposite each other on the wheel. The *split-complementary* scheme involves the division of one of the complementary colors into the two adjacent colors on the wheel. The use of green, blue, and red-orange would be an example of a split-complementary color harmony. *Analogous* harmony utilizes colors adjacent to each other on the color wheel—blue and blue-green or red and red-orange, for example. *Monochromatic* harmony is achieved through the use of a single color varied in intensity and/or value.

The successful use of any of these color harmonies is based on dividing the colors used into a dominant color and subordinate "accent" colors. Particularly is this true of the complementary and split-complementary color harmonies. In general, the dominant color is used over the greater area and is greatly subdued in tone. Much use may be made of neutrals— grays, tans, browns, and metallic colors. The

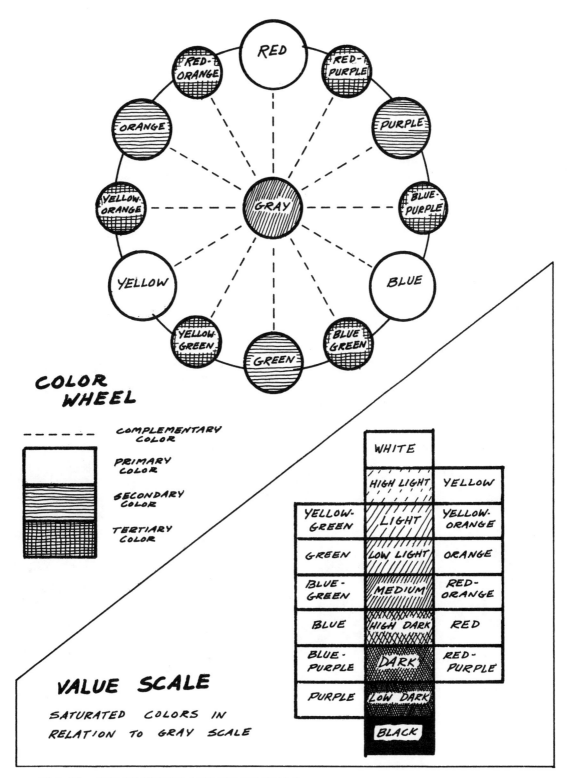

COLOR WHEEL

- - - - COMPLEMENTARY COLOR

PRIMARY COLOR

SECONDARY COLOR

TERTIARY COLOR

VALUE SCALE

SATURATED COLORS IN RELATION TO GRAY SCALE

Plate 13. *COLOR WHEEL AND VALUE SCALE*

accent colors are found principally in small areas such as set dressing, properties, and costumes. To ensure unity in the setting, it is wise to repeat the accent colors in a number of places around the setting.

Color psychology is based on the emotions associated with particular colors: anger and heat with red, mystery and death with black, purity and cleanliness with white, freshness and gaiety with yellow, royalty and luxury with purple, to mention a few. Colors are also divided generally into *warm* and *cool* colors. Red, yellow, and orange are known as warm colors, and blue, green, and purple as cool. Light and dark divisions of color also may be expressive. Light, bright, warm-colored settings are generally appropriate for comedies, whereas dark,

learn about color is to buy a set of paints and start mixing and experimenting, noting successful combinations and mixtures, and discarding failures.

Successful use of the design elements, however, is subject to the principles of design previously mentioned: unity with variety, rhythm, center of interest, and balance. *Unity* (or harmony, as it is often called) is achieved through the use of related elements—using and reusing those that are alike or similar in appearance. As we have discovered, many diversified shapes, forms, and colors may be utilized in a design. We must select those lines, masses, textures, and colors that are similar in quality and then repeat them in a variety of ways and places throughout the setting. Plate 14 illustrates the

Plate 14. *UNITY THROUGH REPETITION OF ELEMENTS: Identical rectangular windows backing the stage provide an almost monotonous sense of unity, relieved by the large circular clock above the center opening.* The Visit *produced by The Goodman Theatre, Chicago. Scenery design by Paul Steinberg. (Photo by Liz Lauren)*

somber, cool-colored settings are very often used for tragedies and serious plays.

It can easily be seen from this brief discussion that the use of color is very important in the designing of scenery. However, no amount of reading about color will make a designer successful in its use. The best way to

use of a single basic shape throughout a setting to achieve visual unity.

However, total unity achieved through repetition of the same element in the same manner throughout the setting is monotonous. We must seek *variety,* either by changing the way in which the device is used—altering the size, shape, or color in some way—or by introducing a different device altogether. Minor variations of the dominant motif(s) eliminate the monotony of identical repeats. The introduction of a completely different motif attracts attention by virtue of its uniqueness, emphasizing the element and, in addition, providing an interest value for the setting that might otherwise be lacking. Unity provides the cohesiveness that binds the setting together, but variety is the spark that gives life and interest. On the other hand, too much variety defeats its own purpose, for it depends upon contrast for full effectiveness. One red apple stands out vividly in a basket of green apples, but is completely lost in a basket containing an equal mixture of red and green apples. Choose carefully the one or two features that should stand out in the setting and allow them to dominate by virtue of their contrast to their surroundings. Recalling the expressive requirement of the setting, make sure those dominant features are the same ones you have selected for being most expressive of the place, period, character, or mood of the setting.

The repetition of like elements, in addition to aiding unity, also affects *rhythm*. Rhythm can probably best be understood by noticing the way in which the observer's eye moves across a design. Features of the design catch the eye and then lead it from one object to another in a particular pattern. Does the eye jump back and forth from object to object in a haphazard pattern? Does it move progressively and rapidly along a series of objects until it finally reaches a stopping point? Does it move for a distance rapidly, pause at an interesting spot, then move rapidly again for a distance, pause, and move on again? This eye movement, slow, random, rapid, or broken, is controlled by the rhythm of the design. The direction of the movement may be circular, straight, diagonal, curved, spiral, zigzag, or any combination thereof. Rapid movement of the eye is achieved through the repetition of like elements, through the line formed by the shape of one or more objects, or through the attitude of one object toward another. The stopping points are our points of visual emphasis. In Plate 14, note how rapidly the eye scans the repeated windows motif until it can find and then pause at the contrasting shape of the central clock unit – a dominant feature. This also serves to illustrate the fact that unity and rhythm may be served by the same devices at the same time. However, two dangers to avoid in the use of repetition are: (1)

too much repetition of identical shapes or colors, which becomes monotonous and loses variety and emphasis; and (2) the use of oversized units with too few repeats, producing a bare and oversized design that lacks interest for other reasons.

Closely related to line and rhythm is *center of interest*. We have already mentioned the importance of points of emphasis in the design; however, for a fully cohesive design, one portion of it should be the dominant feature of interest—the principal resting place for the eye as it travels over the design. This center of interest may be one item in the setting or, more often, it may be a grouping of items in the setting that command attention by virtue of their emphasis and position on stage. Also, the principal lines of movement in the setting —those lines formed by the movement of the eye over a series of objects—should lead to this center of interest. Referring again to Plate 14, the center of interest is the area encompassing the central doorway and the model castle. It is in a dominant position onstage, and the lines formed by the stairs, the stair railings, and the eye movement across the fireplace decoration, window, pictures, and bookcases all lead the viewer to this strong area of interest.

A minor, but still important, principle is the use of terminal accents—emphasis of the edges or ends of the elements in the setting. These are means of adding interest to items within the setting that serve as resting points for the eye, but more importantly, they can form boundaries for the setting itself to prevent the eye from wandering out of the composition. This is the strongest argument for the use of baseboards at the bottom of a realistic setting, and wallpaper borders, picture molding, or cornices at the top. Other items that might be emphasized to serve as interior terminal accents are such things as door and window trim and paneling, stair railings and newel posts, ornate picture frames, and decorative trim around draperies, furniture, or tablecloths.

The final principle, *balance,* refers to the visual balance of one side of the stage with the other. There are two types of balance: symmetrical and asymmetrical, or occult. Symmetrical balance is characterized by the mirror-like duplication of objects and designs on either side of a center line. The setting in Plate 15 is balanced symmetrically. This form of balance produces a setting formal and static in feeling, and is usually reserved for plays that reflect a similar tone of artificiality, formality, austerity, or impersonal coldness. Examples may be found in the comedies of manners written during the age of formalism—the late 17th and 18th centuries.

shape or a bright color. The repetition of like elements—line, mass, texture, and color—on either side of the stage (usually in unequal amounts) will also aid in achieving balance.

Plate 15. *SYMMETRICAL BALANCE: A setting for* All's Well That Ends Well *designed by John Ross for the University of Alabama, Tuscaloosa.*

Asymmetrical balance is the balance of unlike elements—the felt balance of mass against space. It conveys a feeling of greater movement and excitement than does symmetrical balance; and because of this and the feeling of casualness and spontaneity it suggests, it is used for the majority of settings in the modern theatre. Asymmetrical balance is based upon the relative attention value and visual weight of the elements of the design. Because of their color, size, shape, or texture, some features appear to be heavier, or attract more attention than others. The balance of these objects with each other and with others of less weight or attention value forms the basis of asymmetrical balance. Very often, attention value may be used to balance visual weight. An object on one side of the stage that appears large and heavy may be balanced on the other side by a smaller object that attracts a great deal of attention by virtue of a particularly interesting or unusual

The setting in Plate 16 is balanced asymmetrically. Study it and see if you can determine for yourself the ways in which a pleasing balance is achieved.

It should be noted, also, that the arrangement of actors on the stage can forcefully affect the center of interest and the balance of the setting; however, since the arrangement is constantly changing, it is usually not considered in the setting design unless the director plans to group his actors in a particular way throughout the majority of a scene, in which case the composition should compensate for the actors' positions.

Much space has been devoted to the principles and elements of design because of their extreme importance to the successful designing of scenery. However, it is still only a cursory examination. Additional reading sources may be found in the Bibliography following the Appendices at the end of the book.

*An Actor's Nightmare*
*Prelim: Sketch 3/23/89*

Plate 16. *ASYMMETRICAL BALANCE: Sketch of a setting for* An Actor's Nightmare *designed by Richard Durst for the University of Minnesota-Duluth.*

*Practicality*

The practical considerations of a setting fall into two categories: the *use* of the setting by director and actors, and the *construction* of the setting by members of the backstage crew. Actors and director are particularly concerned that the setting be substantial enough to withstand any rough usage incurred in the action of the play. Scenic units that must be stood on must be strong enough to support the necessary weight without swaying, teetering, bending, or (as has happened on some unfortunate occasions) collapsing entirely. Doors should open and close properly without sticking, jamming, or shaking the entire setting, and once closed, stay closed. Nothing will draw attention away from the play quicker than a door that slowly, silently, and mysteriously swings open with no human hand to be seen. In addition, adequate space must be left for passageway between objects and for any action requiring excessive space, such as a dance, a fight, or a chase. Steps and platforms should be arranged so that the actors can move up and down easily while concentrating on their acting, rather than

on the various levels. In short, the setting must be usable without undue stress, strain, or care having to be taken.

Nor can the designer ever ignore the fact that the setting must be constructed within certain limitations: *time, money,* and *labor.* Time and labor are interrelated factors. The setting must be capable of being constructed within a certain limited time—usually a period of three to four weeks, with a work period of usually two to four hours per day in amateur situations. The number and capabilities of the available workers also must be taken into consideration. Most amateur producing groups must rely, for the most part, on volunteers unskilled in stage techniques, who very often appear at random times. Obviously, it is far better to have three or four responsible persons working a regular schedule than to have ten or twenty persons appearing at random times; but it is not always possible to arrange this. The specific number of hours a day that may be used for construction and the number of workers who may be relied upon for regular service must be known in order to avoid designing settings too elaborate to be constructed in the allotted time. It is far better to have a simpler setting than to have one that is obviously only half-completed.

Money, of course, is the dragon that tames the most fanciful designer. Dreams are limited by the resources to purchase them. This is not necessarily a hindrance, unless the designer has a tendency to dream in terms of gold, silver, satin, and lace. Some of the most imaginative settings are constructed of the simplest, most inexpensive materials. It is the manner in which the materials are handled, rather than their initial cost, that determines the creativity of the setting. Nevertheless, a designer must never lose sight of the fact that settings must be designed scrupulously within budgetary limitations.

### Integration

Perhaps the most important requirement of a setting is that it be integrated with all the other elements of the production. This means that the designer must work in close contact with the other members of the production staff: director, costumer, lighting designer, and property master. The style of the production must be established, understood by each person, and then adhered to in each aspect of the production. Colors, textures, and forms must be compared, examined, discussed, and ultimately agreed upon by each person concerned with the design in order that the final product be free of clashing colors or discordant shapes, and that it be lighted in a manner designed to enhance rather than detract from the overall scheme. In all these matters the director has the final authority, and the designer must bow to his wishes. This is really the only means of assuring a unified production in approach, style, and interpretation.

### THE ELEMENTS OF SCENERY

Through the centuries, the requirements of scenery construction for lightness, strength, speed and ease of construction, economy, and ease of joining and handling have resulted in the development of a number of standard scenic units. These scenic units, forming, as they do, the basic structures with which a designer works, may be called the *elements* of scenery. They may be broadly divided into two categories: *flat scenery* and *three-dimensional scenery*.

### Flat Scenery

Perhaps the largest percentage of scenic units falls into the category of flat scenery—scenery that is basically two-dimensional, establishing width and height, but lacking depth or thickness to any appreciable degree. The basic purpose of this type of scenic unit is to create a large surface with a minimum of weight. Within this particular category are two broad divisions: *soft scenery* and *framed scenery*.

*Soft Scenery.* Soft scenery is designed to present a maximum coverage of area with a minimum of weight and a maximum of portability. This type of scenery must depend upon outside sources for support, most often being attached to a pipe or a batten, which is then flown or attached permanently to the ceiling of the stage. The following is a listing of the principal forms of soft scenery:

*Drape* or *Curtain:* This includes a wide variety of forms and styles, but is generally a full-stage arrangement of one or two cloth panels, designed to fly or operate on a traverse track. This material may be hung directly behind the proscenium arch, in which case it is often termed the "Main Curtain" or "Act Curtain"; it may be placed across the rear of the stage and called a "Drapery Cyc"; or it may be placed at any point from the front to the rear of the stage and designed to shut off portions of the stage from audience view, for the convenience of scene changing or to create a greater intimacy.

*Border* and *Teaser:* Narrow panels of cloth suspended horizontally above the stage area and designed to hide the upper portions of the stage from audience view. The teaser hangs directly behind the proscenium and has the additional responsibility of altering the height of the proscenium arch. These units may be constructed of standard drapery materials, or they may be cut from muslin and painted to fit in with a particular setting.

*Leg* and *Tormentor:* Narrow widths of material located at the sides of the stage and serving to conceal the wings of the stage. The tormentors are situated behind the proscenium and are used to alter the width of the opening. These units also may be either drapery or cut-out, painted fabrics.

*Backdrops* (or *Drops*): Generally full-stage-sized expanses of painted muslin or canvas. They are often painted to represent scenes and may, at times, be cut out in places so that the audience can see through to another drop, thereby increasing the effect of distance. Drops may also be constructed of scrim, bobbinet, or other materials for a variety of purposes.

*Cyclorama* (or *Cyc*): A large expanse of light blue- or gray-colored material, usually lighted to represent the sky. This unit may be curved around the back of the stage, or it may simply hang straight across the stage—very often merely a sky-colored backdrop.

*Framed Scenery.* Framed scenery, as the name indicates, is composed of a wooden frame covered with muslin or canvas and painted to represent a specific surface. This type of scenery is by far the most commonly used form and is divided into the following basic categories:

The *Flat:* The basic scenic form. At its simplest, it is a rectangular, cloth-covered wooden frame that may be painted to represent a portion of a wall. There are many variations, including flats with door openings, flats with window openings, flats with fireplace openings, and flats with diverse irregular shapes used to represent everything from slanted roofs to the edge of a forest.

*Ceiling:* A large framed unit designed to cover the top of a realistic interior setting and suggest the ceiling of a room. Usually constructed so that portions of the framing are removable in order to fold or roll the unit for storage, the ceiling has recently fallen into disuse—primarily because of the difficulty of lighting a setting with a ceiling.

*Framed Drop:* A backdrop that has been fitted with a supporting frame to ensure rigidity. As with the ceiling, the framing is usually so constructed that portions may be easily removed for storage purposes.

Although flat scenery may be fitted with a variety of semidimensional pieces such as door and window frames, fireplaces, and moldings of various sorts, these are usually considered accessories to flat scenery and therefore will not be listed with three-dimensional scenery. It should be noted, also, that flats are very often joined together to form three-dimensional shapes, but the basic unit is still flat scenery.

### Three-Dimensional Scenery

Scenic units that exhibit thickness or depth as well as height and width fall into the category of three-dimensional scenery. These units are generally self-supporting structures, and many must also support the weight of one or more actors. The divisions of *weight-supporting* and *non-weight-supporting* (referring to the weight of an actor) form the two classifications of three-dimensional scenery.

*Weight-supporting Scenery.* These units provide the means of altering the level of the stage floor or moving actors from one level to another, as well as a variety of natural shapes that also must support actors. The principal forms are as follows:

*Platforms:* Structures that provide a level playing area at a desired distance above the normal stage floor. These are normally built with a padded wooden top supported by legs that are braced for stability. The size, shape, and height of platforms are limited only by structural feasibility; however, the more useful platforms are constructed to a predetermined standard size and shape and may therefore be used for several productions.

*Steps* and *Stairs:* Any raised level must be easily accessible to the actors, and these units are used for that purpose. The most important criterion for them is that they be comfortable for the actor to traverse—he must be able to ascend and descend easily while most of his concentration is on his acting.

*Ramps:* Flat surfaces inclined from one level to another. These are usually constructed very similarly to platforms—as a matter of fact, they are often formed by altering a standard platform.

*Rocks* and other irregular forms: Occasionally a play will require an actor to move on or across rocks, irregular ground, or other similar natural shapes. These units must be constructed sturdily enough to support his weight and, at the same time, provide a realistically irregular appearance. This is usually accomplished by using a structural framework of sufficient supporting strength, which is then covered by shaped wire and cloth or papier mâché.

*Non-weight-supporting Scenery.* Into this category fall all other three-dimensional units of scenery—those not required to support an actor. These are used for their visual impact and include such things as columns, tree trunks, and rocks. Their construction is similar to that mentioned in discussing weight-supporting rocks, but the structural framework need only be strong enough to keep the desired shape.

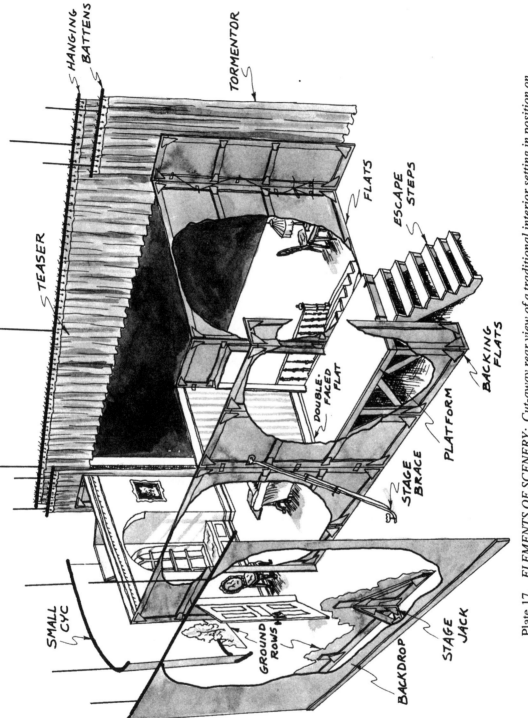

Plate 17. *ELEMENTS OF SCENERY: Cut-away rear view of a traditional interior setting in position on stage, showing the use and placement of several types of standard scenic units.*

These, then, are the basic scenic elements that may be used by a designer. Plate 17 provides an illustration of the use of many of them in a simple interior setting. A designer is not restricted to using these forms—far from it! But they do serve as beginning points from which he may then digress—limited only by the practical considerations of time, money, and material, as well as adaptability to a particular stage. This last is of prime importance, since scenery must fit within the confines of an individual stage. The designer must know the advantages and limitations of his stage thoroughly and must take them into consideration in his designing. The next chapter will deal with the basic stage form, layout, and equipment, and will point out those factors most directly affecting the design of settings.

# chapter II

# THE STAGE

A theatre building is an architectural structure designed primarily for comfortable and efficient presentation of plays to an audience. The shape and form of the building have evolved over hundreds of years to the present proscenium theatre. Even this is in a constant state of modification and alteration—and in some cases complete revision or rejection. In recent years much controversy has raged over which is the best type of theatre, with a number of varieties being propounded—several of which will be discussed in a later chapter. Of all the varieties, however, a good proscenium theatre is still the best equipped and most efficient for providing a total scenic environment for a play.

The proscenium theatre is divided into two distinct areas—one devoted to the members of the audience, and one devoted to play production. The audience portion of the theatre is comprised of the seating area (the "*house,*" as it is known in theatrical parlance), the lobby, box office, toilets, concessions, and other related areas. The play production area ("backstage") is located in the *stage house* and includes the stage and all its appurtenances, the dressing rooms, the greenroom (actors' lounge), and any workshop and storage areas that may be included in the building. (Broadway theatres contain no workshops; educational and community theatre groups, who usually build their own scenery and costumes, very often include these facilities.) The audience and play-production areas meet at a wall containing an opening through which the audience may view the play. This wall is the *proscenium* wall; the opening is the *proscenium opening* and is defined by the *proscenium arch.* This arched wall is the dividing line—on one side is the audience area, or "house," and on the other side is the stage. With the exception of sightlines, which will be discussed later in the chapter, the designer is primarily concerned with the stage portion of the theatre. He must become thoroughly familiar with the stage—its size, shape, advantages, and limitations—before he can effectively design a setting for it.

## STANDARD STAGE LAYOUT AND EQUIPMENT

Proscenium stages are usually quite similar in arrangement and in the types of permanent and semipermanent equipment included; so let's take a verbal tour of a typical stage, noting those items of particular concern to a designer. Plates 18 and 19 will provide a visual accompaniment. Starting from the front of the stage, we see that the stage floor is raised above the floor of the auditorium and may be separated from it by a curved pit, which is often used for seating an orchestra—hence the name *orchestra pit.* The exact size and shape of the pit should be determined, since it may be covered with platforming and used as an additional acting area. Recently constructed theatres very often include mechanical or hydraulic lifts to raise the floor of the pit up to the level of the stage floor for just this purpose. It can be an extremely useful playing area. In the setting illustrated in Plate 7 the orchestra pit has been covered and used for acting.

That portion of the stage floor between the front curtain and the footlights (a row of lights recessed into the front edge of the stage floor) is termed the *apron.* It is usually not more than two or three feet in width, as illustrated in Plate 19. Any portion of the stage floor extending beyond the footlights into the audience is called the *forestage.* The orchestra pit, when covered and used for acting, becomes a forestage. In recent years, the terms "apron" and "forestage" have often been used interchangeably. Stages with extended forestages have come to be known as "*apron stages.*" This loss of distinction between the two areas is a result of the increased tendency for stages to thrust farther and farther out from the proscenium arch and of the disappear-

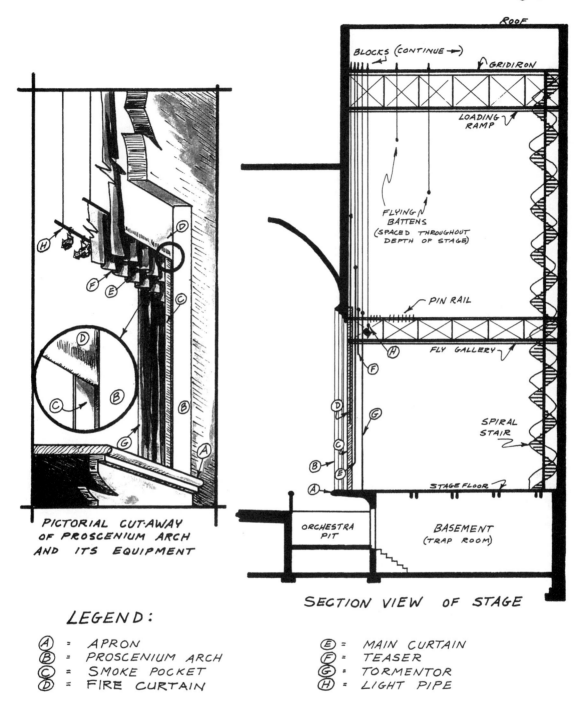

ROOF

BLOCKS (CONTINUE →)

GRIDIRON

LOADING RAMP

FLYING BATTENS (SPACED THROUGHOUT DEPTH OF STAGE)

PIN RAIL

FLY GALLERY

SPIRAL STAIR

STAGE FLOOR

ORCHESTRA PIT

BASEMENT (TRAP ROOM)

SECTION VIEW OF STAGE

PICTORIAL CUT-AWAY OF PROSCENIUM ARCH AND ITS EQUIPMENT

LEGEND:

(A) = APRON
(B) = PROSCENIUM ARCH
(C) = SMOKE POCKET
(D) = FIRE CURTAIN

(E) = MAIN CURTAIN
(F) = TEASER
(G) = TORMENTOR
(H) = LIGHT PIPE

Plate 18. *THE STAGE HOUSE: Side section view and pictorial view showing permanent and semi-permanent structures and equipment in a typical proscenium-theatre stagehouse.*

ance of the footlights from many modern theatres, which has eliminated the line of demarcation between the apron and the forestage. The designer will need to learn the exact shape and size of these areas. He should also determine the size of the proscenium opening (height and width) and the shape and size of the proscenium arch itself (thickness and irregular contours). He should mark on the stage floor a *proscenium line* (PL), a line connecting the upstage edges of the proscenium arch, and should mark perpendicular to this line a *center *line* (CL) indicating the center of the proscenium opening (see Plate 19). These two lines will serve as points of reference for making additional measurements.

opening. The main curtain is usually constructed of a rich, heavy fabric such as velour, but the teaser and tormentors may be made from a variety of materials. They may be the same

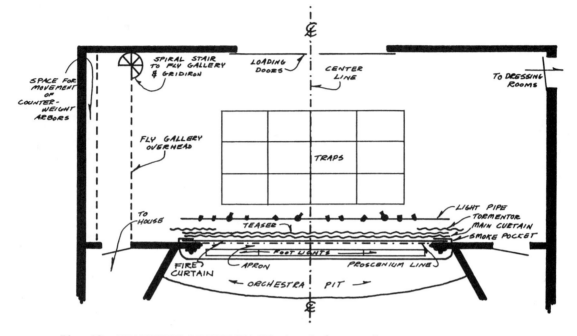

Plate 19. *PLAN VIEW OF THE STAGE: A typical proscenium stage arrangement.*

Directly behind the proscenium is an item of equipment required by the fire laws of most states and large cities—the *fire curtain*. This curtain almost always flies (moves up and down) and is so rigged that fire will automatically bring it down to seal off the proscenium opening and prevent the fire (which usually starts backstage) from expanding to the house. The fire curtain rides in metal grooves attached to the rear of the proscenium arch. These grooves are called the *smoke pockets* and are designed to prevent the fire from spreading around the edges of the curtain.

Moving farther onto the stage, we come across three items that have already been mentioned: the main curtain, the teaser, and the tormentors. The arrangement of these varies somewhat from theatre to theatre, but is quite often as follows: (1) the main curtain, which may fly or open from the center to either side, or both, and which serves to shut off the stage from the view of the audience; (2) the teaser, which is so arranged that it may be raised or lowered to alter the height of the proscenium opening; and (3) the tormentors at either side of the stage and designed to be moved on- or offstage to change the width of the proscenium

material as the main curtain, or they may be constructed in the same manner as flats and so painted and decorated that they form a false proscenium, or *portal*. This device is often used in musicals, with the decorated portal serving as a unifying device for the many varied settings. The designer should make note of the arrangement, placement, type, and size of these elements. He should also determine exactly how much floor space each takes up when in position. The drape of a curtain gives a deceptive amount of thickness—often nine to twelve inches, or more. Too many designers have forgotten this and, as a result, have seen the main curtain lop itself over the front edge of a setting erroneously placed within its line of descent.

Behind these items, there usually hangs either a pipe batten or a metal bridge used for hanging lights. The light bridge, which is partly suspended from above and partly attached to the walls, is included in many of the newer theatres. Older theatres make do with the simple pipe batten. This provision for hanging lighting instruments should be noted by the designer, who will want to know the type of hanging device provided, the space it occupies, and its distance from the proscenium. Settings should sit far enough back so as not to hinder the lighting from this position.

All of the pieces of equipment mentioned so far may be termed semipermanent equipment, with the only exception being the mandatory fire curtain. They may all be altered, replaced, or even removed entirely if the demands of the show require it. In addition, they are all related to the proscenium opening—being designed to close it off or to alter its size or shape. The pictorial inset on Plate 18 provides a view of the proscenium arch and its accompanying equipment.

Once past the proscenium, we find ourselves in the stage house proper. Our first concern will be to determine the exact amount of floor space available; measurements should be taken to determine the distance from the proscenium line to the back wall of the stage, and the distances from the center line to each side wall. The areas between the edges of the proscenium arch and the side walls of the stage are known as the *wings* and are used primarily as storage space for properties and scenery used in the current production and for the location of such backstage operations as the stage manager's post and, very often, the lighting and sound control boards. The location and size of such equipment should be very carefully noted. Also to be noted are any obstructions that might intrude into the stage area—pillars, posts, pipes, stairways, and the like. We should also note the openings onto the stage from dressing rooms, shops, and audience areas, as well as the loading doors from the outside. It is particularly important to learn the measurements of the loading doors (height and width). It is a sad designer who builds a piece of scenery only to learn too late that it is too large to fit through the loading doors and must either be dismantled and rebuilt inside or discarded entirely. This can be avoided by always keeping in mind the means of access to the stage.

The stage floor itself is made of soft wood to facilitate securing of scenery, and may be provided with a number of *traps*. These are removable doors cut into the floor to provide access to the room below the stage (often called, fittingly enough, the *trap room*). Not all stage floors are equipped with traps; but if provided, they can be extremely useful for such plays as *Street Scene, The Madwoman of Chaillot,* and *Hamlet,* all of which need some form of opening or space below floor level. If traps are available, their size and position should be measured and also the distance to the floor of the room below.

Some theatres may have several types of stage machinery built into the stage floor. There might be a revolving stage, a circular portion of the stage floor that can be turned mechanically or electrically; or there may be wagon stages, rolling platforms large enough to hold full-stage settings, which roll on- and offstage by means of built-in tracks. A stage that incorporates wagon stages must have adequate wing space to store these large platforms out of sight of the audience. Other theatres may have portions of the stage floor, as well as the orchestra pit, built onto hydraulic lifts so that they may be raised or lowered to any desired level at any time—even while a play is in progress. The designer must become familiar with any of these forms of equipment that may be at his disposal: where they are situated, their size, and method of operation.

Shifting our attention overhead, we see that there is considerable height to the stage. A good proscenium theatre will include a stage house whose total height is two and one-half to three times the height of the proscenium opening. The height is necessary in order to provide enough space to *fly* full-size scenery—to move the scenery by raising it above the stage floor and storing it high enough to be completely out of sight of the audience. This storage area above the stage is termed the *fly loft*.

The majority of structures and equipment above the stage floor are related to the flying of scenery. In order to appreciate their purposes fully, it will be necessary to gain some understanding of the operation of flying systems.

## FLYING SYSTEMS

There are two principal types of flying systems in use today: the *rope system* and the *counterweight system*. Both are based on a very simple principle—the idea that you may raise an object by tying a rope to it, running the rope up over a pulley and then down again. When you pull down on the free end of the rope, the object rises; and when you release the rope, the object comes down (see Plate 20, part A). In the theatre more than one line is used—three to five may be necessary, depending on the width of the proscenium opening (the wider the opening, the more lines necessary). These lines are spaced parallel to the proscenium opening at equal intervals across the opening. They run straight up from their position to pulleys above the stage, over the pulleys, and across to the side of the stage, over a second set of pulleys, and then run together down the side wall of the stage. These lines, making up a *set of lines,* are attached to the same wooden or pipe batten or scenic unit and, when pulled together, will raise the batten or unit to which they are attached (see Plate 20, part B). Both the rope system and the counterweight system use this basic idea, and differ of pulleys as lines in the set. Each set of lines requires one head block and the same number of loft blocks as lines in the set. This is true no matter whether the lines belong to a rope system or a counterweight system.

### The Rope System

The rope system is the oldest form of flying system. It includes very little more than the

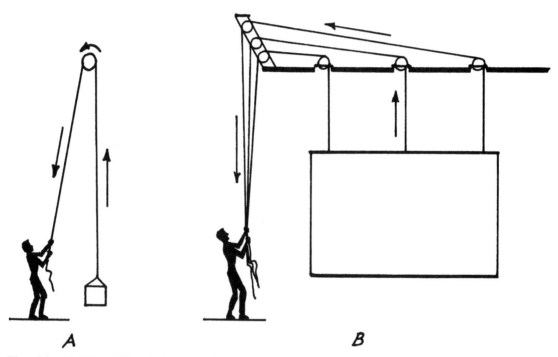

Plate 20.   *THE PRINCIPLE OF FLYING SYSTEMS: (a) the basic pulley principle; (b) the pulley principle as adapted to theatrical flying systems.*

only in the refinements added to make the operation easier and more efficient. Plates 21 and 22 will aid in understanding their operation.

Before going into the explanation of each system, one particular structure needs to be introduced: the *gridiron,* or *"grid,"* as it is more often called. The grid is a metal framework situated six to eight feet below the roof of the stage house and used to support the pulleys used in the flying systems. The grid has three to five open *channels* running from the front to the rear of the stage, perpendicular to the proscenium, spaced approximately ten feet apart (see Plate 22). Across these channels are attached *loft blocks,* the pulleys for the lines. The lines run from the loft blocks over to the side of the stage, at which point is found the *head block,* a single unit containing the same number

basic system described earlier. The lines used are ½"- or ¾"-diameter manila rope. A stage that uses the rope system will usually contain a narrow platform mounted twenty to twenty-five feet up the same side wall of the stage as the location of the head blocks. This platform is the *fly gallery* and contains, on the side facing the stage, a railing in which are set a series of wooden or metal belaying pins (yes, they are the same type of pins as those used on the old-fashioned sailing vessels—see Plate 21). This is the *pin rail,* and the lines coming down from the head blocks are tied off onto the belaying pins. The pin rail actually contains two sets of pins, as you may have noted in the illustration. The bottom set of pins is used to hold the scenery in its playing position. This means that the scenery, when attached to the lines, is set into the position it will take when

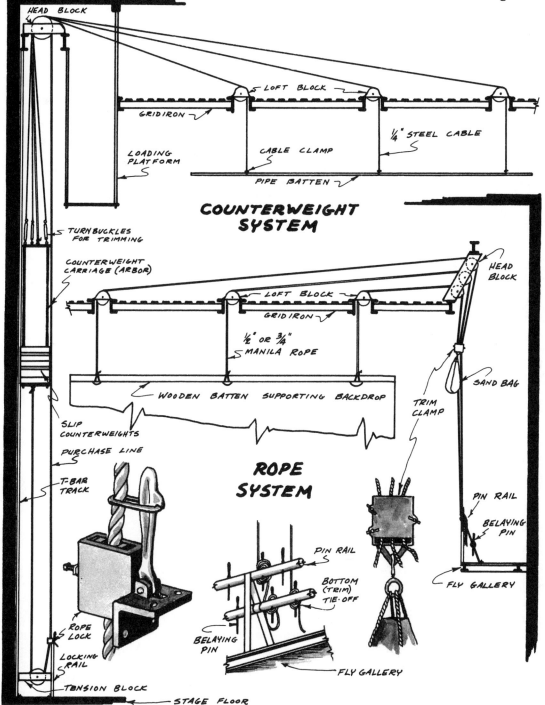

HEAD BLOCK

LOFT BLOCK

GRIDIRON

LOADING PLATFORM

CABLE CLAMP

¼" STEEL CABLE

PIPE BATTEN

**COUNTERWEIGHT SYSTEM**

TURNBUCKLES FOR TRIMMING

COUNTERWEIGHT CARRIAGE (ARBOR)

LOFT BLOCK

GRIDIRON

HEAD BLOCK

½" OR ¾" MANILA ROPE

SAND BAG

WOODEN BATTEN SUPPORTING BACKDROP

TRIM CLAMP

SLIP COUNTERWEIGHTS

PURCHASE LINE

T-BAR TRACK

**ROPE SYSTEM**

PIN RAIL

BOTTOM (TRIM) TIE-OFF

BELAYING PIN

PIN RAIL

BELAYING PIN

FLY GALLERY

ROPE LOCK

LOCKING RAIL

TENSION BLOCK

FLY GALLERY

STAGE FLOOR

Plate 21. *FLYING SYSTEMS: Diagrams of the parts and operation of the counterweight and rope flying systems.*

it is in audience view—the correct height and the correct relationship to the stage floor. (Usually the scenery will rest parallel to the stage floor, but not always.) This playing position is achieved by trial and error. The designer sits out in the house and directs the men on the fly gallery to raise or lower one line or another until the scenery is at just the right position, called *trim,* and then instructs them to make a *"bottom tie."* The lines will be tied off on the bottom pin where they will remain throughout the run of the show, unless the

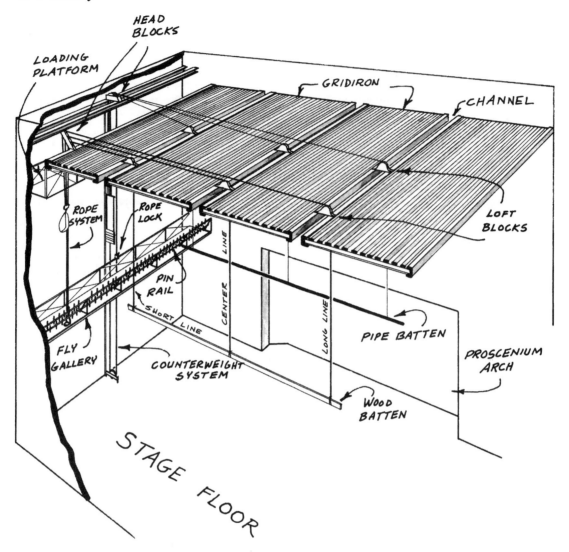

Plate 22. *A TWO-SYSTEM STAGE: Cut-away view of a stage equipped with both counterweight and rope flying systems, showing the location of the equipment in relation to the stage house.*

trim needs to be altered. When the scenery is pulled up out of sight to *high trim,* the lines are tied off onto the top pin. To lower the scenery into playing trim, the lines are untied from the top pin and the scenery is lowered until stopped by the bottom tie—at which time the scenery should be in its correct playing position.

To facilitate the process of "trimming" scenery, each line in a set is given a name. This naming is related to the placement of the fly gallery. The line that comes down nearest the fly gallery is termed the *short line;* the next line is the *center line;* and the line farthest from the fly gallery is the *long line.* In a five-line system, the names are short line, short-center line, center line, long-center line, and long line.

One further step in the flying of scenery is concerned with the problem of weight. Scenery that is to be flown is often quite heavy—at times requiring four to six men to lift it. Obviously, it will not do to have this number of men struggling at a set of lines each time the scenery must be raised or lowered. Ideally, one man should be able to handle each set of lines, which means that, in most cases, he will need some form of assistance other than additional manpower. This is done by adding weight in the form of sandbags to the lines where they come together below the head block. Once the scenery has been trimmed, a metal *trim clamp* is secured over the lines (see Plate 21), keeping the scenery in trim (always horizontal to the stage floor) and providing means for attaching the sandbags. Enough weight is added so that the pulling power of only one man is needed to raise the scenery.

The rope system has several disadvantages. The ropes expand and shrink with changes in the humidity, making it difficult to maintain trim. Ropes wear out fairly rapidly and must be constantly checked for signs of wear, so that they may be replaced before they become so worn as to be dangerous. The weighting of scenery by sandbags is a difficult and time-consuming process involving a great deal of manpower, since the scenery must be hauled up to high trim to be weighted (see Plate 23).

On the plus side of the column, the rope system is the least expensive to install. In addition, each line in a set may be isolated and used individually or, if so desired, the three lines may be spaced at irregular intervals across the depth of the stage and used to fly three separate items at the same time or to fly an odd-shaped scenic unit.

### The Counterweight System

The counterweight system has succeeded in solving most of the disadvantages of the rope system. (Constant reference to Plate 21 will aid in understanding the explanation of this system.) In the first place, the lines used are

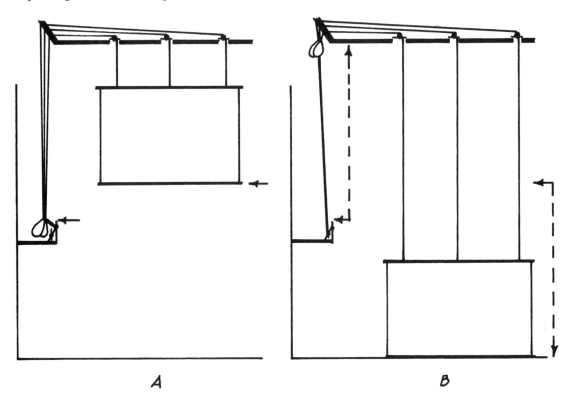

A                    B

Plate 23. *THE ALLOTTED MOVEMENT OF SANDBAGGED SCENERY: (a) scenery at height trim for sandbagging (the scenery must be manhandled or winched up to this position for weighting); (b) scenery in playing trim, showing distance of movement allowed by travels of sandbags.*

Scenery can never be completely counter-balanced in this system, since the scenery must always remain heavy enough to pull itself to the floor (you cannot very well push *up* on the sandbags to make the scenery go *down,* and there would be no other way if it did not go down of its own accord). Finally, there is no way to control the sway of the sandbags as they move up and down, and this can constitute quite a danger.

wire cable, which will not shrink or stretch and lasts much longer than rope. These cables are permanently fastened to a pipe batten by means of cable clamps. As in the rope system, the lines run from the batten up and over the loft blocks, and then across to and over the head block. Once past the head block, however, differences begin to appear. Instead of continuing on down to be tied off at the pin rail, the lines are attached to a metal frame called an *arbor,* or *carriage*. The lines are not fastened directly to the arbor, but are attached to turnbuckles that are, in turn, fastened to the arbor. The turnbuckles serve to shorten or lengthen each line to adjust the trim of the batten. The arbor is designed to hold metal weights, which are used to counterbalance the weight of the scenery attached to the batten. Stage weights come in a variety of sizes ranging in weight from ten to thirty or forty pounds. Combinations of the weights may be used to balance equally any piece of scenery.

The path of the arbor is controlled by one of two means: A T-bar track fastened to the stage wall, or wire cable guides stretched between the stage floor and the grid. The arbor moves along one of the two devices mentioned, and sway is thereby eliminated from its movement.

Control over the up and down movement of the arbor (which, because of its close attachment, also controls the up and down movement of the scenery) is achieved through the *purchase line*. This is a rope line, one end of which is attached to the bottom of the arbor, from which point it runs down to the stage floor, around a pulley there, back up through a rope lock, and then all the way up to the head block, which it circles and then returns down to be attached to the top of the arbor. This purchase line, in effect, forms a circle, with the arbor serving as the connecting link between the two ends of the line. The pulley on the floor is constructed with springs so that it will automatically compensate for expansion and shrinkage in the purchase line and thus keep a constant tension on the line. For this reason, it is known as the *tension block*. The *rope lock* does just what the name indicates—locks the purchase line in position so that it cannot move, which in turn keeps the arbor from moving, which in turn keeps the scenery from moving. Pulling down on that portion of the purchase line leading directly from the bottom of the arbor lowers the arbor and thereby raises the scenery. Pulling down on the portion of the line coming down from the head block raises the arbor, which in turn lowers the scenery. Because the arbor may be moved both up and down by means of the purchase line, the scenery need no longer outweigh the balancing weight in order to descend to the floor. This means that it may be exactly counterbalanced, making the operation of the unit a good deal easier.

Counterweight systems provide a *loading platform* situated near the head blocks and just below the level of the gridiron. When the scenery is on the floor and the arbor is up at the level of the gridiron, weights may be placed in the arbor from the loading platform, thus eliminating the necessity for manually hauling the scenery up to high trim in order to balance it.

Disadvantages of the counterweight system lie in the increased initial installation cost and the fact that the lines are permanently attached to a batten, which precludes the possibility of using one of the lines individually or scattering the lines to various parts of the stage, as may be achieved without difficulty with the rope system.

While the counterweight system is probably the prevalent rigging system in use today, an increasing number of theatres are employing varying degrees of motorized rigging. Motorized winches of various sorts are often employed to raise and lower lighting battens and full-stage curtain battens—normally the heaviest line-sets found in a theatre. When budgetary restrictions allow, theatres may employ motorized equipment for other flying purposes. Automated winches controlled from a central control station may be used as spot lines located at any given point above the stage, or they may be employed to raise and lower entire line-sets. While early motorized rigging had problems with consistency and dependability, modern systems have become very reliable, accurate, and dependable, and are considered by many to be the "state of the art" in rigging equipment.

The designer should know what type of flying system, if any, is incorporated into the stage, how many lines are taken up with other types of equipment such as lights, borders, legs, curtains, and cycs. He will want to know whether there is a fly gallery, on which side of the stage it is situated, and its height from the floor. He will need to know if the gridiron is sufficiently high to allow full-height scenery to be flown out of sight. Some theatres, unfortunately, have been mistakenly constructed with insufficient height in the stage house to allow this, which necessitates complicated rigging methods in order to utilize the flying system with any degree of effectiveness.

Once he has found out all he can about the stage, its size, shape, and equipment, the designer must concern himself with the view the members of the audience have of the stage. To determine this fully, he must acquaint himself with the audience *sightlines*.

SIGHTLINES

By determining which seats in the house provide the most extreme views of the stage, the designer can plan his setting in such a way as to place all of the important elements of the setting in a position where they can be seen by everyone in the house and can, at the same time, plan his masking so that those persons seated in the most extreme positions cannot see past the scenery into the backstage areas. Plate 24 illustrates these *critical seats*.

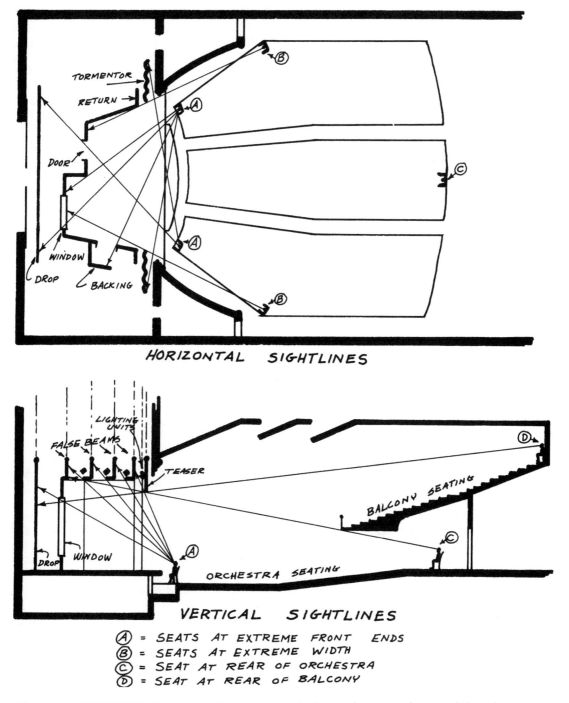

HORIZONTAL SIGHTLINES

VERTICAL SIGHTLINES

Ⓐ = SEATS AT EXTREME FRONT ENDS
Ⓑ = SEATS AT EXTREME WIDTH
Ⓒ = SEAT AT REAR OF ORCHESTRA
Ⓓ = SEAT AT REAR OF BALCONY

Plate 24.  *SIGHTLINES: Plan view and section view of a theatre showing audience sightlines from extreme (critical) seats.*

The two seats that usually provide the most extreme views of the stage are those at either end of the front row in the orchestra (labeled "A" in the illustration). Persons sitting here can see farther into the wings and up into the fly loft than from any other seat in the house. If the designer plans his masking so as to block the view from these seats, he can be assured that his masking will work for everyone else in the house.

The two seats at the ends of the rows at the widest point in the house (labeled "B" in the illustration) provide views that may be will mask the fly loft from seats "A." If there is a balcony, then seat "D," the last row in the top balcony, must be considered in setting the trim. The teaser must be high enough to allow a person sitting in this seat to view all of the important action and areas of the stage. Two-balcony theatres and theatres with very high or steep balconies pose a great problem in this respect, since total view from the balcony and total masking from seat "A" may not be possible. In such a case, it is better to allow seat "A" to see a portion of the fly area than to hinder the view from seat "D."

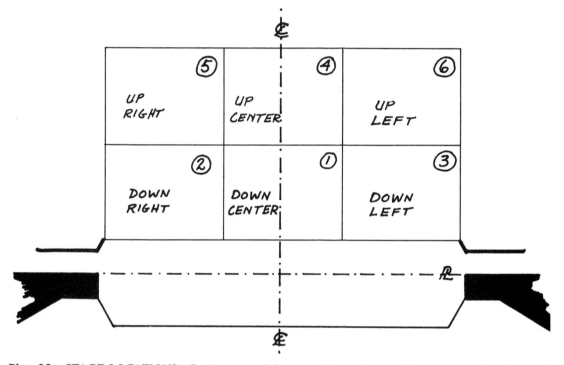

Plate 25. *STAGE LOCATIONS: Basic areas of the stage, lettered according to stage directions and numbered in order of relative dramatic importance (according to many theorists).*

blocked to some degree by the proscenium arch or by the tormentors, thus limiting the stage area that can be used for necessary scenery or action. If all the important areas can be seen from these seats, they are also visible from all other seats.

Seat "C" in the center of the last row in the orchestra provides probably the best overall view of the setting. Unless there is a balcony, this seat is usually used for setting the trim on the main teaser. The teaser is adjusted so that a person sitting in this seat can just see the top of the rear wall of the setting below the bottom of the teaser. All other borders are then positioned in relation to this trim so that they

The designer should measure the exact placement of these critical seats in relation to the proscenium opening—their distance from the proscenium and their position to one side or the other of the edge of the proscenium. In addition, he should determine the eye level of a person sitting in these seats in relation to the stage floor. Balcony seats can present a problem in this respect, unless an architectural section drawing of the theatre can be obtained. Otherwise, the height position of the balcony seat and the rear seat in the orchestra may have to be gauged by eye, rather than by accurate measurement.

Before concluding this discussion of the

stage and its equipment, it might be well to introduce some theatre terminology related to the areas of the stage.

### STAGE AREAS

The stage is broken up into a number of arbitrary areas whose names are used in describing positions and for giving directions as to movement on the stage. The area marked off by the sightlines as being in view of all members of the audience is known as the *acting area*, the *playing area*, or *onstage*. That portion of the stage that is beyond the view

farthest from the audience—is *upstage*. These terms come to us from the days of the Renaissance when the stage floor was slanted, the upstage portion literally being higher than the downstage portion. The acting areas then become named *down-right, down-center, down-left, up-right, up-center*, and *up-left*, as can be seen in Plate 25. As noted on the diagram, certain of the areas are stronger dramatically than others. The designer should remember this and avoid placing in weak areas scenic elements important to the action of the play.

The stage area may also be subdivided in terms of *planes*, receding areas parallel to the proscenium (see Plate 26). These areas are

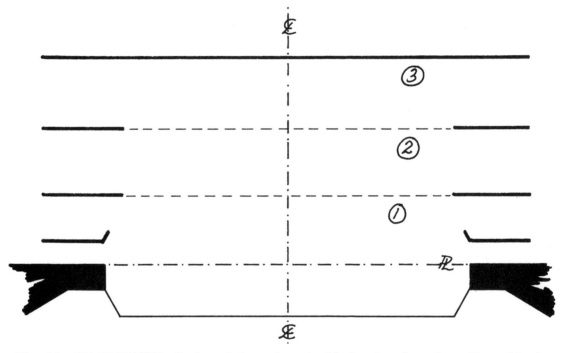

Plate 26. *STAGE PLANES: Horizontal planes determined by location of portals or side masking legs, numbered from downstage to upstage.*

of the audience is called *offstage*, or *backstage*, although "backstage" generally connotes more than just space, including in its meaning all of the technical equipment and personnel necessary to run a production.

The acting area is further divided into individualized areas for more specific descriptions of the space. These are described in terms of stage directions. For instance, *right* and *left* on the stage refer to the actor's right and left as he stands facing the audience. The front of the stage—that part nearest the audience—is termed *downstage;* the rear of the stage—

determined by the positions of legs or portals. The plane between the first set of legs and the proscenium is known as *number one*, or "in one"; the plane between the first set of legs and the second set of legs is *number two*, or "in two"; and so forth. When theatre folk speak of playing a scene "in one," it is this subdivision of the stage to which they are referring.

Anyone—not just designers—but anyone who is planning to work in the theatre in any capacity should become familiar with stage terminology and stage layout and equipment.

These are the language and tools of the theatre person and should be common knowledge to him. The designer, in particular, must make a careful study of the stage layout and equipment and the sightlines of the theatre and then, after taking accurate measurements, make out scaled drawings of his theatre such as those pictured in Plates 19 and 24. The section view of the stage illustrated in Plate 18 would also be helpful, but is not as essential as the other two types of drawing. These can then be used as he designs the setting(s) for the theatre, following the general design procedure that will be outlined in the following chapter.

# chapter III

# THE DESIGN PROCESS

As a preface to this chapter, I should perhaps mention that there are no hard and fast rules pertaining to the procedure for designing a setting. Each designer works out a sequence and method that is particularly efficient and comfortable for him, and he may vary that sequence from production to production. The following outline is a very general, common-sense procedure that is not intended to detail all of the conferences, planning stages, and steps that actually occur in the design process. As an illustration, the procedure for designing one of the settings for a production of *Lu Ann Hampton Laverty Oberlander* by Preston Jones will be discussed, with examples of the necessary developmental sketches, drawings, plans and materials.

The process of designing a setting, starting from the very beginning and continuing until the completed setting is ready for opening night, logically divides into two general steps: (1) the *conception of the design*, in which the design idea is created, altered and enlarged upon, and finally approved; and (2) the *realization of the design*, in which the approved design is finally converted into the completed setting.

## CONCEPTION OF THE DESIGN

The creation of a stage setting is restricted by the requirements of the media. As we have discovered, the scenic designer is a collaborative artist and must work within certain boundaries—the limitations of the stage, the requirements of the script, and the requirements of the director. Before a designer can develop a workable design, he must become fully conversant with the requirements of that particular production. After he has studied the stage in the manner described in the preceding chapter and knows its advantages and limitations, he must learn the requirements of the script and the director.

*Reading the Script*

The obvious starting point for any design is the playscript. Within this one source are contained the kernels of all ideas that will later develop into the realized design. The designer will find that he must read through and study the script until he knows it as well as do the director, the stage manager, or the actors. Usually, however, the first reading of the play is primarily for enjoyment and to learn the basic story. Also, at this time, he gets an idea of the period, locale, style, and atmosphere of the play. Further readings will provide insight into the number and types of settings and the specific technical requirements of each individual scene.

This information should not necessarily be gained from the set descriptions provided at the beginning of each scene or act (many playwrights do not provide enough information here to be of much value, anyway). Some designers will deliberately ignore any reference to the setting in the stage directions, preferring to form their own ideas from the action of the play and the dialogue. Whether this extreme approach is totally valid is debatable; however, the idea behind it has significance to any designer—that the designer's ideas must be evolved without strict adherence to the setting descriptions of the playwright, who is, after all, more interested in the story and the characters and who may, in addition, be an extremely poor judge of what is and is not practicable and feasible in settings, particularly in view of the specific stage to be used. The designer should be more concerned with the requirements of the action and the guidelines for the setting contained within the dialogue of the play. Specific pointers that may be found in the script for various types of settings will be discussed in later chapters.

From the script the designer will learn the story, the period, locale, and style of the play. He will find out about the characters in the play – although much will have to be read "between the lines" in order to make a full character analysis. He will also begin to discover the specific scenic requirements of the play: the number and types of settings, the entrances, levels, necessary furniture for each setting, and the problems, if any, that may be involved in moving from one setting to another.

I found *Lu Ann Hampton Laverty Oberlander* to be a realistic comedy/drama set in a "small frame house in a small farm town" in west Texas. The setting requires the porch of the house to be utilized, as well as an interior living room containing "Sears-catalogue-type" furniture—sofa, table, chairs, radio, etc. Exits from the room lead to the kitchen and to other parts of the house, including bedrooms. This setting was used for Act I, set in 1953, and also for Act III, set in 1973. (For this discussion, the setting for Act II will be omitted.) The house belongs to a working-class woman with teenage children with no time or money to lavish on more than basic upkeep of the house. (In Act III the generations change, but the situation remains the same.) The cast is not overly large, and the stage for the production is sizeable, so space should not be a problem.

Armed with information from the script and some preliminary research, the designer should develop some preliminary ideas about the nature of the setting before meeting with the director to discuss more specifically the various aspects of the production.

*Conferences with the Director*

Often discussions with the director will involve all the designers for the production and, possibly, other personnel such as choreographer, musical director, and some members of the technical staff. These discussions may occur at periodic intervals for several days or weeks until the design is finally conceived and approved. Ideas are evolved, hashed over, and then dismissed or enlarged upon. The designer should develop his own ideas concerning the design possibilities and not rely on the director to provide him with fully detailed lists of style, mood, and specific requirements for the show. Theatre is a collaborative effort, and the designer should be prepared to contribute concrete ideas concerning the visual aspects of the show and to discuss, evaluate and alter these ideas in collaboration with the other contributing artists of the production. The most skilled and imaginative directors with whom I have worked provide concepts or metaphors for the show, suggesting that the setting should be "simple, yet decorative" or that it should look like a "child's toy" or a "Chinese painting" or even, in one instance, should suggest the quality of

"marginality"—characters living on the fringes of events, alternately caught up in the swell of important actions and then deposited out of the mainstream. It is up to the designer to translate this into concrete visual terms and ultimately into a realized setting.

Those aspects about which the director will frequently be more specific are the required playing areas, and the physical needs for each scene in terms of acting space, levels, furniture and set properties, and entrances/exits. In those instances where a director might be hazy or uncertain about these elements, the designer should continue to question and probe until agreement is reached about the physical requirements of each scene and, where possible, the stylistic and atmospheric aspects of each scene as well.

Ultimately, though, each development idea for the setting should be approved by the director before proceeding into the next phase of the design process. As the overseer of, and the person ultimately responsible for, the entire production, the director should be kept fully informed of all major ideas and approve the final design before the realization phase is begun.

The director of *Lu Ann...* and I already had worked together on numerous productions, so we were familiar with each other's working habits and preferences. We were able to skip much of the "Well, what do you want to do about this?" process necessary when director and designer are new to each other. The director was not insistent on a totally real representation of a west Texas house. We agreed that the porch and a certain amount of the exterior of the house should be more predominant than indicated in the script and that some external elements suggestive of west Texas were important. Specific arrangements of the space and the means of changing into the setting for Act II became my responsibility—subject to his final approval.

A continuing process in the development of a design is that of learning as much as is necessary about the locale and time period of the play.

*Research*

No designer can be familiar enough with each period or region in which a play may be set to be able to design scenery conveying the basic attributes of that place or period. Therefore, he must spend a great amount of time researching the play. This research includes both written and visual sources. He will read as much as possible about the social, economic and political happenings of the time and place, and the people who lived there; to better understand that characters of the play, he will familiarize himself with the beliefs, attitudes, customs, habits, and everyday lives of the people of that period. At the same time, he will be looking for as much visual material as he can find on the subject. Photographs, drawings, and paintings will all provide possible sources of inspiration. The recent outpouring of pictorial books on every imaginable subject has been a great boon to the designer in that respect. Magazines provide much material, both written and pictorial. It is a wise designer who makes an organized collection of pictures clipped from magazines that may be used for future reference. The best reference, of course, is for the designer to have actually visited or seen the place in question. Much can be observed and experienced through an actual visit that could never be realized through pictures. In order to increase remembrance, it would be helpful to take photographs or slides of the places visited.

Research should be both general and specific. The designer should seek basic architectural, decorative, and natural earmarks of the particular region or period; he should also find specific details such as door trim design, wallpaper, gable decoration, and tree shapes and foliage groupings. For *Lu Ann...* I looked for specific details pertinent to Texas architecture and decor. I have visited Texas (first-hand experience is always best) and returned with images of windmills scattered everywhere, and the prevalence of Victorian "gingerbread" architectural details—even on the smaller frame houses. My principal resources for this play became photographic essays on the everyday aspects of Texas life and people. One particular book focused on the "Lone Star" image in decor and architecture, an image of particular importance in developing the final design.

### The Design Idea

Throughout this period of reading, conferences, and research, the designer is searching for this design idea. Where does it come from? It is difficult to be specific, particularly since I can speak authoritatively only about my own designing. Usually in reading a play I get a strong feeling of atmosphere or style—hazy mental images or feelings about the setting and how it should look. At times this image or feeling is clearer than at others. When reading *Man of La Mancha,* for instance, I definitely felt the play required a setting strong in texture with a definite Spanish quality. I was interested to note from an article in a trade magazine that Howard Bay and Patton Campbell, the setting and costume designers of the Broadway production, felt the same way (even though spe-

cific interpretations of the general feeling would probably be quite different). *Iguana* evoked a strong image of sweating palm leaves, bamboo, and moldering, paint-flecked wood.

The real difficulty comes in trying to recapture this mental image or feeling in actual visual symbols—lines, masses, textures, and colors. This is where reading, research, and conferences with the director prove to be of great value. From one of these sources may come a verbal or visual symbol that will crystallize what has been, up to now, a hazy image. This symbol—what Mordecai Gorelik calls the "dramatic metaphor" of the setting—may come from some action or dialogue in the script, from a remark made by the director, or from a portion of a painting, drawing, or photograph discovered during the research. It may take the form of a particular style, a specific decorative detail, an architectural feature, or something not quite as definite; but, whatever it is, it "says" something that seems to be particularly appropriate to that particular play. Symbols that have worked for me have included: for *The Fantasticks,* a rural American front porch; for Brecht's *A Caucasian Chalk Circle,* a Russian child's toy; and for *The Crucible,* rough-hewn vertical planks.

For *Lu Ann...,* windmill, and "Lone Star" images and memories of wonderful plains sunsets were prominent in the final design concept: a fragmented setting of "gingerbread" details, a portal with Lone Star Images, and a streaky sky with a windmill silhouette to compliment the somewhat fragmented script, allow easier transition to Act II, and feature the exterior symbols more prominently. It may take a number of premininary sketches (see Plate 27 for one example) and drawings before the mental image can be fully translated into visual forms that will be theatrically practicable, but once accomplished, the resultant setting seems to be "right" for that particular production (although it would probably be discordant with a different interpretation of the same play).

The design idea must be made clear not only to the designer, but also to the director and other members of the production staff. In order to achieve this, the designer makes a visual presentation of his ideas in the form of *floor plans* and *sketches* or *models.*

### The Floor Plan

The floor plan is a drawing showing a top view of the stage with all of the setting in position and of an exact size in relation to the stage itself. To do this accurately, the drawing must be in scale—each line in the drawing measured to be a proportional representation of the actual size of the item the line describes. The scale most often used in theatrical floor plans is ½″ = 1′0″, which means that each one-half inch in the drawing represents one foot in actual size. A line three inches long in

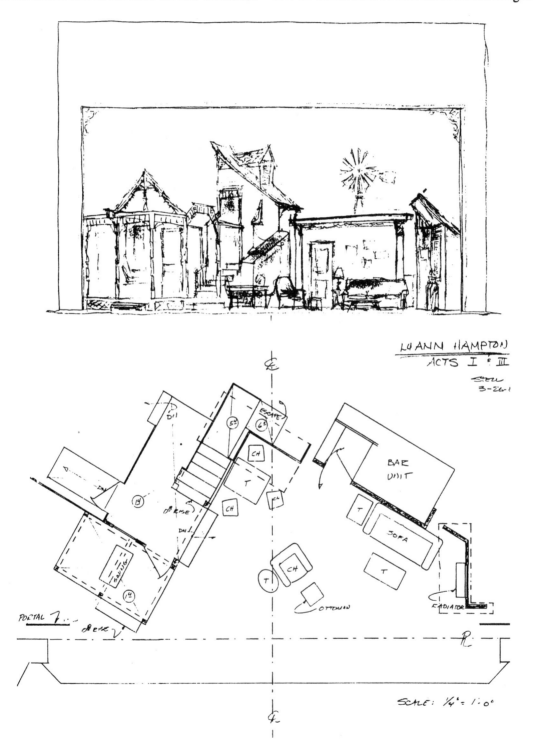

Plate 27. *PRELIMINARY SKETCH FOR* LU ANN HAMPTON LAVERTY OBERLANDER: *A rough free-hand sketch combined with a small scaled floor plan are used to show the director and other interested parties the status of the design concept about mid-way through the development process.*

the drawing represents six feet of actual length. Each item in the drawing is measured to precisely conform to the same scale. In addition, standard symbols are used in the drawing to represent specific architectural structures.

precisely how much of the action can be seen by all members of the audience. Although drafted before the USITT Symbols had been published, the final floor plan for *Lu Ann...* shown in Plate 28 utilizes

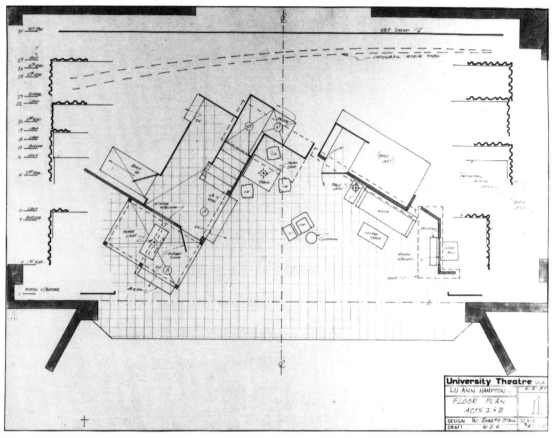

Plate 28. *FINAL FLOOR PLAN: A carefully drafted plan shows in detail all aspects of the proposed setting.*

cific architectural structures. Standard drafting symbols which have been developed by the U.S. Institute for Theatre Technology can be found in Appendix B.

By use of the scaled drawing and the standard symbols, the designer is able to relate clearly to the director and other interested persons the exact size, shape, and arrangement of the setting. The director can then see where doors, windows, walls, and furniture will be placed and can determine exactly how much space he will have in which to work. The one-foot grid listed indicates that the floor plan is lined off into 1′ squares to enable the director to readily estimate distances and space. In addition, the critical seats will be indicated on the floor plan, so that the director can know

symbols which are very similar and shows the type of information conveyed by this means.

*Sketches and Models*

The floor plan explains the arrangement and size of the setting, but cannot show how the setting will look to the audience—the picture they will see when they look at the stage. For this purpose, the designer must rely on perspective sketches (sometimes called "renderings") or scaled models of the setting. At times, both devices are used.

The designer usually makes countless small pencil sketches during the process of designing the setting, but these are primarily visual notations for himself—not very often used to convey information to someone else. When he

Plate 29. *COLORED RENDERING FOR* LU ANN HAMPTON LAVERTY OBERLANDER: *This rendering shows the setting designed for Acts I and III of the production. A separate rendering illustrated the setting for Act II.*

feels ready to depict his idea of the setting in a form that is clear to others, he will often rely on a colored rendering (painted perspective sketch) of the setting as it would appear to a member of the audience seated in the ideal seat in the theatre (usually the center of the orchestra seating). The rendering is not to scale and will *not* serve as a guide to the carpenter or painter for the actual preparation of the setting, but is intended to show only the appearance of the setting when completed and lighted. The rendering may be a carefully detailed drawing prepared using me-chanical perspective, or it may be a looser free-hand interpretation of the design; and many different types of art media may be used in its preparation, according to the taste of the designer. The final result, however, must be a clear representation of the completed setting. Plate 29 shows a final rendering for *Lu Ann Hampton Laverty Oberlander*. In it an attempt was made to suggest the lighting and mood for one scene from the play, and human figures were included to clarify the scale of the setting.

A model of the setting can depict the ap-

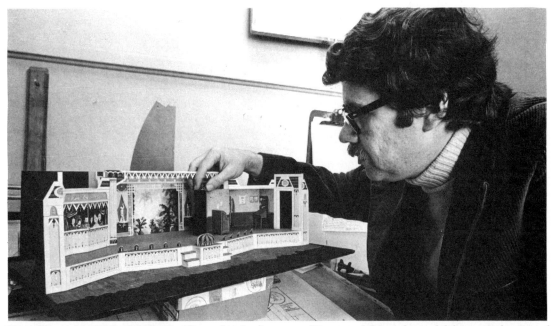

Plate 30. *A MODEL SETTING: The author is shown working on a 1/2" scale model for a production of* Fashion *produced by the University of Georgia.*

pearance and arrangement of the setting with greater clarity than can a drawing—particularly for the designer who is somewhat unskilled at artistic rendering. Because it is done to scale in each element, the relationship of walls, levels, and spaces can be clearly understood. If it takes the place of the colored sketch, the model is usually painted as the setting will be painted. Otherwise, it may have the architectural and decorative details only inked onto the model. In either case, this is a working model—not intended for public display—and as such, does not require the care and delicacy needed for a presentational model. Very often the furniture is omitted or shown in a flat, cutout form. The model is constructed from materials selected for ease of workability rather than strength. Cardboard, paper, and balsa wood are the most commonly used materials. These are cut out, shaped, painted, and set onto a solid base of thin plywood or Masonite by means of tape or glue. A good example of a relatively simple model made from just such materials is shown in Plate 30 (Page 56), while Plate 31(below) shows a more complex model constructed for a multi-setting musical.

It is through the use of the floor plan and the sketch or model that the designer is able to secure the director's approval of the design concept. Once this approval has been granted, the designer must transfer his attention to reproducing the design idea in a full-sized setting.

### REALIZATION OF THE DESIGN

If a design is to be fully realized, those persons who are concerned with the construction, painting, or rigging of the setting must fully understand what the designer has in mind. To this end, the designer makes *construction drawings,* which are much like the blueprints of an architect.

#### Construction Drawings

A setting is not constructed as a single structure, but is broken down into a number of units that are constructed separately and then, on set-up day, are fastened together to form the completed setting. The construction drawings are scaled drawings showing in detail the number, types, sizes, shapes, and exact method of construction for the scenic units. The basic

Plate 31. *MODEL FOR A MULTI-SETTING SHOW: A 1/2" scaled model for a setting of* Oliver! *is being used to explain to junior high school students the operation of this complex production. Models can be particularly helpful in clarifying the proposed scene changing methods for complicated multi-setting shows.*

# CONSTRUCTION DRAWINGS

SCALED REAR VIEWS OF ALL UNITS PLUS ANY ADDITIONAL VIEWS NEEDED TO PROVIDE ALL INFORMATION NEEDED FOR CONSTRUCTION

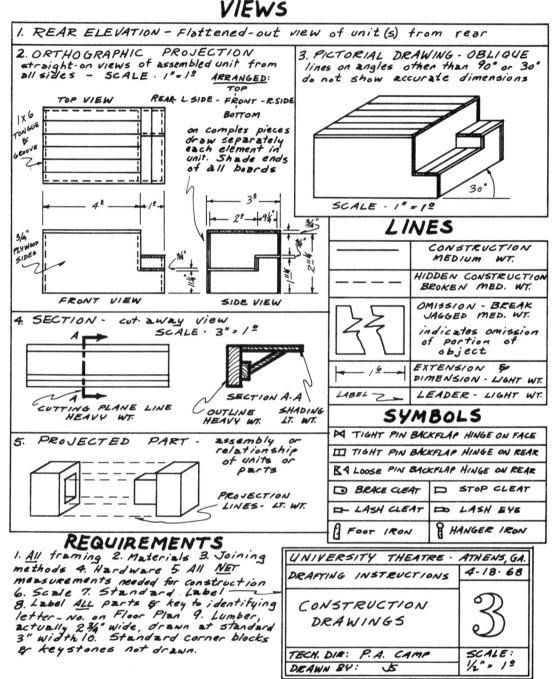

## VIEWS

1. REAR ELEVATION - Flattened-out view of unit(s) from rear

2. ORTHOGRAPHIC PROJECTION
straight-on views of assembled unit from all sides - SCALE · 1"=1° ARRANGED:
TOP
REAR - L. SIDE - FRONT - R. SIDE
BOTTOM
on complex pieces draw separately each element in unit. Shade ends of all boards

TOP VIEW
1X6 TONGUE & GROOVE
3/4" PLYWOOD SIDES
FRONT VIEW
SIDE VIEW

3. PICTORIAL DRAWING - OBLIQUE
lines on angles other than 90° or 30° do not show accurate dimensions
SCALE · 1" = 1°
30°

4. SECTION - cut away view
SCALE · 3" = 1°
A
A
CUTTING PLANE LINE HEAVY WT.
SECTION A·A
OUTLINE HEAVY WT.
SHADING LT. WT.

5. PROJECTED PART - assembly or relationship of units or parts
PROJECTION LINES - LT. WT.

## LINES

| | |
|---|---|
| ———— | CONSTRUCTION MEDIUM WT. |
| — — — | HIDDEN CONSTRUCTION BROKEN MED. WT. |
| (jagged) | OMISSION - BREAK JAGGED MED. WT. *indicates omission of portion of object* |
| ⊢—1°—⊣ | EXTENSION & DIMENSION - LIGHT WT. |
| LABEL | LEADER - LIGHT WT. |

## SYMBOLS

| | |
|---|---|
| ⋈ TIGHT PIN BACKFLAP HINGE ON FACE | |
| ⊞ TIGHT PIN BACKFLAP HINGE ON REAR | |
| ⋉ LOOSE PIN BACKFLAP HINGE ON REAR | |
| ▱ BRACE CLEAT | ▭ STOP CLEAT |
| ▱ LASH CLEAT | ▱ LASH EYE |
| ▯ FOOT IRON | ⎆ HANGER IRON |

## REQUIREMENTS

1. All framing 2. Materials 3. Joining methods 4. Hardware 5. All NET measurements needed for construction 6. Scale 7. Standard Label 8. Label ALL parts & key to identifying letter-no. on Floor Plan 9. Lumber, actually 2¾" wide, drawn at standard 3" width 10. Standard corner blocks & keystones not drawn.

| UNIVERSITY THEATRE · ATHENS, GA. | |
|---|---|
| DRAFTING INSTRUCTIONS | 4-18-68 |
| CONSTRUCTION DRAWINGS | 3 |
| TECH. DIR: P. A. CAMP | SCALE: ½" = 1° |
| DRAWN BY: JS | |

Plate 32. *CONSTRUCTION DRAWING GUIDE: Views, lines, symbols, and requirements for construction drawings.*

drawings are the front and rear elevations, detail drawings, section views, orthographic projections, and pictorial drawings. Plate 32 is a guideline sheet for construction drawings, giving the lines, symbols, types of drawings, and a detailed list of requirements.

Plate 33 shows front elevations drafted for *Lu Ann...* Note the careful dimensioning of all elements and the use of enlargements to clarify portions of the drawing. The rear elevation shows the back, or construction side, of the units and is used by the carpenters. It indicates the exact size, shape,

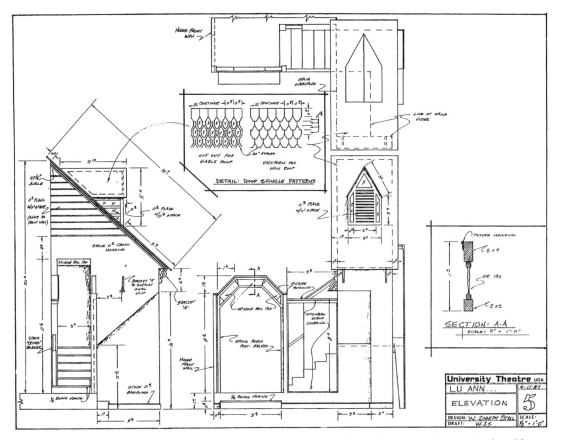

Plate 33. *FRONT ELEVATIONS: One of a number of pages of front elevations showing in detail how a portion of the setting for* Lu Ann... *should look when completed.*

Elevation drawings are the principal means of describing the setting to the construction crew. An elevation is a scale view of the setting flattened out and divided into the construction units. It shows the exact size and shape of each unit, as well as any openings or other constructed elements attached to the unit. The *front elevation* presents the face of the units and is used primarily by the painters. It includes all of the painted detail drawn to scale and is very often colored. When not colored, it must be accompanied by paint samples and instructions as to the specific painting techniques to be used. It must be complete enough to serve as a detailed guide for the painters.

and placement of all framing members, the methods of constructing openings and unusual structures, and the means by which the units are to be fastened together and supported. Flats are usually made from lumber designated as 1″ x 3″; however, the actual measurements are ¾″ by 2¾″. This discrepancy is not usually indicated on the elevations—the lumber is drawn a full 3″ width. The position and type of all hardware to be used is illustrated, and notations are included to make clear any unusual construction methods or materials. If the means of joining the framing members are standard in that particular shop (*i.e.*, the use of corner blocks and keystones) and the standard method is to be followed for the units in the drawing, then the exact means of joining may be omitted, as they have been in Plate 33, which shows rear elevations for a production of *The Night of the Iguana.*

The remaining types of drawings are used to

ject. This technique involves the systematic arrangement of a number of drawings, each shows one specific view of the object. Together, these individual views can provide a complete picture of the object. The views most often used are the top, front and side views, illustrated in Plate 35, which details

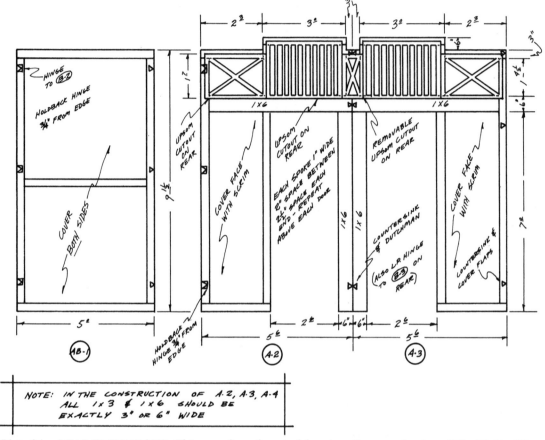

Plate 34. *REAR ELEVATIONS: This page from the set of drawings for a production of* The Night of the Iguana *shows exactly how this portion is to be constructed and joined. Careful dimensioning and additional notations make clear to the carpenters the desires of the designer.*

explain or clarify more complicated scenic units or methods of construction. The *detail* drawing is an enlarged view of a unit, or a portion of a unit, and is used to depict what might be unclear because of its small size in an elevation drawing. Elevations are usually drawn to a scale of $\frac{1}{2}$" = 1'0". Details are drawn to such scales as 1" = 1'0", 3" = 1'0", or even life size. A *section* drawing is a cut-away view showing the inside of an object. It is used to clarify interior construction or exterior contours of an object. Plate 35 shows a detail drawing and a section drawing used for *Night of the Iguana.*

*Orthographic projection* is a method of describing fully the shape and size of a three-dimensional ob-

the construction of the wagon unit for a production of *Mother Courage.* This type of drawing presents accurate information about all necessary sides of the unit, yet it may be very difficult for the beginner (or even the experienced hand, on some occasions) to visualize the unit as a whole. In this case, the designer has included research sketches to help illustrate the desired result. In other cases, *Pictorial Drawings*, which are three-dimensional draftings of scenic units, may be included to supplement the orthographic projection—or sometimes as the only method for describing a particular element.

Shows which require any degree of detailed scene painting call for *Paint Elevations*, which give to the scenic artist a clear idea of the color and techniques to be used in painting the scenery. An example of a paint elevation is shown in Plate 36. Such elevations are usually accompanied by paint chips which show all the principal colors to be mixed for the show.

sioned sketches, since he will always be on hand to explain the sketches to his co-workers. If, on the other hand, he turns the job of construction over to a master carpenter or technical director, then he must provide com-

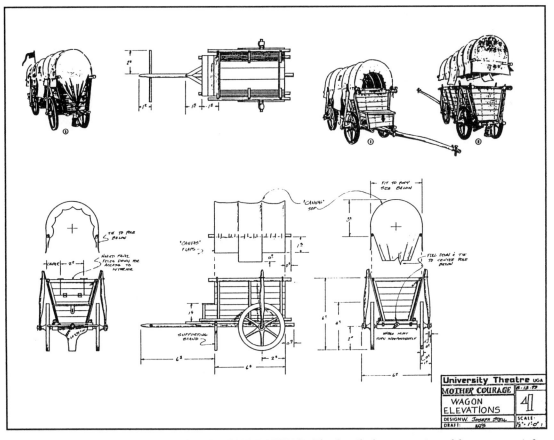

Plate 35. *ORTHOGRAPHIC PROJECTION DRAWING: The detailed construction of the wagon unit for a production of* Mother Courage *is shown by means of the multiple views of orthographic projection. Research sketches have been included for additional clarification.*

In order to make clear and accurate construction drawings, a designer must have a good understanding of drafting techniques. The Bibliography includes several books on drafting in general and one book on stage drafting in particular. These would greatly aid the serious designer in the improvement of his technique. In the meantime, study the illustrations provided in this chapter and see if you can determine the materials and methods of construction indicated in the drawings.

It is not always possible, or necessary, to make a complete set of construction drawings for each setting. When the designer is also in direct charge of the construction, he may forgo scaled drawings in favor of freehand, dimen-

plete and accurate plans. Much depends on the degree of supervision the designer will be expected to assume.

### Construction, Set-up, Dress Rehearsals

Depending upon the size and sophistication of the producing organization, the construction responsibilities of the designer may range from constructing the scenery himself with little or no help, to turning full construction responsibility over to a technical director and merely providing general supervision and advice and answering questions. In the smaller producing companies, the designer usually has a direct hand in the construction; but even if the construction responsibility is delegated to someone

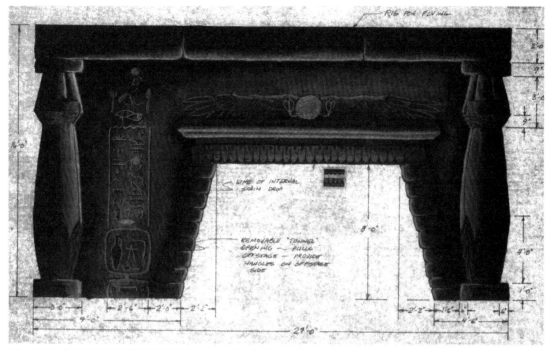

Plate 36.  *PAINT ELEVATIONS: Settings which demand complex scene painting techniques, such as this production of* The Mystery of Irma Vep, *require that the designer prepare detailed Paint Elevations showing the colors and methods to be used to achieve the desired effect.*

Plate 37.  *THE COMPLETED SETTING:  A view of the completed setting for Acts I and III of* Lu Ann Hampton Laverty Oberlander *which clearly shows the porch, roof, and background scenic elements.*

else, he will want to keep a close watch on the progress and realization of his plans. To his dismay, many a designer has found out too late that some construction worker has made a careless error that will mean rebuilding a whole unit, thereby wasting valuable time and materials. Particularly is this likely to happen when the work is being done by unskilled labor, as so often happens in educational or community theatre.

The painting, particularly, requires the designer's attention. Unless he is very fortunate in his helpers, he will find that he is the most skilled painter in the group and must give close supervision and detailed instructions to the members of the painting crew. Often it happens that, either by desire or necessity, he winds up doing the detail painting himself.

Once the setting is constructed and painted, the designer must be available to supervise the set-up, help plan and rehearse any scene shifts, and check during technical and dress rehearsals for any necessary repairs or alterations. The set-up date is usually scheduled a week or ten days prior to the opening of the show. This gives an opportunity for the director and actors to become familiar with the setting and to rehearse the action within its limitations. On the set-up day, the set pieces are brought together in the theatre and secured in position. The sequence for a set-up is generally as follows:

1. Lay out the floor plan of the setting on the stage floor, or at least the key points of the setting.
2. Hang and adjust any scenery that is flown—ceilings, backdrops, etc.
3. Secure any platforms, steps, or ramps in position.
4. Place the wall, door, and window units in position and secure.
5. Secure the backings in position.
6. Add the furniture and set dressing.

Any minor adjustments that are found to be necessary in terms of arrangement, position, and fastening are made during this time. These adjustments are *only minor adjustments*. Major changes should have been made in the planning or early construction stages. Both from the point of view of time and money, it is too late now to make any major revisions.

The designer works with the stage manager and the stage carpenter to plan the shifts for the show. These are worked out into a move-by-move and man-by-man scheme that is then rehearsed until the changes are smooth and rapid. A discussion of the

Plate 38. *ANOTHER VIEW OF THE COMPLETED SETTING: This view of the setting for* Lu Ann... *focuses on the interior portion of the setting. This view and the previous one clearly illustrate the importance of good stage lighting to a completed set design.*

planning of scene shifts is contained in Chapter VI.

During the tech rehearsals and dress rehearsals the designer is on hand to see that all goes well with the scene changes and to check for minor repairs or adjustments in the setting. These will include such things as light leaking through cracks or joints in the scenery, portions of the scenery that were overlooked by the paint crew, floppy canvas that will need to be back-painted, and doors that need to be oiled or adjusted for easy operation. Anything of this sort noted by the designer or director during a rehearsal should be corrected before the next rehearsal, so that by opening night the setting will be fully ready, and the designer will be free to await nervously the audience reaction to his latest creation. Plates 37 and 38 show the completed setting for Acts I and III of *Lu Ann Hampton Laverty Oberlander*.

This general procedure for designing applies to all settings. However, lest the beginning designer be completely discouraged at being confronted with this array of drawings, let me repeat that they are not always necessary—particularly not in a small operation. What is necessary is careful preplanning and organization to eliminate costly last-minute changes and additions. Even though all the scenic units may not be specified in terms of detailed construction drawings, the designer must know how many and what kind of units are necessary for each setting. If he knows this, can clearly depict his ideas for the director, and can succeed in getting the units constructed and painted to conform to his ideas, he will be able to meet his responsibilities as a designer. Construction drawings are an additional means of clarifying design ideas and construction procedures and solving difficulties before going into actual construction, but it is not always practical or desirable to spend the time required to produce them. Exceptions to this might be in the case of a stagecraft, design, or shop course in which the design and drawings could be incorporated into a class project.

In the next four chapters specific planning procedures and considerations, as well as construction and painting techniques for various types of settings, will be discussed.

# SECTION II:
# DESIGNING THE ONE-SET SHOW

# chapter IV

# INTERIORS

A majority of the plays produced in the past half-century have used scenery so designed as to give the impression of a realistic room, with all of the walls, doors, windows, furnishings, and decorations we would expect to see there. This type of setting, however, is only a relatively recent development in the overall history of the theatre. For nearly three hundred years, beginning in the 16th century, scenery consisted primarily of a series of painted wings arranged in pairs parallel to the footlights, combined with a painted backdrop upstage and a series of painted borders overhead. Plate 79 illustrates a stylized reconstruction of a setting from this era (see also Plate 39, part A). As a result of the discovery of the principles of perspective drawing, the wings and drops could be painted to give the illusion of vast distance. And they were. It was the heyday of the scenic painter. Interiors and exteriors, Heaven and Hell, palace and dungeon—all were presented in incredibly detailed two-dimensional magnificence by such designers as the Bibienas, Inigo Jones, and Giacomo Torelli, to name a few.

Then, during the 19th century, it was discovered that by turning the wings so that their edges met and formed a solid wall and inserting doors and windows into these walls, a reasonably accurate representation of a room could be obtained. A ceiling was added to replace the painted borders, and the "box setting" was born (See Plate 39, part B). With the advent of Realism and Naturalism in the latter part of the 19th century, as ushered in by such playwrights as Ibsen, Chekhov, Gorki, and Shaw, and such directors as Stanislavsky and Belasco, the painted detail gave way to realistic detail—actual pictures, curtains and decorations; three-dimensional moldings; solid, workable doors and windows; and utilitarian, everyday props. This produced the realistic box-set interior, which remains a predominant form of setting, in spite of recent breakaways from Realism into such byways as

Expressionism, Symbolism, Epic Theatre, and the "Theatre of the Absurd." Plates 39, 40 and 41 are examples of modern, realistic box-set interiors—one a poor urban synagogue, the other a rural southern church.

Today, after designing a seemingly endless succession of interiors, a scene designer may feel as if he had become an interior decorator. However, there is a difference between his creating an interior setting and an interior decorator's designing a room. Although many of the principles used are the same, and the stage designer must have much the same background as the interior decorator, the purposes are entirely different. The interior decorator attempts to create a room, or rooms, in which certain people will feel at home *as long as they live there,* or until they feel inclined to change—he is designing for day-to-day living. The stage designer, on the other hand, seeks to capture not only the personalities of certain characters (which is extremely important) but also the spirit of the particular dramatic circumstances of the play. He is *not* designing for day-to-day living; he is portraying the *moment*—evoking the specific emotional quality of *these* people in *this* situation at *this* time. If he succeeds, the design will have an intrinsic character that will make it totally unsuitable for any other play.

To achieve this, the designer must completely immerse himself in the people, the place, and the situation. Out of this immersion will come the dramatic image, distilled from all the information, ideas, feelings, and visual impressions he has absorbed from the script, the director, and his research. He must, in addition, take into account certain specific problems, requirements, and considerations of the realistic interior setting.

### SPECIAL PROBLEMS, REQUIREMENTS, AND CONSIDERATIONS

Over and above the dramatic and aesthetic requirements mentioned in Chapter I, the

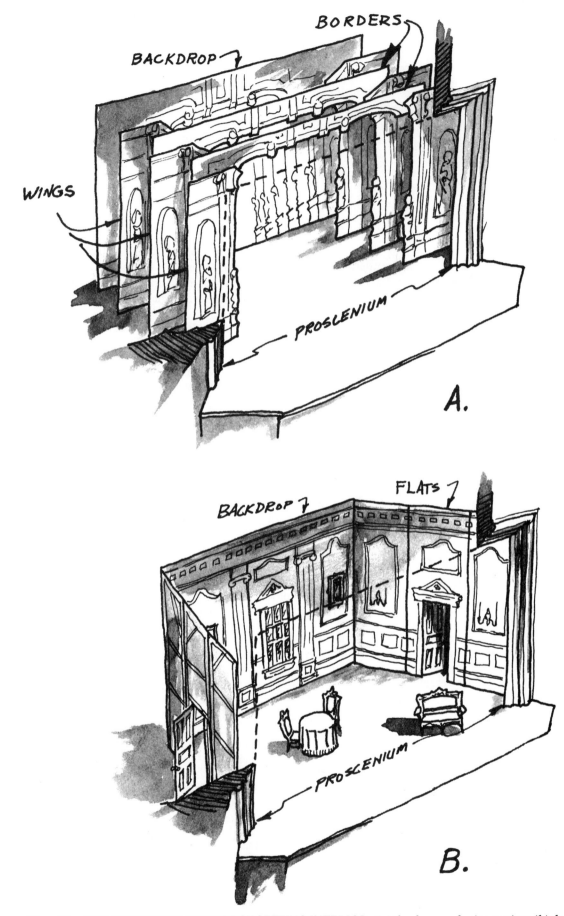

Plate 39. *THE EVOLUTION OF THE BOX SETTING INTERIOR: (a) the drop-and-wing setting; (b) the wings turned in to form walls.*

realistic interior setting must meet a number of other demands necessary to create the illusion of "reality."

1. *The elements of the setting must be so arranged as to give the impression of an architecturally realistic room of the proper period.* Walls, doors, windows, stairs, arches, paneling, molding, rafters, lighting, heating, and plumbing must all be positioned in a structurally feasible manner. Fireplaces must have allowances for the necessary chimneys; walls must

*room is located.* The relationship of this room to the other areas of the building must be made evident through the arrangement of the elements of the room and the placement of proper backings behind windows and doors. It should be clear where each door leads and, not only that, each door should be so placed that it could logically open to that area in the overall plan of the building. It is unlikely, for instance, that a door to a hallway would be found on the same wall as a window through which can

Plate 40. *A REALISTIC BOX-SET INTERIOR: Much of the effectiveness of a realistic interior setting rests in careful attention to architectural detail combined with appropriate furniture and set properties. Note the detailed attention paid to those items in this setting for* The Tenth Man *designed by David Hays for the Broadway Production at the Booth Theatre, NYC.*

have thickness; paneling and molding must be realistically arranged; provisions must be made for lighting and heating of the proper period (electricity and central heating are, after all, fairly recent innovations); stairs need banisters and space enough to reach their supposed destination (they must *appear* to reach the proper level, even if they do not actually do so in the setting). In addition, all of the architectural elements should be appropriate to the particular place and period.

2. *The setting should provide a clear impression of the whole building in which the*

be seen an exterior. Fireplaces and windows should be considered in the same manner. Are they placed where they ordinarily would be found in a room of that sort in a building of that type and period? It becomes obvious that before a designer can realistically design a single room he must have a clear idea of the organization and arrangement of the building in which the room is situated. It may even be necessary to draw a floor plan of the entire building in order to fully understand the arrangement.

3. *Adequate and appropriate offstage mask-*

*ing and space must be provided.* Areas behind windows, doors, and above walls (if there is no ceiling on the setting) must be masked to prevent the audience's seeing backstage areas, equipment, and personnel. These backings should be indicative of the area into which the windows or door supposedly open. In addition, adequate space must be left for actors awaiting an entrance, for the placement of lighting instruments to light the backings, and for the actors to cross from one side of the stage to

in order to achieve variety in his movement and seating of the actors; and he will be grateful for any others you can manage to squeeze in. The furniture should be arranged, however, in a manner that is logical to the room and to interior decorating principles. Sofas, for instance, are usually placed parallel or perpendicular to a wall (perpendicularly, they may serve as partial room dividers), and chairs are placed in an arrangement with the sofa that will provide comfortable seating for conversation.

Plate 41.  *A REALISTIC BOX-SET INTERIOR: Although the country-church interior of this setting is fully realistic, a somewhat stylized portal is used to suggest the exterior architecture of the church and provide masking for the wings.* Smoke on the Mountain, *produced by the McCarter Theatre, Princeton, NJ. Scenery by the author.*

the other out of sight of the audience (*cross-over*).

4. *The furniture must be "open" to the audience, must form conversation areas, and must allow adequate space for movement.* To be "open" to the audience, chairs, sofas, and other seating units must be so placed that an actor sitting on any one of them is at least partly facing the audience—in profile at the very minimum. At the same time, the seating should be arranged into at least two conversation areas—areas in which two or more persons can sit and converse comfortably. A director needs a minimum of two conversation areas

Fireplaces create central conversation areas. Furniture is grouped around them—rarely facing away from them. When a fireplace is on an upstage wall this can create a difficulty in arrangement, which might be solved by arranging chairs or loveseats facing each other on either side of the fireplace and angled just enough so that the occupants can be slightly facing the audience.

Other considerations in arranging furniture are: furniture rarely blocks paths between doors; space must be allowed for free movement around and between furniture (a minimum of two feet and preferably three or more feet between objects); important entrances should not be blocked by furniture from audience view; and it is wise to avoid placing tall furniture (such as lamps and highbacked chairs) downstage where they might conceal part of an actor upstage. At all times, avoid cluttering the stage area with nonessential furniture. It is vastly more important that the actors have space to move than it is to fill the stage with furniture.

Obviously, the fulfilling of these four requirements can present some problems for a designer. The first problem is that he must fill all of the requirements within only three walls —the fourth wall being occupied by the proscenium arch and the audience. All doors, windows, arches, stairs, and fireplaces must somehow be fitted into these three walls. At times, this can be a major engineering feat. At the same time, however, these same three walls can become very dull and uninteresting if they remain simply three straight walls. Variety must be added in the way of jogs (narrow flats used to make a break in an otherwise flat surface), angles, alcoves, steps and levels, or slanted ceilings. However, in adding these interest features, the designer must keep in mind that any architectural change or addition he makes must be logical and feasible within the limitations of that particular kind of room.

From the aesthetic point of view, the designer finds himself handicapped in the decorative and expressive use of the elements of design. The use of line, mass, texture, and color is limited to the architectural and decorative realities of the place and period. And yet he must somehow provide the proper mood and atmosphere for the play. Sounds impossible, doesn't it? Actually, it is this very multiplicity of requirements, limitations, and problems that makes the designing of an interior setting interesting and challenging and keeps it from falling into the realm of repetitious interior decoration. Successful interiors require as much information as possible from the playscript, director and other designers. There is specific data the designer should expect to learn from each of these sources. In the following sections, we will discuss this information, how to find it, and how to use it. To learn how, we will analyze, research, and evolve a setting for the play *Lawyer Lincoln* by Betty Smith and Chase Webb.

Since that script is not immediately available, however, we will present here a summary of the basic information.

*Lawyer Lincoln* occurs on a spring evening in 1849, in Sis Beaseley's boarding house in a small town in Illinois. This was a time in Lincoln's life when he traveled over the Illinois Circuit, spending his days arguing cases and his nights joking and skylarking.

The setting is described as a "large cheerful room which has been made to serve as both living and dining room." There is a door to the outside, a door to the kitchen (through which the parlor may be reached), and an exit to upstairs rooms. There is a fireplace with a "blazing log fire." The furniture called for includes a three-legged stool near the fireplace, a high-backed settee (or "settle"), a long boarding table with two straight chairs upstage and a narrow, backless bench downstage, a sideboard, an old-fashioned chest, and a couple of other chairs scattered about the stage.

As the play opens, Sis Beaseley is discovered alone onstage. As she moves around the stage, a face appears in an upstage window. Startled, she runs to look out the window while, behind her, the outside door opens and her bashful son Nate Beaseley enters. Soon young and pretty Keenie Jackson enters (also from outdoors), and we learn that Nate is sweet on Keenie and wants to marry her. Unfortunately, he cannot afford the honeymoon which Keenie insists she must have—and which Nate's handsome rival, Curly Allen, can afford. Shortly after Keenie leaves and Nate goes out to slop the hogs, Judge Davis and Lawyer Craig come down from upstairs.

Judge Craig is annoyed by Lincoln's apparent lack of respect for his profession—he would rather be swapping yarns at the stable than spending time with his fellow attorneys. When Lincoln arrives, he is taken to task by the Judge for "wasting time" with his continual anecdotes and jokes. At the same time Sis seeks Abe's advice on "how a feller can get hisself up to the altar" with the girl of his (and his mother's) choice. Intrigued by the problems of young romance, Lincoln makes a bet with Judge Craig: if Abe succeeds in getting Nate to propose and Keenie to accept, the Judge is never again to lecture him about wasting time; if he loses, Abe will devote all his time to his profession and give up his tale telling.

Lincoln soon arranges a "payin' job" for Nate—as a juryman. After Abe exits to arrange a meeting between Nate and Keenie and Sis enters the kitchen, the Judge sets about to win the bet. He admonishes Nate that, as a juror, it is strictly against the law for him to talk to anyone at all. Nate, unversed in legal matters and fearful lest he lose his new-found job, agrees to remain completely silent at all times.

Abe returns with Keenie, her mother and several other ladies, one of whom is a "spare, eager, man-hunting spinster." Judge Davis and Lawyer Craig realize that they are in danger of being accosted by the spinster and attempt to escape up the stairs, but are stopped by Lincoln. After some verbal interaction, the ladies exit through the kitchen to the parlor, and the Judge and lawyer make their belated exit upstairs. This leaves Lincoln onstage with Nate and Keenie.

During the ensuing scene Lincoln attempts to moderate between Nate who stubbornly refuses to speak and Keenie *who will accept nothing less than a full spoken proposal from Nate. There is a great deal of jockeying for position during this scene—both physically and verbally. Lincoln is puzzled by Nate's refusal to speak and attempts to act as a surrogate for both parties. Finally, when Lincoln convinces Keenie that she should come over and kiss him (Lincoln), Nate can stand it no longer and breaks his silence, from which Lincoln discovers the trick that Judge Davis has attempted. While Nate and Keenie kiss enthusiastically, the remainder of the cast appears onstage. In celebration of the happy occasion, the full cast joins in singing with an optional folk dance. At the end, after all the others have left, Judge Craig admits defeat and promises never to criticize Lincoln again—if Abe will help him get rid of an "extremely jealous widow back in Springfield."*

These, then, are the principal elements and actions of the play. Our analysis will help to determine specific elements which will have a direct bearing on the scenic design. First, though, we will discuss script analysis in general.

READING THE SCRIPT

From the script we must gain the answers to the following questions:

*General:*
What is the style of the play?
What is the mood of the play?
What is the theme of the play?
What mental image or feelings did you derive of the setting?

*Setting:*
In what country and region of that country does the play occur?
In what period (year) does it occur? What season? What time of day? Do any of these change during the play?
What sort of room does the setting represent? In what sort of building?
How many doors are required? Where do they lead? Is there any special action relating to them?
How many windows, if any, are needed? Does anyone look out of them? Must anything (anyone) be seen through them?
What furniture is necessary? How many must sit at one time? What else is needed in the way of tables, cupboards, desks, bars, etc.?
What are the other setting requirements? Fireplace? Stairs? Levels? Balcony? Built-in cabinets, bars, or bookcases?
Are there any other clues as to the setting, its arrangement, or its contents?

*Characters:*
How many people in the play?
How many people live in this room? What type and relationship? Bachelor(s)? Husband and wife? Children? How many and how old?
Who is the dominant character? Who is most likely to have had the greatest influence on the decoration or use of the room? Who else might affect the contents or decoration of the room?
What is their financial status?
What is their intellectual level?
What are their backgrounds? Education? Culture? Environment?
To what do their tastes and hobbies run? Books? Records? Hunting? Fishing? Sports? Politics? Parties? Bright or muted colors? A quiet chat by the fireside or beer and poker with the boys?
What are their personal characteristics? Neat? Fastidious? Sloppy? Crude? Happy? Melancholy? Brave? Cowardly? Moody? Reticent? Gregarious?

It is not always possible to answer all of these questions (particularly those relating to character), but it is necessary to answer as many as possible. Nor will all the answers be contained directly in the script. Much will have to be deduced from small, hidden "clues," or by reading "between the lines." A designer must be part detective and part psychologist in order to obtain all the answers he needs. This will be illustrated, I think, when we begin our study of *Lawyer Lincoln.*

Within the script there are three sources of information: the opening description of characters and setting, the stage directions, and the dialogue.

1. *Opening Description:* Bernard Shaw, Eugene O'Neill, and Tennessee Williams often provide page-long, detailed descriptions of the setting, which must be reasonably faithfully followed. Shakespeare and Federico García Lorca give such directions as "a room in a castle," "a hall," "another hall," or "a yellow room," which do not offer much information. Other playwrights fall somewhere between these two extremes. This opening description usually gives some idea as to the general setting—arrangement, number of doors and windows, placement of furniture, and essential properties. It is well to take these descriptions with a strong grain of salt until you have had an opportunity to judge the needs of the play in relation to the limitations of your particular stage and the demands of your director. The opening

descriptions are probably the least reliable source of information about the setting, but may provide a good introduction to the characters in the play.

2. *Stage Directions:* Stage directions provide information as to the action of the play—who does what, when. Again, these may be detailed or skimpy, depending on the particular playwright. Certainly, action necessary to the plot or meaning of the play will be indicated in the stage directions—burning the incriminating papers, fighting the deadly duel, discovering the body, fainting, kissing, or even entering and exiting. Beyond these essential actions, however, the director is quite likely to ignore the stage directions and substitute his own action. For that reason, the designer should pay really close attention only to those stage directions that materially affect the action, meaning, or outcome of the play.

The actions contained therein can dictate much about the arrangement of the setting, particularly in relation to doors, windows, and fireplaces. Does one character exit while another enters from a different source? The doors should be situated on separate, or opposite, walls. Is there a "grand" entrance? It works better upstage center. An important exit? One of the side walls is the best location for the door. And then there are the innumerable variations: someone enters without being seen by persons onstage; someone onstage is hidden to another person entering; and so on *ad infinitum.*

Windows and fireplaces assume varying locations depending on their usage. If an actor must play a long scene looking out a window, then the window had best be on one of the side walls so he can play the scene with some portion of his face turned toward the audience. If someone or something is to be seen through the window, however, it must be on the upstage wall so that the audience has a better chance of seeing. If a fireplace is to be used for an important piece of action, such as the burning of papers, it should be on one of the side walls so that the actor is close to the audience and can face them as he performs the business. However, if he must conceal what he is doing, the fireplace works best on the upstage wall.

Other things to watch out for are fights, dances, chases, and others scenes requiring a great deal of space; dining-table scenes, which require careful planning and arrangement of the table and chairs (this is always a problem, but round tables or tables placed at an angle to the proscenium make it easier for a director to position his actors without winding up with a "Last Supper" tableau); and special tricks or devices, such as hidden panels, falling ceilings or walls, or elevators and dumbwaiters. In addition, the information provided in stage directions concerning the reactions of various characters to specific situations may provide a meaningful clue to the personalities of these characters.

3. *Dialogue:* This is probably your most reliable source of information. The characters will speak about themselves, about the others in the play, and about the setting. Much can be learned about the personalities of the characters and about the setting in this manner. People will talk about going outside, to the kitchen, to the hall, or the bedroom; they may speak about "grandpa's portrait over the fireplace" (telling us about the portrait and the fireplace at the same time); they may complain about the uncomfortable, straight-backed chair; or they may make some other direct comment about the room, its furnishing, or its decorations. Search the script carefully for these spoken clues to the setting, for as surely as you get careless you will paint paneling on the walls and learn too late that the leading character makes constant reference to the *wallpaper* pattern. It only takes one such oversight to make a designer scrutinize the script with a magnifying glass.

Using these sources of information, let us now answer for *Lawyer Lincoln* those questions established in the beginning of this section.

*What is the style of the play?* Basically realistic, with no deviations from realistically feasible or logical situations or actions.

*What is the mood of the play?* Light, warm, comic, somewhat suspenseful, but with no tragic or strongly dramatic overtones.

*What is the theme of the play?* How about, "Love and Lincoln conquer all," although this sort of play relies more on the humor of the situation than on an underlying theme.

*What mental image or feelings did you derive of the setting?* Coziness, warmth, cheerfulness, simplicity, wood beams and stone fireplace, frontier rusticity (this has to be a personal reaction for each designer; yours may be entirely different).

*In what country and region of that country does the play occur?* A small town in the state of Illinois, U.S.A.

*In what period (year) does it occur? What*

*season? What time of day? Do any of these change during the play?* An evening in the spring of 1849. No change.

*What sort of room does the setting represent? In what sort of building?* A combination living-dining room in a boarding house.

*How many doors are required? Where do they lead? Is there any special action relating to them?* Three doors or entrances: one to the kitchen, one to the outside, and one to upstairs. When the ladies of the Harmony Class arrive, Judge Davis and Lawyer Craig attempt to bolt upstairs, which means that these two openings should not be too close together. Later, the judge and lawyer are still attempting to go upstairs and are detained by Miss Sophrony while the other ladies exit through the kitchen. For best movement purposes, these openings should be on opposite sides of the room. Even later, Nate moves from the settee toward the kitchen door while Keenie goes from the settee to the outside door and calls Lincoln, who stops Nate before he gets out the kitchen door. This requires that the settee, kitchen door, and outside door be so arranged that Keenie can go from the settee to the outside door and get Lincoln before Nate can move from the settee out the kitchen door.

*How many windows, if any, are needed? Does anyone look out of them? Must anything (anyone) be seen through them?* One window, through which Sis Beaseley (and the audience) must see a face peering. Then, while Sis is looking out the window, Nate comes in the outside door behind her back. The window must be on the upstage wall and there must be space between the window and the outside door so that Nate will not walk directly into Sis when he enters.

*What furniture is necessary? How many must sit at one time?* At one time, Judge Davis, Lawyer Craig, Sis, and Lincoln are all onstage simultaneously. During this scene any or all of them may sit, which means that there must be provision for at least four people to sit. A settee is mentioned in the script; a table on which Nate eats is necessary (with benches or seats of some sort, obviously); and a cupboard from which Sis obtains eating utensils must be provided. Anything else is extra.

*What are the other setting requirements?* A fireplace is mentioned, but is not absolutely essential to the action. The stairs to upstairs seem to open directly out of the room, rather than from a hallway. Is it possible that the stairs could come directly into the room itself with no door between? This is something to be answered when we begin our research.

*Are there any other clues as to the setting, its arrangement, or its contents?* At one point Sis indicates that the parlor can be reached from this room only through the kitchen, giving rise to a question about the overall arrangement of the house. Where is this room situated within the house so that its only connection with the parlor, or with the rest of the house, is through the kitchen? We must learn about the arrangement of rooms in houses of this period in order to answer this question.

*How many people in the play?* Nine (an important consideration, because large-cast plays require more open stage area and seating facilities).

*How many people live in this room? What type and relationship?* Two people actually live in the house—Sis Beaseley and her son, Nate. Evidently her husband is dead, since we learn nothing about him and he does not appear in the play.

*Who is the dominant character? Who is most likely to have had the greatest influence on the decoration or use of the room? Who else might affect the contents or decoration of the room?* Lincoln is, of course, the dominant character in the play, but he is only a visitor in the house. Sis Beaseley, being the homemaker, would be the dominant influence on the room. Nate, because he also resides permanently in the house, would probably have contributed to the contents or decoration of the room.

*What is their financial status?* They could probably be considered to have a middle-class income for that era. If they were rich, they would not be likely to be taking boarders; but if they were poverty-stricken, they would hardly have a judge and lawyers as boarders.

*What is their intellectual level?* This is hard to judge from the script alone, but they would seem to be about average in this respect. One would guess that they prefer many activities over reading or philosophical discussions. Notice, also, Nate's naiveté about jury duty.

*What are their backgrounds?* Not much is indicated in the script. To form any definite conclusions on this, we will have to rely on our research.

*To what do their tastes and hobbies run?* Sis would seem to be involved with household and church-related activities. She probably enjoys cooking and housekeeping chores and is the faithful attender of all the church social and work activities, the quilting bees, and bake sales. Nate would probably be interested in farm affairs and activities and, for recreation, enjoy hunting and fishing and "gallivanting" with the other young men of the town; although he should by no means be considered a "hell-raiser."

*What are their personal characteristics?* Sis appears to be the warm, eternally cheerful, calmly efficient type of woman whom everybody thinks of as an aunt. She would be a neat, tidy person who likes to have around her evidences of the people she loves—pictures and mementos. Nate is a cheerful, hard-working, but shy young man who probably has the tendency of all young men to strew the room with his belongings.

Such information as this is essential to the creation of an effective setting for the play. The next step would ordinarily be consultation with the director to verify our conclusions and seek his ideas. We have no specific director for this show, however, so, having discussed the general requirements of a director in Chapter III, we will move into the next source of information: research.

### RESEARCHING THE PLAY

From researching the play, just as from reading the script, we must find the answers to several specific questions relating to the place and period in which the play is set.

What would be the historical and social environment of the type of people included in the play?

What would be their background?

What are the architectural characteristics of the type of building(s) indicated in the play?

What are the arrangements of the interiors of these buildings?

What are the characteristics of the rooms of the buildings? How do the walls, doors, windows, ceilings, floors, and stairs look?

What type of furniture is used? How is it arranged? What are its particular characteristics?

What conclusions may be drawn that apply to the particular persons or places in the play?

As mentioned in the previous chapter, if the people, place, and time are not included in our own exeriences, we must learn as much as we can about them through written and visual sources. Prime sources for information about the historical, social, and environmental conditions of the time and place are such books as

histories, travelogues, and personal diaries or biographies of people who lived in that time or place. Good reference books for visual research on interiors are generalized sources, such as: *An Illustrated History of Furnishing* by Mario Praz (George Braziller, Inc., New York, 1964); *Three Centuries of Furniture in Color* by H.D. Molesworth and John Kenworthy-Browne (The Viking Press, New York, 1972); *Interior Design and Decoration* by Sherrill Whiton (J.B. Lippincott Co., New York, in constantly updated editions); and *The Grammar of Ornament* by Owen Jones (Studio Editions, London, 1986). Also, such wide-ranging magazines as *American Heritage, Horizon, National Geographic, Smithsonian,* and *Historic Preservation* (from The National Trust for Historic Preservation) can be of extremely important value to a designer. Facsimile re-publications of turn-of-the-century of *Sears Roebuck Catalogues* and *Montgomery Ward Catalogues* and others are prime reference sources for the everyday articles of early Americans. Recent decades have produced an astounding variety of truly excellent sources on both general and specific periods and locales. Many of these are available at discount bookstores for *very* reasonable prices. And, of course, you will find that many of these excellent titles are also available at most good libraries.

In addition to such general reference volumes as have been mentioned, the designer will want to consult sources relating directly to the room, building, period, and region specified in the play. In researching *Lawyer Lincoln,* for instance, the following books provided much important information:

*The Story of Illinois,* Theodore C. Pease, Chicago, A. C. McClurg & Co., 1925.

*Growing Up With Southern Illinois, 1820 to 1861,* from the memoirs of Daniel H. Brush, edited by Milo M. Quaife, Chicago, Lakeside Press, 1944.

*Illinois in the Fifties,* Charles B. Johnson, Champaign, Ill., Flanigan-Pearson Co., 1918.

*Abraham Lincoln, The Prairie Years* (Vol. 1 of three volumes), Carl Sandburg, New York, Dell Publishing Co., Inc., 1960.

*Old Illinois Houses,* John Drury, Chicago, Illinois State Historical Society, 1948.

*The Homes of America,* Ernest Pickering, New York, Thomas Y. Crowell Co., 1951.

*The Early American House,* Mary Earle Gould, Rutland, Vermont, Charles E. Tuttle Co., Inc., 1965.

*The Treasure House of Early American Rooms,* John A. H. Sweeney, New York, Viking Press, 1963.

*Early Domestic Architecture of Connecticut,* J. Frederick Kelly, New York, Dover Publications, Inc., 1963. (The relevance of this particular book will be pointed out later.)

Using such sources as these, we can now answer the research questions about *Lawyer Lincoln* as follows:

*What would be the historical and social environment of the type of people included in the play?* At the time of the play, Illinois was a young state whose inhabitants were just

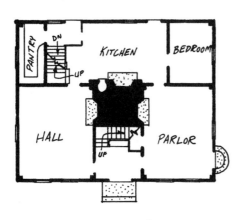

PLAN A.

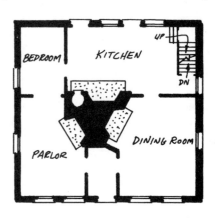

PLAN B.

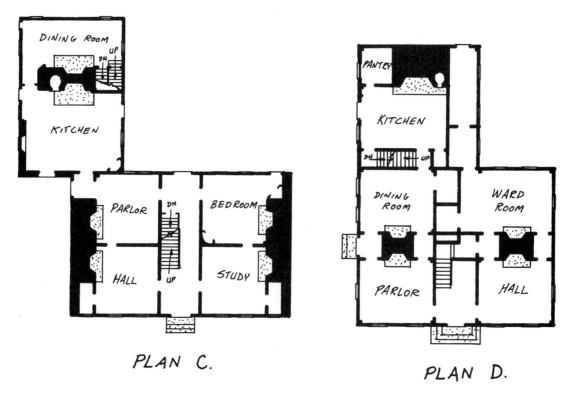

PLAN C.

PLAN D.

Plate 42. *RESEARCH SKETCHES: Floor plans of early New England houses.*

beginning to develop roots after the first dangers and labors of settlement. Although the town involved in the play is a county seat (otherwise court would not be held there), it would still be very small and rural, with all of the principal business activities being related to farming and the social activities predominantly related to the church. A town of this sort would not have an overabundance of stores, and the ones there were would be primarily stocked with staples: food, clothing, and farm equipment. Such things as furniture would probably either be constructed by each homemaker or have been brought with the family when it originally arrived.

*What would be their background?* Illinois was settled by people from all of the early states —the southern portion being settled primarily by persons, from the Southeastern states, and the northern settlers coming primarily from Pennsylvania, Ohio, New York, and the New England states. The eastern section of Illinois (where Lincoln rode circuit court) was settled by people from all the regions mentioned; so, since no indication is given in the script, we have our choice as to the background of the Beaseley family. Because available reference material is somewhat more abundant for the New England states, let's assume that they came from that area, where they were probably farmers or storekeepers who saved up enough money for the trek west, carrying whatever they could of household furnishings and belongings. Presumably they would have migrated to Illinois sometime between 1820 and 1830 (when that area was settled) and settled into primitive surroundings that gradually became more civilized as the years passed, the dangers lessened, and more settlers arrived. Sometime during this period, Sis's husband must have died or been killed.

*What are the architectural characteristics of the type of building indicated in the play?* At that time in Illinois history the variety of houses was immense, ranging from the crudest log cabins to veritable mansions. Each settler, when he advanced beyond the log-cabin stage, usually built the same type of house with which he had been familiar prior to migrating west. Because we have decided the Beaseleys migrated from New England, their house would resemble those found in their home state. (Now the relevance of *Early Domestic Architecture of Connecticut* becomes clear.) Those houses were generally simple, two-storied, frame or brick structures with all of the rooms clustered around one or more fireplaces—the only sources of heat in a cold climate. The houses were usually symmetrical in shape and arrangement, although later additions sometimes destroyed this symmetry.

*What are the arrangements of the interiors of these buildings?* Several floor plans of New England houses are illustrated in Plate 42. Notice how the fireplaces very often serve more than one room. Floor plan C illustrates an arrangement that might explain why the parlor can be reached only through the kitchen from the room in the setting—it could be a room in a later addition to the original house. We should also pay attention to the arrangement of stairs; in doing so we find that the stairs often rise out of an individual room— usually occupying a corner of the room.

*What are the characteristics of the rooms of the buildings?* Simplicity is the keynote here. Walls were of plaster or simple paneling. Ceiling beams were often exposed. The fireplace was large, constructed of stone or homemade brick, and very often capped with a heavy mantel. Doors, windows, and moldings were also simple—necessarily so, since they all had to be constructed by hand craftsmen. Plate 43 shows several good sketches of interior elements of the period.

*What type of furniture is used? How is it arranged?* Following our basic assumption concerning the Beaseleys' migrating from New England and bringing much of their household goods with them, we can assume that the furniture would be of an early New England vintage. This furniture was simple but carefully crafted wooden furniture, frequently employing turned arms, legs, and backs. Plate 44 provides a few samples of this type of furniture.

Usually, in a room of the sort described in the play, the furniture was arranged so as to take advantage of the heat of the fireplace. Tables, chairs, and settees were placed as close as possible to the fireplace.

*What conclusions may be drawn that apply to the particular persons or places in the play?* Having chosen to provide our characters with a New England background, we find that the characteristics of the architecture, furniture, and decorations of that place and period coincide quite nicely with our earlier general feelings about the setting. It is entirely possible to stay within the characteristics of the period and still achieve the warmth, coziness, cheerfulness, and simplicity, complete with wood beams,

Plate 43. *RESEARCH SKETCHES: Interior details of early New England houses.*

Plate 44. *RESEARCH SKETCHES: Early American furniture.*

fireplaces, and frontier rusticity originally envisioned. The fireplace should be large and set in the wall between this room and the kitchen so that it can serve both rooms. The stairs should lead directly into the room with no separating door. The architecture and decoration should indicate a rural New England background.

### Planning the Setting

The first step in planning the setting is to decide on the style. This has usually been somewhat predetermined by the script and the discussion with the director, but the final decision is made now. *Lawyer Lincoln*, for instance, has been determined to be basically realistic, but the setting could move in several directions. It could be a completely realistic setting, "a slice of life", like that shown in Plate 40. It could also be designed using some aspect of stylization which allow exaggeration of one or more design elements in order to express a stronger comic flavor. It can be further simplified in one of the ways to be discussed in Chapter IX. For the sake of this particular discussion, however, let us say that we want *Lawyer Lincoln* staged in a full-stage realistic setting.

We have already found a dramatic image that seems to be feasible—the simple coziness of a fireplace and wooden beams—so it is time to start putting something on paper. The question now arises, "Which do you work on first—floor plan or rendering?" This must be answered by each designer for himself. In designing an interior, I usually sketch out a number of floor-plan ideas and then sketch a perspective view of each plan to see if it looks well. That might be a good procedure to follow until you can find a method of your own.

Before drawing out any floor plans, however, let us set down a brief summary of the information we have found about the arrangement of the room.

1. The window must be on the rear wall, which means that the outside door should probably also be on that wall.
2. The fireplace is shared by this room and the kitchen, so it and the kitchen door should be on the same wall.
3. There must be space, or separation, between the outside door and the stairs.
4. There must be space, or separation, between the kitchen door and the stairs.
5. There must be space between the outside door and the window.
6. The seating for Nate and Keenie should be near the outside door and some distance from the kitchen door.
7. There should be a dining table with seats, a cupboard, and some other form of seating.
8. There should be one or more oil lamps, or other means of artificial lighting, since the action occurs during the evening.

Using this information, together with the information we have gleaned from research, we now make several thumbnail sketches of possible arrangements of the room. Plate 45 shows several sketches of this type. Let us analyze each of them and see how well they meet our requirements.

Sketch No. 1 is based directly on the house arrangement labeled "Plan C" in Plate 43. It presents a visually interesting aspect of the room—a corner—that takes us away from the essentially dull three basic walls of a box setting. However, it would not meet the requirements of the play very well. Keenie and Nate would be likely to use the settee by the fireplace for their scene, which places them much too close to the kitchen door. Even if they should use the table and benches, the action in which Keenie calls Lincoln from outside before Nate can depart through the kitchen door would be a near thing. Also, the scene in which the judge and lawyer exit upstairs while the ladies go out into the kitchen would be difficult—both doors being on the same wall making for awkward action here. In this case, the corner setting does not seem to be feasible, although it might work well for some other play.

In Sketch No. 2, the stairs have been moved all the way across the room, and the outside door is placed farther center. The plan is now much more workable for the action of the play. The settee is in a much better position in relation to the outside door and the kitchen door. However, the stairway still presents problems. The stairwell tends to block the outside door from the view of the right side of the audience, and the escape (offstage access) for the stairs is in a bad position. The actors have to go almost up to a full second story before they can be out of the audience view, and this means constructing quite an elaborate platform structure. What would happen if we kept the stairs in the same corner of the setting, but turned them around to face in the other direction?

Sketch No. 3 has done just that, and it presents a much more practicable setting. It also creates a good conversation area around the settee downstage of the stairs. Being set off by the stairs makes this area more intimate than before, which is appropriate for the scene between Nate and Keenie. Incidentally, you might notice that the oil lamp has moved from its position on the table in the two earlier sketches into a hanging position. On the table, it would hide actors upstage of it. This set has a pleas-

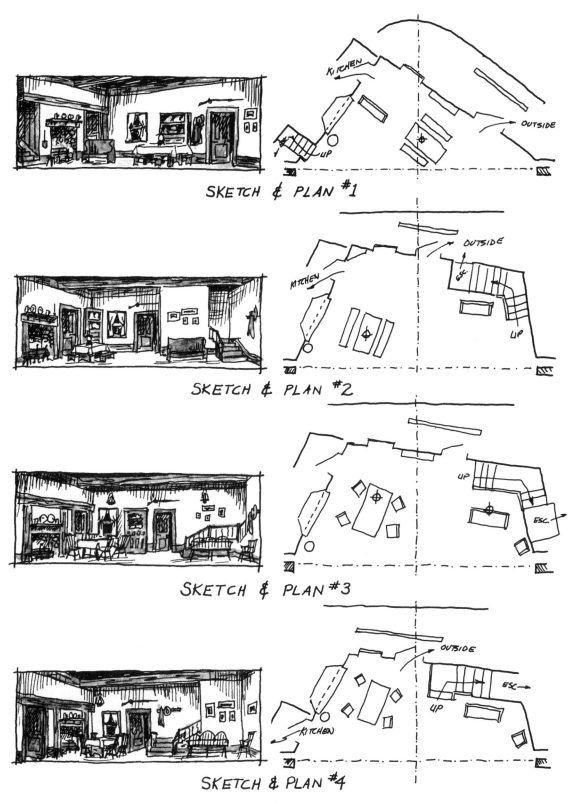

SKETCH & PLAN #1

SKETCH & PLAN #2

SKETCH & PLAN #3

SKETCH & PLAN #4

Plate 45: *THUMBNAIL SKETCHES FOR* LAWYER LINCOLN

ing appearance and seems workable. Are there any problems that would prevent us from using it? On second analysis, we do note one problem. With the entrance to the stairs too near the outside door, there is going to be a bad traffic jam when the Harmony Class ladies enter while the judge and lawyer are trying to go upstairs. Also, all three entrances are now upstage, so anyone exiting has to move upstage to do so. A director might not like this idea, so let's try again.

In Sketch No. 4, the kitchen door has been moved downstage of the fireplace, and the stairs are turned so that they lead downstage, providing a separation between the outside door and the stairs. This also opens up the stair landing as a possible acting area. This seems to be the most workable arrangement yet. There is one problem, however. To achieve this arrangement in the sketch, we have had to omit the cupboard. Still, it may be possible to work the cupboard back in when we draw the floor plan out to scale. If we can work it back in,

then this would seem to be the best choice for a design, so on we go to the scaled floor plan.

First, we draw in to scale the proscenium arch, the proscenium line, and the center line. Allowing space for the main curtain, teaser, tormentors, and first light pipe, we start drawing in the side walls of the setting. These were placed at angles to keep them well within the sightlines, so we will start by drawing in one side wall at an angle that looks workable. The length of the wall is found by marking off the sizes and placement of the structural elements that must be included in the wall. For instance, we know that the kitchen door and the fireplace are in the stage right wall. A door is usually three feet wide and the fireplace, which is larger than normal, would probably be about five feet wide. Allowing 1' to 1½', at the very least, on either side of these items gives us a wall 11' to 14' in length. If we are careful, perhaps we can squeeze a corner cupboard into the upstage corner.

The other walls are worked out in the same

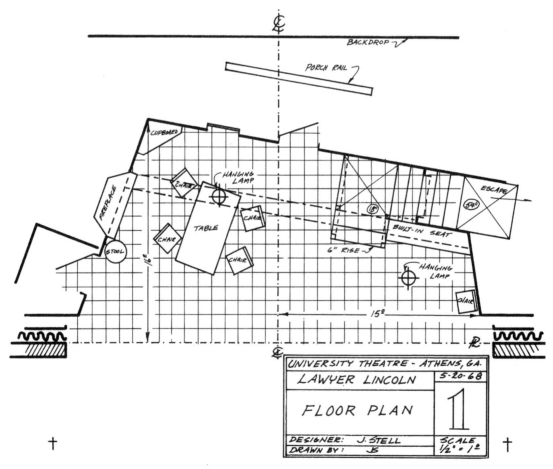

Plate 46: *SCALED FLOOR PLAN FOR* LAWYER LINCOLN

way—putting in the essentials, seeing how much space is left or how much more space is needed, then shifting and adjusting until the arrangement is satisfactory. Other changes may be found necessary. For instance, the settee is found to require a large amount of space. By eliminating it and adding a built-in seat below the stairs, such as we saw in Plate 43, we can salvage a bit of space that can be used for the

this as our dominant line and use the vertical line as a secondary line (standard room construction dictates certain uses of these lines, so we may as well use them to our advantage). We must choose those realistic elements that can be used to accentuate the horizontal or vertical line and then arrange them into a composition in which the horizontal line dominates. Plate 47 shows the result.

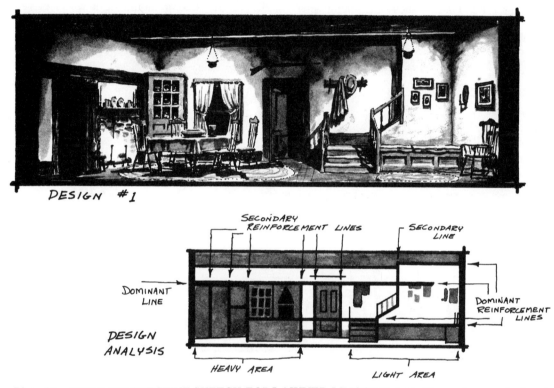

Plate 47. *FIRST PERSPECTIVE SKETCH FOR* LAWYER LINCOLN, *including a chart analyzing the composition.*

corner cupboard. We should also check to be sure we have provided sufficient backing behind doors and windows. The completed floor plan is shown in Plate 46. Now we are ready to develop a more detailed perspective drawing.

It is time now to consider more carefully the elements of composition. The final composition is determined, to a great degree, by the floor plan, so we will have kept the ideas of balance and center of interest in mind while we were working; but now we are primarily concerned with the picture presented to the audience and, consequently, must deal specifically with the elements of composition. What is to be our predominant line? Because of the warm, simple, down-to-earth quality of the play, the use of horizontal line is indicated. We can take

Does it work as a composition? Let's analyze it and see. Referring to the design analysis chart, we see that the horizontal line is, indeed, the dominant line with the vertical line serving as the secondary. Note the way in which this is achieved—through the use of horizontal beams, horizontal elements, and the placement of items on the wall in such a way as to form a horizontal eye movement. Note, also, the way in which the horizontal and vertical are used in a variety of ways to achieve interest, and the inclusion of a few diagonals for additional interest. So we can say that the use of the element of line works in this rendering. What about balance? Is the setting balanced? Here we find a problem. Stage right with its cluster of interesting objects and dark color far outweighs stage left—both in interest value and weight. It looks as if we will have to make some alterations. We need to lessen the weight on stage right and add more weight and interest on stage left without harming the effective use of line already achieved. If we cut down on the heavy beams around the fireplace, make the window smaller, add paneling along the stage-left wall and the wall behind the seat, and alter the wall hangings, perhaps we can achieve a balanced setting. Plate 48 shows the setting after

feeling, we will choose light and warm colors. The wood area should be a warm brown of a medium, rather than dark, value. The walls should be light enough to offer contrast to the wood color, but not white. White is usually a bad choice for walls on stage, because it picks up so much light that the actors appear to be almost silhouettes. The walls should be dark enough that the actors can be seen in front of them—at least as dark as skin tone. The walls for our setting should be a warm beige,

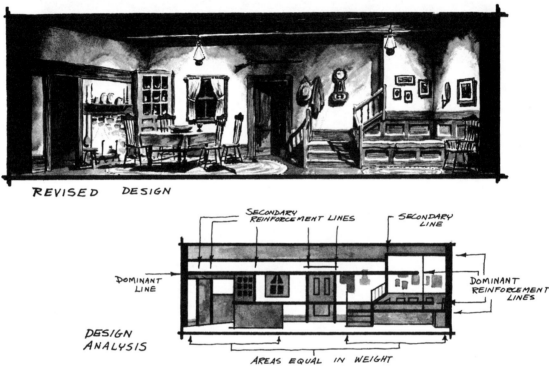

Plate 48. *REVISED PERSPECTIVE SKETCH, with design analysis chart.*

the changes have been made. The alterations have made tremendous improvement. Balance has been achieved, and the stage-right and stage-left areas, while still structurally the same, have gained much more interesting visual shapes.

Textures for the setting are already determined, to a great extent. The wood in the beams and the stone in the fireplace have been decided upon. The only remaining area of great importance is the wall area. Realistically, this should be plaster and, from an expressive point of view, it would add to the roughhewn, frontier quality desired; so plaster is the choice for the walls.

Color, now, is the big factor. Through it we can make our setting either cold and depressing or warm and cheerful. Since we need the latter

which might have subtle hints of yellow or orange worked into the texture to give them a bit of spice—not enough to be obvious, however. The rocks in the fireplace should also be of a warm or brownish tone, as opposed to a cool or bluish gray. We can pick up accents of brighter color in the furniture and dressing of the setting, as well as in the costumes. Reds, yellows, and oranges, and even blues or greens, could work as accent colors, so long as they are not *too* vivid.

This, then, completes the design for *Lawyer Lincoln*. It is now ready to be approved by the director, worked into construction drawings, and then constructed, painted, set up, and used. It is, however, not the only way in which the play can be designed. There are as many other valid interpretations and designs as there are designers and directors. Any play can be designed in a number of ways. Note, for instance, the entirely different interpretations of *The Night of the Iguana* as illustrated in Plates 2 and 73.

In this discussion, the design process has been very much condensed. All of the arrangement and design decisions can involve much soul-searching and brain-racking before the final design evolves; but the steps are basically the same for any setting. Always the floor plan must be tested and analyzed in terms of the requirements of the action of the play, and the pictorial composition must be considered in terms of the elements and principles of design. Only in this way can you arrive at a setting that is workable and pleasing to the eye.

A few other points should be considered be-fore we leave this section on planning the design. You may have noticed that in all of the sketches for *Lawyer Lincoln* the upstage wall was *raked*—placed at an angle rather than being parallel to the proscenium line. This can help to achieve interest in an interior setting; it can assist the director in designing his movement; and it can also aid in balancing an asymmetrical design. It is not used 100 percent of the time—nor should it be—but it should be considered as a possibility for any interior setting.

Whether to use a full ceiling on the setting should be another consideration. While a full ceiling is architecturally logical and can provide a realistically "completed" appearance to the setting, it severely hampers the lighting of the show. Several alternatives to a full ceiling include the use of split

Plate 49. *SETTING WITH A VARIED UPPER WALL LINE: Skeletal rafters provide visual interest above the setting and establish a rationale for varied wall heights in this setting for* Night Must Fall *designed by Carl Lefko for Radford University Theatre.*

Plate 50. *ARCHITECTURAL ELEMENTS FILLING SPACE ABOVE A SETTING: Roof profiles, window silhouettes, and fragmented walls, together with a stylized "seasons" projection compose the space above this basically realistic interior. Setting for* A Former Gotham Gal *at the University of Georgia. Design by the author.*

Plate 51. *INTERIOR DESIGNED WITH A STYLIZED UPPER PROFILE: The "block" appearance of the scenic units carried above this interior locale suggests the architecture of skyscrapers and apartment buildings in this setting for* The Boys Next Door *designed by Tom Tutino for the University of Western Kentucky.*

ceilings, false beams, louvered ceilings, or black borders to mask overhead and conceal lighting instruments. More visually interesting solutions rely on taking liberties with architectural realism for the upper parts of the setting. One variation is to break up the realistic but relatively uninteresting horizontal top edge of the walls by extending certain elements above the natural horizontal wall line. Windows and doors are architectural elements which provide some rationale for extension above the wall break. Tops of walls above staircases may follow the diagonal of the stairs (see Plate 3). Portions of roofs, flown windows, and other selected architectural elements may be used to fill in above the wall break and provide aesthetically pleasing solutions which also keep the fly area clear for lighting instruments. Plate 50 shows one solution, making use of several elements listed above, in addition to a projected background which suggests exterior conditions. Plate 51 illustrates a more simplified and stylized approach.

Last, but certainly not least, we must think in terms of practicality. This takes various aspects. One is that the designer should think in terms of stock scenic units—either designing as many units as possible that may be placed into stock and used for future productions, or using as many units from available stock as possible. The visual effectiveness of the setting should never be sacrificed in order to use only stock units; but at the same time, the designer should know what stock is on hand and avoid planning a completely new construction when usable stock items are available.

Another aspect of practicality is that the scope of the production should be in proportion to the play itself. For instance, *Lawyer Lincoln* is a one-act play, with a performance time of approximately thirty to forty-five minutes. It will probably be presented on a program with one or more other one-acters. Because of this, the setting we have designed is too elaborate for practical considerations. It was done this way to illustrate the process of designing an interior setting, but in proportion to the size of the play it is too expensive and time-consuming. Our setting is in the scale of a three-act production. The play had better be presented in a more simplified form such as one of those illustrated in Chapter IX. The time, money, and effort spent on any production should be carefully balanced with the length of the play, number of performances, learning experience for students (which, alone, can often justify a full-

Plate 52. *INTERIOR WITH FRAGMENTED ELEMENTS: Suspended silhouette windows are framed by simple textured panels and separate door units, providing a sense of unity with variety in this setting for* The Cherry Orchard *designed by Carl Lefko for Radford University Theatre.*

Plate 53. *SIMPLIFIED REALISTIC INTERIOR SETTING:    The Broadway production of* Hughie, *designed by David Hays for the Royale Theatre.*

scale production), or importance of the production, to determine the desired elaborateness of the treatment.

Thus far, we have been talking only in terms of interiors. A majority of interiors are designed in a more or less realistic manner. However, interiors may also be stylized, and then the style and mood of the play become the vital factors. When liberated from the reality of a setting, the designer can use the elements of composition in a more expressive manner. Plates 9 and 52 illustrate two variations of stylized interior settings, while Plates 53 and 54 show different degrees of simplification. In Plate 51, the stressing of the horizontal and vertical lines, plus the careful composition of elements, provides an almost geometrically abstract design and gives a strong feeling of starkness. A stylized treatment for an interior setting should not be overlooked. It frees a designer from many of the restrictions of realism.

No matter what form the interior setting may take, there are always a number of standard scenic units that are commonly associated with its design. Since a designer must be thoroughly acquainted with the forms of scenery, the construction of those

Plate 54.    *INTERIOR WITH EXTREME SIMPLIFICATION: This interior is suggested primarily through very simplified wall units, with careful furniture selection, swagged draperies and decorative detail on the tops of the walls serving to create a suggestion of period and atmosphere.   Sketch of a setting for* Les Liaisons Dangereuses *designed by Tom Tutino for the University of Western Kentucky.*

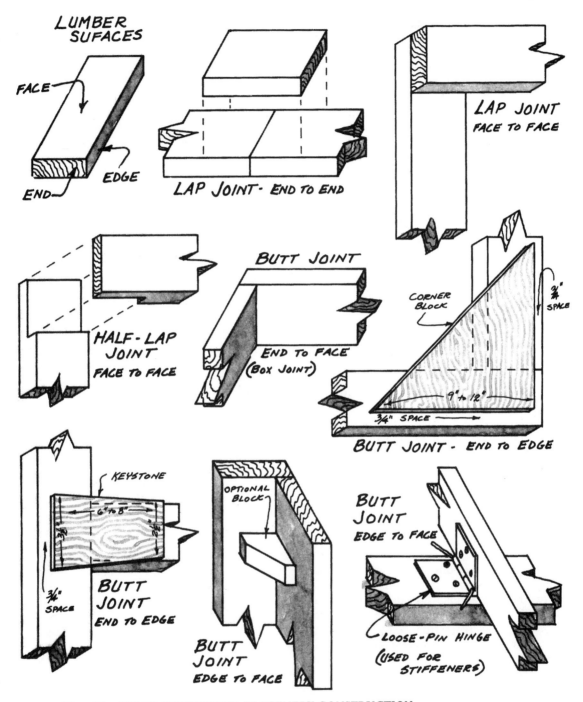

LUMBER SUFACES

FACE

END

EDGE

LAP JOINT - END TO END

LAP JOINT FACE TO FACE

HALF-LAP JOINT FACE TO FACE

BUTT JOINT END TO FACE (BOX JOINT)

CORNER BLOCK

BUTT JOINT - END TO EDGE

KEYSTONE

BUTT JOINT END TO EDGE

OPTIONAL BLOCK

BUTT JOINT EDGE TO FACE

BUTT JOINT EDGE TO FACE

LOOSE-PIN HINGE (USED FOR STIFFENERS)

Plate 55. *WOOD JOINTS USED IN SCENERY CONSTRUCTION*

particular units is examined in the next section.

### CONSTRUCTION TECHNIQUES

Scenic construction uses lumber as the primary framing material, and with a few exceptions, standard carpentry methods are employed.

Plate 55 illustrates a number of standard wood joints. The lap joint, end-to-end, is used in the theatre for lengthening battens. The face-to-face lap joint is used for legging platforms and for off-stage framing. The half-lap joint is used for double-faced flats, window sashes, door shutters, and any other construction in which both sides must be usable. Boxes and platform framing are constructed with the butt joint, end-to-face. The edge-to-face butt joints are used for reveals (thickness pieces) and for stiffeners.

The two joints peculiar to stage construction are the end-to-edge butt joints using the corner blocks and keystones. In these joints particularly, care should be taken to square the pieces of lumber at the joints before applying the corner blocks or keystones, which should be laid so that the exposed grain crosses the joint and, also, should be held back ¾" from all outside edges. They are fastened with scenery nails or clout nails (see the nail pattern shown in Plate 56). Scenery nails are used for temporary (one production) construction; clout nails are used for stock scenery and scenery that is to be flown. When using clout nails, insert a metal clinching plate under the joint, place the wedge-shaped point *across* the grain of the lumber, and drive the nail at a slight angle for best results.

In selecting lumber to be used, sight down the length of the lumber to be sure it is straight, and then check for knots, cracks, or splits that might weaken the completed structure. Pieces of lumber to be used for long expanses of framing should be as straight and as free from flaws as possible. Always square the ends of the lumber with a combination square or framing square before starting to do any measuring. When measuring, it is good practice to "measure twice, cut once" to eliminate costly errors.

### Flats (Plate 56)

Whenever possible, flats should be constructed to a standard size and shape. The standard height for flats should be the height that is most usable in your particular theatre—usually one or two feet higher than the normal proscenium opening, where the height of the ceiling permits—and may range from 8′ for small stages to 14′ or 16′ for large stages. The maximum width is usually 6′ because of the limiting widths of covering materials and the ease of handling. The minimum width is 1′ (for units of less width, wide pieces of lumber can more easily be used), and the range between this width and 6′ includes every six inches, i.e., 1′6″, 2′0″, 2′6″, 3′0″, etc. A good selection of widths makes the designing of a setting from stock flats much simpler.

The parts of the flat are the *rails,* the top and bottom horizontal pieces; the *stiles,* the outside vertical pieces; the *toggle rails,* the inside horizontal pieces that keep the stiles

the same distance apart; and the *corner braces,* which are placed between the rails and stile on the same side of the flat to ensure rigidity. The steps in constructing a flat are as follows:

1. Cut all rails, stiles, and toggle rails from 1″ x 3″ lumber—the two rails the full width of the flat; the two stiles the full height of the flat minus the combined width of the two stiles.
2. Butt the ends of the stiles against the rails. (Extending the rails the full width of the flat makes them runners for sliding the flat across the floor without the danger of splitting the lumber.) Check for a right angle with a framing square and fasten with corner blocks, as described earlier.
3. Insert the toggle rails between the stiles, spacing them no farther apart than 4′0″. Double-check the width of the flat at each toggle. Check for right angles with a framing square and attach with keystones.
4. Cut the corner braces from 1″ x 2″ lumber, with approximate 45-degree cuts on the ends. Insert them between the stile and rails at the top and bottom on the same side of the flat and attach with specially cut keystones.

The framing of door and window flats is executed in a similar manner. The placement of the toggles determines the position of the opening in both units, with additional vertical framing members forming the sides of the opening; however, the outside framing is constructed as indicated above (see bottom of Plate 57). In constructing the door flat, it is a good idea to construct the bottom rail the full width of the flat and cut the door opening out later. This makes it easier to ensure rigidity and right angles during the initial construction. The door flat also has a sill iron—a strip of ¼" x ¾" strap iron—placed across the bottom of the flat to hold the door square when the bottom rail has been cut out. Remember, also, to maintain the ¾" holdback in the placement of the corner blocks and keystones around the door and window openings to allow for the addition of reveals (thickness pieces). Arches use curved sweeps cut from ¾" plywood or 1″ x 12″ lumber, which are inserted into the tops of door or window openings and secured with nails or keystones.

To cover a flat, the flat frame is laid face up, the covering material (canvas, scenic cloth, or muslin) laid over the face with approxi-

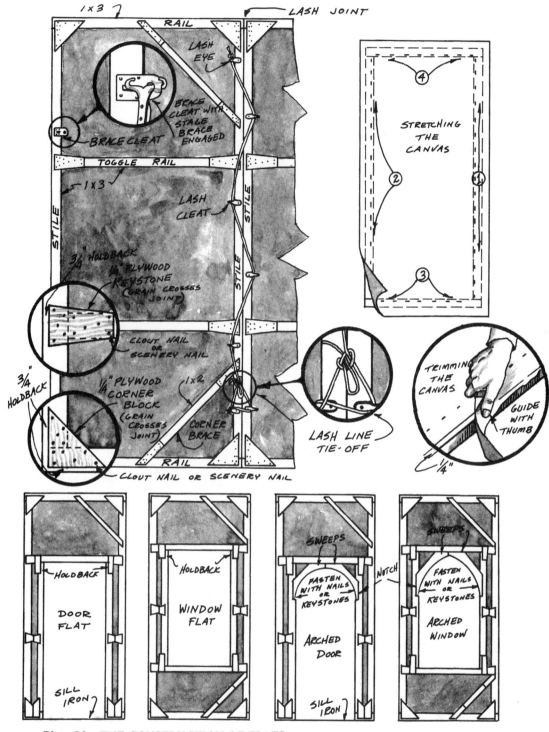

Plate 56. *THE CONSTRUCTION OF FLATS*

mately 2″ overlapping each edge. Starting from the center of one of the stiles, staple ¼″ from the inside edge of the lumber at 6″ intervals from the center to one end and then from the center to the other end of the stile. Slack should be taken out of the cloth as you move along, but it should not be stretched so tightly that it puckers around the staples. It is important at this time to keep the weave of the material straight along the edge of the flat. Move across to the opposite stile and repeat the process. In this case, however, the material must be stretched across the flat as well as along the length. Here, also, the slack should be taken out of the material, but it should not be pulled taut. Muslin should be allowed more slack than canvas, because it will shrink more when painted. The stretching process is completed by moving to either end of the flat and stretching along the rails, working from the center of each rail to the ends, as was done on the stiles. It may be necessary to remove staples and adjust the material to take out wrinkles that may have developed. Do this *now*. Any other time will be too late.

When the cloth is smooth and even, the edges are glued to the frame. Using wheat paste (wallpaper paste) or white polyvinyl glue (Elmer's, Sobo, etc.) thinned slightly so it may be brushed on, secure the cloth to the lumber between the staples and the outside edge of the lumber. Make sure that all of this area is securely fastened—be careful not to slight any portion of the lumber with your paste. Glue only to the outside frames of the flat—*do not glue the cloth to the toggle rails.* When the glue is dry (six to ten hours for wheat paste, thirty to forty-five minutes for polyvinyl glue), trim the cloth ¼″ in from the outside edge with a sharp knife—utility knife or mat knife.

Doors and windows are covered in much the same manner. Secure the material to the outside edges in the manner described above, and then secure it around the window or door opening, stapling on the lumber edge away from the opening so that room is left for gluing. Door and window flats may also be covered in pieces—separate pieces of material for top, sides and bottom areas to be covered. In this case, all overlap within the unit must be confined to the wood frame elements and secured with glue—you cannot trim this part with a knife.

In recent years more and more flats are made of hard-surfaces—covered with plywood or *luan* panels. This strengthens the unit, eliminates the flapping of canvas when doors are slammed, and allows more types of decorative detail to be attached—vacuformed and foam elements which would not secure well to a cloth surface, for example.

*Stage Windows and Doors (Plate 57)*

Stage window and door units are usually constructed separately from the flats for ease in storage, although in some cases they may be attached directly to the flats. There are three primary parts to the units: the *casing*, which is the decorative trim around the door or window (when the unit is attached directly to the flat, the casing is often painted onto the flat face); the *reveal*, or thickness piece—used to give the illusion of thickness to a wall; and the actual window or door itself—the window is composed of two *sashes*, and the door is termed a *shutter* (no pun intended).

The lumber used for the casing and reveals is determined by the design requirements. The casing may be highly decorative with applied moldings, or may be very simply widths of lumber. The width of the lumber used for the reveals determines the apparent thickness of the walls and should be consistent in all door and window units in the same setting. The average thickness of a wall is 6″, so 1″ x 6″ lumber is usually used. However, for very thick walls, as might be needed for a medieval or Spanish setting, the reveals can be made from lumber as wide as 12″ or more.

The reveal portion is cut to size and fastened together in a box-like construction. The casing pieces are cut to allow for necessary overlap and secured to the edge of the reveal with finishing nails. The casing pieces are attached to one another with small keystones applied on the offstage side. In the construction of the door frame there is, obviously, no casing applied to the base of the door. The reveal of the door may include a batten across the bottom to serve as a threshold, or the bottom may be secured with sill irons; however, it should be secured in some way.

The window sashes employ 1″ x 2″ or 1″ x 3″ lumber for the outside frame, and 1″ x 1″ lumber for the cross-pieces (*muntins*), and are joined with half-lap joints. The top sash is made to fit securely within the reveal and is nailed into the reveal on the offstage side. The bottom sash should be ⅛″ to ¼″ less in width than the window opening so that it will have clearance to move up and down. A 1″ x 1″ guide strip is attached along the sides of the reveal flush with the face of the top sash. The bottom sash is placed into position, then a second set of guide strips is attached to hold it in position. Clearance of ⅛″ is allowed between the bottom sash and the second set of guide strips, which allows the bottom sash to move freely in the grooves thus formed. The sashes may be left completely open or may be

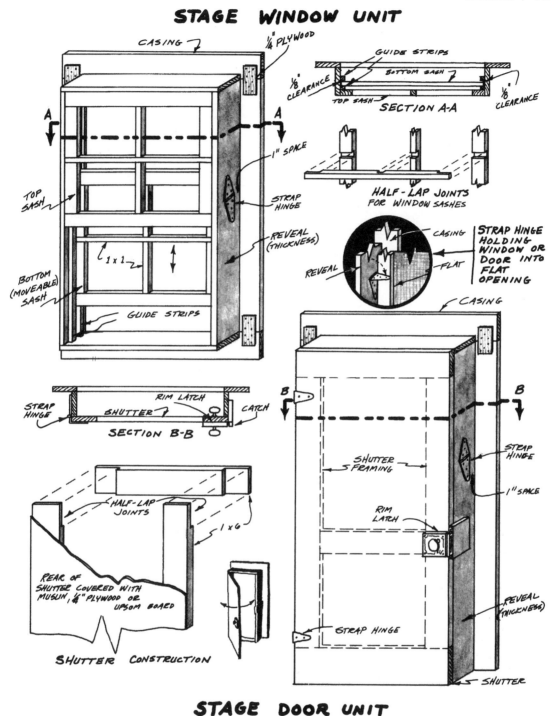

**Plate 57.** *THE CONSTRUCTION OF STAGE WINDOW AND DOOR UNITS*

covered on the rear with plastic, screen wire, or painted cheesecloth, to suggest glass.

Door shutters may be constructed as plain-front doors or as recessed-paneling doors. Plain-front doors are constructed in the same manner as flats with the surface covering being either canvas, upsom board, or ¼" plywood. For recessed paneling, the framework is usually constructed of 1" x 6" lumber half-lapped together and covered on the rear by one of the same materials just mentioned. The shutter may be made to fit behind the reveal or within the reveal—if behind, it is made 1½″ larger than the door opening; if within the reveal, it must be made ¼″ to ½″ smaller than the opening, and 1″ x 1″ stop strips must be attached within the reveal to keep the shutter from swinging forward. (Stage doors should, if possible, open offstage.) The shutter is lifted ¼″ to ½″ off the floor and attached with strap

## PLATFORMS

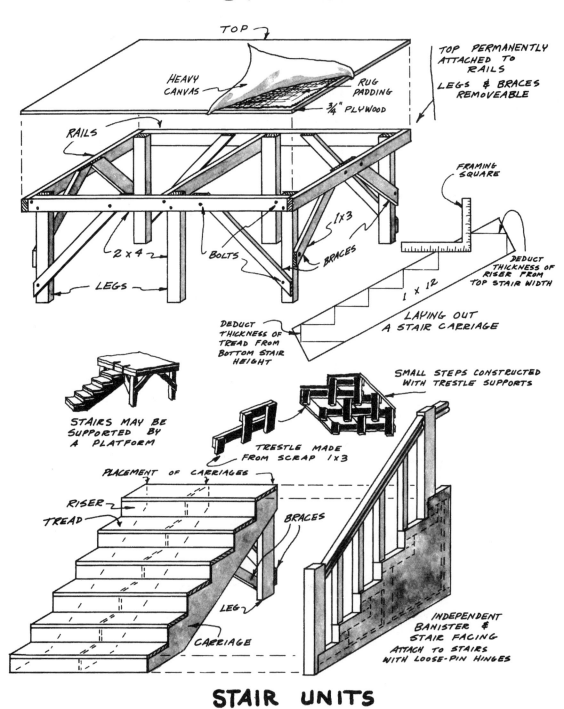

## STAIR UNITS

Plate 58. *THE CONSTRUCTION OF PLATFORMS AND STAIR UNITS*

hinges (usually on the upstage side). A rim latch with knobs and catch is attached to the offstage side of the door, approximately 3' from the floor.

The window and door frames are nailed or screwed in position after insertion into the opening in the flat (remember, when constructing the flat, that the opening must be made large enough to accommodate the insertion of the frame). When the frame must be removed quickly during a performance, a strap hinge is secured to the outside of the reveal two thirds of the distance up the side. Only the bottom flap of the hinge is attached, leaving the top free to fold down behind the flat when the frame is in position, thus holding the frame in the flat.

*Platforms (Plate 58)*

A platform is constructed using ¾" plywood for the top and 2" x 4" lumber for legs and rails. The top is cut to size (or often, used as is) and covered with rug padding, which is in turn covered with heavy canvas carried around the edges and tacked underneath. The rails are joined with box joints, and sufficient cross supports are added so that no area of plywood greater than 4' x 4' goes unsupported. The legs are cut to the desired height and joined to the rails with bolts. Any platform 1' high or higher needs the additional support of diagonal braces, which are bolted to the legs and rails. If you are very careful to drill all of the legs and diagonals in exactly the same pattern, they may be interchangeable, enabling any platform to be used at any height with any legs.

Many technicians and authors will offer the *parallel* platform as the most desirable means of elevating an area. The parallel is a platform so constructed as to permit it to be easily folded for storage. The parallel, however, has several disadvantages: once it is constructed, its height cannot be altered, necessitating a large number of units to provide variety in heights; it is rarely as stable as the rigid type of platform; and it does not resist wear and tear as well as the rigid platform. The platform with interchangeable legs, when the legs are removed, stores in as small an area as a parallel and has the further advantages of extreme stability and complete adaptability as to height.

*Stairs (Plate 58)*

Stairs are composed of three parts: the *treads,* the portion on which a person steps (usually 12" in width); the *risers,* the vertical portion separating the treads (usually 6" to 8" in height); and the *carriages,* the supporting pieces to which the treads and risers are attached. The carriage is usually cut from lumber 1" or 1½" x 12" after being laid out with the aid of a framing square, as shown in Plate 59. The treads are cut from 1" x 12" lumber or from ¾" plywood. The risers may be made from upsom board, ¼" plywood, or ¾" lumber, depending on the degree of stability and support required of them. The stairs may be supported by legs and diagonal braces or by being attached to a platform. Banisters and facings (masking for the edges) may be attached directly to the stairs or may be constructed as an independent unit, which is then loose-pin-hinged to the stairs.

Small stair units—two, three, or four steps high—may be constructed using trestle units made from scrap 1" x 3" lumber in place of cut carriages. The 1" x 3" pieces are cut to size, joined with lap joints, and braced as necessary for stability. This is a good way to use up small lengths of 1" x 3", which seem to accumulate after flat construction.

*Joining, Stiffening, Bracing (Plate 59)*

Scenic units may be joined to one another in a variety of ways, of which the following are perhaps the most used. In a permanent setting (one which does not change during a production), units may be nailed, screwed, or bolted together. Care is required, however, or this may result in damage to the units when they are disassembled and hinder their usefulness as stock units. *Lashing* (illustrated in Plates 57 and 60) and *hinging* are perhaps the most useful methods of joining units. Lashing is useful not only in one-set shows, but also in cases in which units must be quickly and easily joined and separated during the course of a performance. Units may be tight-pin-hinged to fold for more compact handling and storage. When hinged on the face in this manner, the joints are usually covered with a *dutchman—* a 4" to 6" wide strip of muslin with torn, *not cut,* edges secured with wheat paste over the hinges and the joint. When painted, the torn edges blend with the covering material and give the appearance of an unbroken wall. Loose-pin hinges may be placed on the face (in which case the flaps are usually countersunk, covered, and painted) or on the rear of the unit, and are used when the units must be separated for portability during construction,

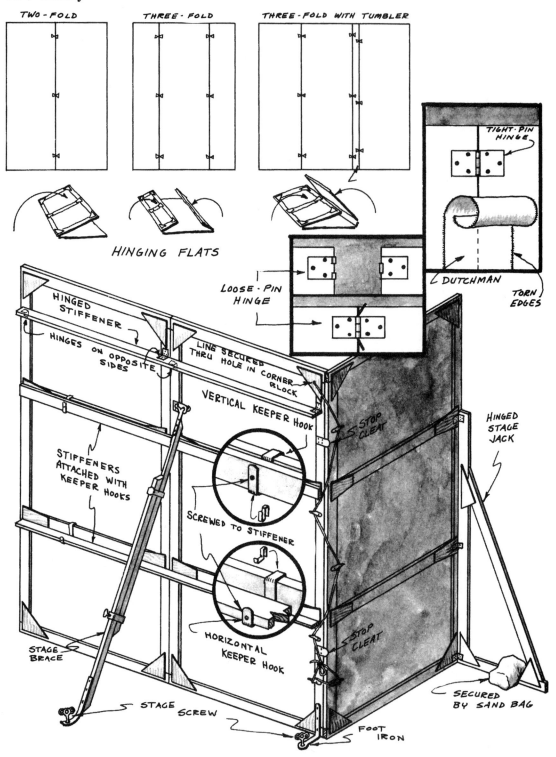

Plate 59. *JOINING, STIFFENING, AND BRACING TECHNIQUES*

set-up, or performance. Long walls may also be formed from several flats secured together by battens nailed, screwed, or bolted across the rear of the units. The joints in this type of unit should also be dutchmanned.

Stiffening is necessary to keep large units from bending or buckling. Battens holding several flats together also serve as stiffeners.

Stiffeners work best, however, when the lumber is placed edge to face rather than face to face. For this reason the hinged stiffener and the stiffener using the horizontal keeper hook provide greatest support. Tight-pin-hinged stiffeners and stiffeners nailed, screwed, or bolted to the units are permanent. Loose-pin-hinged stiffeners may be removed for transport or storage. Stiffeners attached with keeper hooks may be removed at any time—even during performance, if necessary.

Bracing scenic units to keep them upright is accomplished through one, or all, of three basic methods: support from above; attachment to the floor; and angled bracing from the floor up to the rear of the unit. A unit may be suspended from the flies or, if there are no flies available, tied off to the ceiling. A unit can be attached to the floor by use of the *foot iron* or by nailing the unit to a batten that has been secured to the floor. Angled bracing is obtained through use of the *stage brace*, which provides adjustable bracing, or through use of the *stage jack*, a triangular-shaped frame—both means of support being attached to the stage floor by means of a *stage screw*. In situations in which screws and nails may not be driven into the floor, the stage jack must be used and secured by means of a sandbag, as shown in Plate 59.

Any expanse of flat scenery must be braced at one or more places along its length. Any portion of the scenery that is subject to contact or movement occurring during the action of the play should be braced. Doors should be braced on one side, or, if possible, both. However, wherever flats are joined at right, or near right angles, braces are not necessary, since this particular arrangement of flats supports itself. Lashed joints should not be braced, because this would hinder speedy fastening and separation of the joint.

These are just a few of the techniques used in the the construction of interior settings. They are, however, some of the most used. More detailed information concerning these and other stagecraft techniques may be found in the books listed in the Bibliography. Specific information regarding tools, hardware, and materials will be found in Appendix B.

PAINTING TECHNIQUES

Scenic painting uses a number of materials and techniques not found in any other form of painting. The materials are discussed in Appendix B. A brief discussion of the techniques applicable to interior settings follows.

*Mixing*

All paints are composed of *pigment*, which provides the color; *binder*, which holds the pigment to a surface; and *solution*, which suspends the pigment and binder and allows them to be brushed or sprayed. The older scenic paints are powdered pigment only and must be mixed with a glue binder and water solution. Granulated or flake glue mixed with water and then heated in a double boiler until the glue becomes liquid has been the traditional binder for centuries. More recently, however, white glues such as "Elmers" have more often been employed as the binder. Whatever binder is used, the glue/pigment/water relationship must be carefully tested. If the pigment dusts off when it has been painted onto a surface and dried, there is too little glue; if the painted area glistens or crackles, there is too much glue. Because this type of paint is given to rapid spoilage, a few drops of preservative, such as oil of wintergreen, is frequently added to the mixture.

Creating desired colors with dry-pigment paints is usually done with the dry pigment alone, since this type of paint is considerably darker when wet than when dry. When the solution evaporates, however, the paint returns to a color approximating that seen in the dry color.

Casein, vinyl, and acrylic paints, on the other hand, contain all the elements already mixed—usually in a concentrated form which must be diluted to a usable painting consistency. Here the colors must be mixed wet and tested on a scrap of material identical to that which is to be painted. Only when dry can the true color be seen. Generally, the procedure is to: (1) thin the concentrated color(s) to a consistency which may be easily mixed—but not necessarily as thin as the desirable painting consistency (usually the consistency of rich milk); (2) mix and test the color until the desired tint or shade has been achieved (a hint: when attempting to mix a very pale color, add *small* amounts of the color to white rather than adding white to a color—you will save gallons of wasted paint by that method); (3) dilute with water only enough of the finished color to paint a given surface—don't mix it all up at once. This is particularly true of dry-pigment and protein paints which are prone to rather rapid spoilage (with an accompanying disagreeable odor).

Some general suggestions: (1) write down and retain the formula for each color mixed (e.g., 5 parts white, 1 part red, 2 parts yellow ochre); (2) mix enough paint initially to cover all necessary surfaces—nothing is more frustrating or time consuming than trying to match a previously mixed color; (3) always keep at least a small amount of each mixed color for touch-up during the performances—especially longer running shows.

### Sizing and Base Coating

The first paint coat to be applied to a flat is the size coat. This is very little more than pure size water

### Texturing

Occasionally a flat coat, such as a base coat, will provide the final surface for a unit, but more often the surface is given a broken, irregular appearance, which gives an illusion of greater depth and looks better under stage lighting. The texturing methods most used for interior settings are as follows:

BLENDING (Plate 61): This is a method for subtly altering colors in a setting. Two colors are applied side by side and, while still wet, the edges are

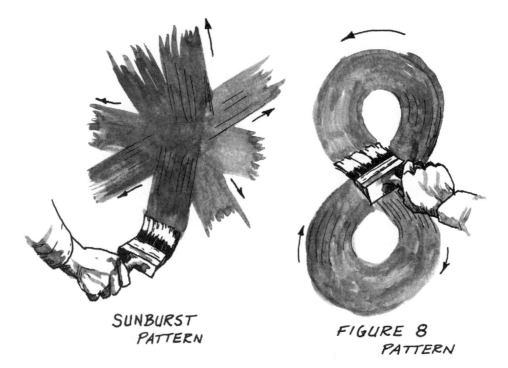

SUNBURST PATTERN

FIGURE 8 PATTERN

Plate 60. *BRUSH PATTERNS FOR APPLYING BASE COAT: to achieve an even surface coating.*

mixed with enough pigment to add sufficient color to be able to see where you have painted. Its purpose is to shrink the covering material and seal the porous surface to make later coats easier to apply. The size coat is worked thoroughly but rapidly into the material with a large brush.

The base coat is the first actual painting operation aimed at achieving the final color of the setting. It usually provides the general color for the setting, serving as a base on which later overpainting is to be done. It is generally a single color laid on the surface lightly and rapidly with a wide brush, which is stroked in all directions to provide an even coating (see Plate 60); however, it may be applied in several colors with a blended or "scumbled" technique (see below).

blended together until there is no discernible line of demarcation. This may be used for darkening the tops or corners of a setting, or for the painting a sky in which colors shade smoothly into one another.

SCUMBLE (Plate 61): Also a blending technique, except the colors are placed in a random pattern and then blended into one another to achieve a mottled appearance. It provides a useful background for old plaster, stone, or stucco.

ROLLING (Plate 61): A rag or sponge is dipped into paint, squeezed out, and then rolled over the surface in random directions. This provides a rough-textured effect useful for stone, stucco, plaster, and brack. Different effects may be achieved by varying the pressure on the sponge or rag, using a variety of materials (burlap, muslin, terrycloth, etc.), or by

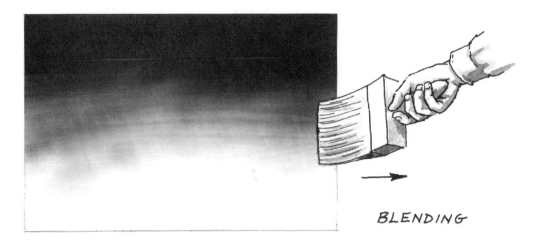

BLENDING

SCUMBLE

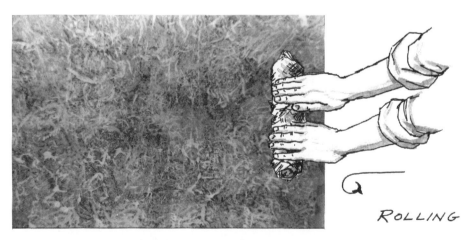

ROLLING

Plate 61.   *TEXTURE PAINTING TECHNIQUES*

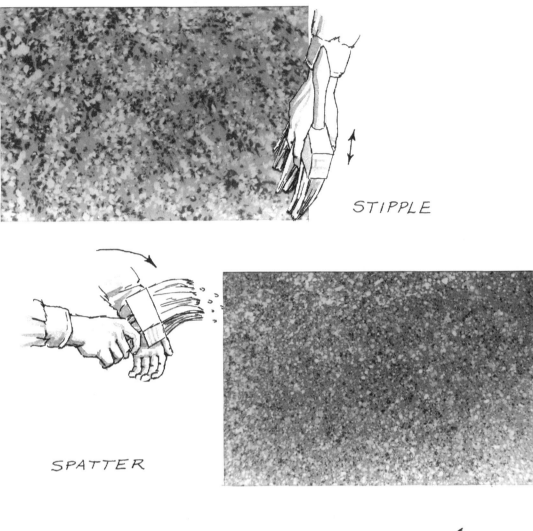

STIPPLE

SPATTER

DRY BRUSH

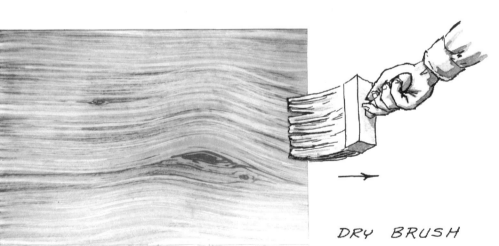

Plate 62. *TEXTURE PAINTING TECHNIQUES*

rolling in specific patterns.

STIPPLE (Plate 62): A technique using the tips of a brush, sponges, rags, crumbled paper, a feather duster (or anything else that happens to be handy and effective), dipping them lightly into the paint, and then touching them lightly to the surface, altering the angle and shape with each subsequent contact. This can provide a wide variety of textures depending upon the material used, and may be useful for stucco, stone, brick, plaster, or mottled wallpaper.

SPATTER (Plate 62): Perhaps the most used and most usable technique. A brush is charged with paint, drained or shaken to remove the

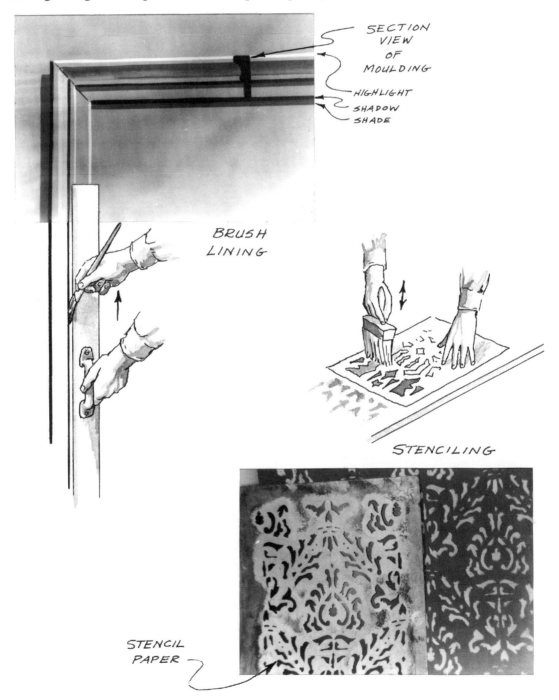

Plate 63. *LINING AND STENCILING TECHNIQUES*

excess, and then snapped smartly in the direction of the scenery, imparting droplets of paint onto the surface. The direction of the spatter should be changed constantly in order to achieve even distribution. The size of the dots depends on the type of brush, the amount of paint in the brush, the density of the paint, the smartness of the motion, and the distance of the brush from the surface (the closer to the surface, the smaller the drops). Spattering may be used to shade or shadow portions of the scenery, to blend areas of varying colors, to cover flaws in underpainting, to subtly alter the color of the setting, or to provide a surface texture of less roughness than any of the techniques mentioned above. A variety of colored spatters applied to the same surface will blend together visually, but may be brought out by strongly colored lights, thus altering the appearance of the setting.

DRY BRUSH (Plate 62): Used to provide a grained appearance such as in wood, bark, rough-woven cloth, or the striations in cast or cut stone. A brush is drained of most of its paint and then the tips of the bristles are lightly drawn over the surface, keeping the pressure even and avoiding sudden stops and starts. Wood may be simulated by tilting the brush from one side to the other and leaving holes into which knots may be painted. Cloth may be simulated by dry-brushing horizontally and vertically to provide a woven appearance.

Actual textures may be achieved by mixing sand, cork, asbestos powder, or sawdust with paint that has extra glue and then brushing or modeling the resulting mass onto the surface.

*Lining Techniques (Plate 63)*

Brush lining is the painting technique used to fake moldings, panels, and architectural details that are not constructed. To be successful at this technique, the painter must study perspective and the effects of light on real architectural detail. Also, the detail must be simplified and theatrically oriented. Lining requires a minimum of three colors: *highlight,* which is lighter in value than the base color; *shade,* which is several steps darker in value than the base color; and *shadow,* which is the darkest color used—often close to black in value. Us-

Plate 64. *DETAIL OF SCENERY PAINTED WITH NEWSPAPER STENCIL, DRY BRUSH GRAINING, AND BRUSH LINING*

ing the placement of a light source (window or lamp in the setting) as a guide, determine from a cross-section of the molding those portions closest to the light and those farthest away. Highlight indicates parts closest to the light, shadow the parts farthest from the light, and shade those parts only partly hidden from the light. Lining employs the wooden straight-edge and long-handled lining brushes in order to achieve straight, even lines—a necessity for successful lining.

*Stenciling (Plate 63)*

Repeated patterns such as those found in wallpaper are generally simulated onstage through the use of stencils. One full motif plus portions of adjacent motifs are cut into stencil paper with a sharp knife or razor blade. It is a good idea to cut two identical stencils to lessen the wear on one and to provide a replacement in case the first stencil becomes damaged. For additional support, the stencil may be attached to a box constructed of 1' x 2' lumber. Vertical, horizontal, or diagonal lines are snapped onto the surface to be painted wherever necessary to indicate the successive positions of the stencil. The stencil is held against the surface in those positions, and paint is sprayed, sponged, stippled, or dry-brushed through the openings onto the surface. Be careful to wipe off excess paint that may accumulate on the face of the stencil after each application. The wallpaper pattern in the setting in Plate 40 was applied in this manner.

Another method of stenciling depends on the availability of a Cut-Awl tool. Using the Cut-Awl, the pattern is cut out of a large stack of newspapers at the same time. The newspapers are spread over the entire surface to be patterned in such a way as to cover all of the area except the design to be stenciled. Then a heavy coating of spatter is applied over the entire surface. When the paper is removed, the stencil pattern will have been spattered onto the surface, giving a hazy, rough-appearing wallpaper. The wallpaper pattern shown in Plate 64 was achieved in this manner. The wood effect was achieved through dry-brush graining, together with brush lining, and all shadows are painted effects.

Needless to say, skill at scenic painting cannot be acquired through reading. Practice and experimentation are the only means by which you can hope to achieve any degree of success. However, this brief discussion of techniques may at least give you some idea of how to start. In addition, here are three general scene-painting suggestions: (1) all the painting should be exaggerated—done in bold and free manner in order to carry to an audience seated far enough from the stage to be unable to discern small, fussy details (bold and free does *not* mean sloppy, however); (2) usually texture of some sort is needed to liven up what might otherwise be a dull, flat surface; and (3) most settings are shaded darker at the top and in the corners in order to focus attention into the acting area.

This chapter has gone into the designing of interiors in some depth. Subsequent chapters will deal with other types of settings in less detail—noting principally the ways in which the design considerations, requirements, and processes differ from those we have examined in this chapter, as well as discussing additional stagecraft techniques.

Plate 65. *THE MARRIAGE OF FIGARO*: Act Two, Scene One from The Moscow Art Academic Theatre. Designed by Golovin. The post revolution extravagance is apparent by the lavish gold texture used on the walls and furnishings.

The interior setting is our strongest reminder of the realism prevalent during the late 19th and early 20th centuries. Even after the introduction of the realistic box setting, however, exterior settings continued to be of conventional drop-and-wing construction, such as that shown in the stylized re-creation in Plate 79. When attempting to revamp this form of exterior setting, the realists soon found, to their dismay, that—try as they might—they could not reproduce nature as realistically as they could architectural structures. The remark that "only God can make a tree" is particularly apropos to attempts to re-create nature onstage. Supposedly realistic exteriors still appeared artificial and contrived, and the advent of motion pictures, using natural surroundings as backgrounds, simply pointed up this artificiality. There had to be some other answer.

Stylization and Simplified Realism (or perhaps, more accurately, *Suggested Realism*) seemed to be the answers. Illusion and atmosphere have become the key words. We now seek to capture the *essence* of an exterior without having to picture the *totality*. Two prominent theorist-designers from the turn of the century have guided us along this path—Adolphe Appia and Gordon Craig. They suggested the use of simplified settings that would emphasize the actor and, therefore, the play; the employment of highly suggestive objects, which through their expressiveness could conjure up in the imagination of the audience a vision of the reality and atmosphere of the place represented; and the fusion of setting, lighting, costume, movement, and sometimes music to create a strong, unified approach to a single interpretation of the play (see Plate 66). Appia, in particular, emphasized the combined use of lighting and setting to create the necessary atmosphere. Even though the two areas are presented in separate volumes in this series, they cannot be separated in actual practice. Scenery and lighting complement each other; and, more and more, lighting is taking the

place of elaborate settings. A scenic designer should not—in fact, *cannot*—design a setting without considering at the same time how that setting is going to be lighted. This is borne out by the number of outstanding designers who design both setting and lighting: Robert Edmond Jones (who, perhaps more than any other one designer, is responsible for turning theory into fact), Norman Bel Geddes, Lee Simonson, and, in more recent times, Jo Mielziner, Donald Oenslager, Howard Bay, Will Steven Armstrong, and David Hays, to mention just a few. The *essence* of an exterior must be re-created through the combined use of setting and lighting, designed creatively to *suggest* rather than *duplicate*.

In an interior setting, the realistic approach is often the easy way out—it frequently requires less imagination to produce a serviceable (though uninteresting) realistic interior than to turn to stylization in an attempt to portray more expressively the character and atmosphere of the place. In an exterior setting, the reverse is more often true. The problems of designing a realistic, or semirealistic, exterior setting, although relatively few numerically, are enormous from the practical point of view. Let us take a moment and examine those particular problems and requirements.

## SPECIAL PROBLEMS AND CONSIDERATIONS

All of the problems are directly related to the overall problem of re-creating within a limited space the limitless space and variety characteristic of nature. Simply stated, they are (1) the problem of sky and distance, (2) the problem of side and top masking, and (3) the problem of the duplication of natural forms —foliage, trees, and rocks.

### Sky and Distance

Sky onstage must be suggested through the use of the cyclorama, which we discussed in

SKETCH OF A DESIGN BY
ADOLPHE APPIA FOR
TRISTAN - 1923

SKETCH OF A
DESIGN BY
ADOLPHE APPIA
FOR
LITTLE EYOLF
1924

SKETCH OF A DESIGN
BY E. GORDON CRAIG
FOR HAMLET: THE
GHOST SCENE - 1907

Plate 66. *THE DESIGNS OF APPIA AND CRAIG*

Chapter I. The amount of sky that can be presented to the view of the audience is limited by the size of the available cyc. There are cycs in the form of a partial dome (see Plate 67) that are ideal for the production of exteriors because they can present an apparently unlimited expanse of sky to the view of the audience. However, the size and shape of this type of cyc severely limit the use of other forms of stage machinery—including flying; this, in turn, limits the overall use of the stage for other types of productions. Another form of cyc hangs vertically but has sides that curve downstage almost to the proscenium and is tall enough to obviate the necessity for overhead masking. The setting in Plate 68 makes use of this type of cyc. However, this also has disadvantages. Unless the stage house is tall enough to permit the unit to fly out of sight, or unless the sides can fold in in some way, it

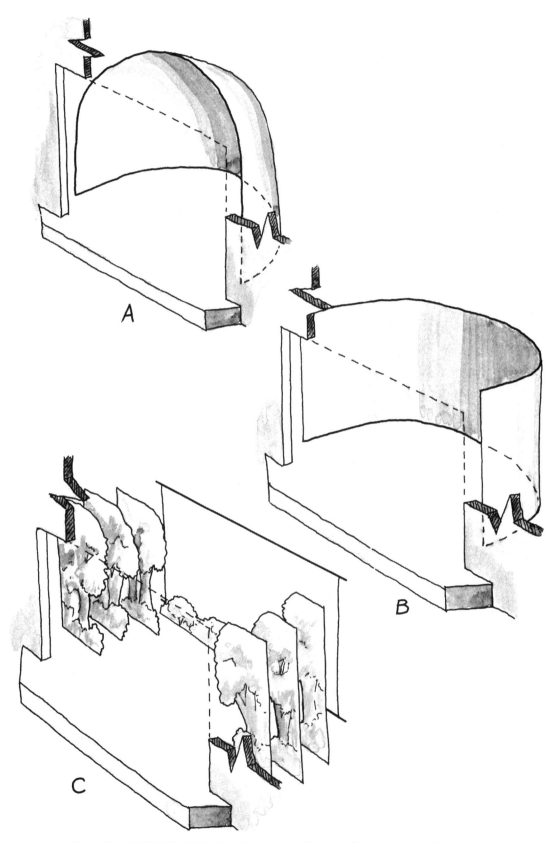

Plate 67.  *CYCLORAMAS:  (a) domed cyc;  (b) curved cyc:  (c) straight cyc*

hampers the movement of scenery between the playing area and the wings during multisetting productions. Shortening this type of cyc to permit flying necessitates overhead masking of

mentioned in Chapter I, much can be done through the overlapping of masses—each mass becoming perceptibly smaller the farther it is placed from the audience—note how effectively

Plate 68.  *CURVED CYC BACKING AN EXTERIOR SETTING: In this setting the sky cyc serves as the principal means of suggesting an exterior expanse beyond the principal architectural units.* Family Portrait *designed by A.S. Gillettte for the University of Iowa.*

some sort. Shortening the sides of the cyc necessitates side masking. By far the most common type of cyc is the straight, sky-colored backdrop that requires the use of both top and side masking. The problems of masking the edges of a cyc in a realistic manner are discussed in the next section.

Any form of cyc must be well lighted in order to give the appearance of a sky. Wrinkles appear in even the best cloth cycs, and must be properly lighted in order to be invisible to the audience. This requires that space be left for lighting instruments at the top and bottom of the cyc. Unless you are fortunate enough to have your bottom cyc lights built into the stage floor, they too must be concealed in some way from audience view.

The illusion of distance on any stage of normal depth, and particularly on shallow stages, requires careful consideration. As was

this is used in the setting in Plate 69. Cut-drops suggesting successive lines of tree trunks are designed for just this illusion. Scrim, a loosely woven fabric resembling cheesecloth, may be used to heighten the effect of distance. Hung in successive layers in front of a lighted cyc, it creates the misty, hazy feeling of distance. If, in addition, lights are directed onto the scrims in a variety of ways, a series of atmospheric effects can be achieved. Even one scrim can add enormously to the effect of distance.

All of this, however, requires stage space. An area of 3′ to 5′ downstage of a cyc must be left clear for lights. Masking for these lights, plus one or two scrims and/or other scenic units provided to suggest distance, may require an additional 5′ to 6′ of space—particularly if lighting is used between the units. Altogether, it is quite possible to use as much as 8′ to 12′ of the upstage portion of the stage just

Plate 69. *OVERLAPPING PLANES USED TO SUGGEST DISTANCE: The overlapping layers of ground rows and buildings together with the receding telephone poles combine to create the flavor of a distant rural community in this setting for* Picnic *produced at the University of Georgia, with scenery by Paul Camp.*

for creating effective sky and distance—all of which severely limits the available playing area.

*Side and Top Masking*

As indicated above, unless you are equipped with a cyc that is wide enough or curves downstage far enough and is high enough to obviate the necessity for concealing the side and top edges, you will be faced with the problem of masking. The big question here is, "What can be used that will add to rather than detract from the reality of the setting?" If the play is set in the middle of a city or the middle of a forest, the answer is simple—buildings or trees. Few plays, however, lend themselves to so easy a solution. Many do require one building of some sort onstage, and this can be placed in such a way as to mask one side of the stage and conceal one edge of the cyc; but the question remains as to what to do with the other side of the stage. Another building or a succession of tree trunks are the most obvious answers, but it is not always possible or valid to use these. Beyond these, you must look for any element that is appropriate to the setting

and can be designed in such a way as to be large enough, high enough, and so arranged as to serve its masking function. Piles of crates, cartons, or bales; haystacks; trellises; hangings of material such as fishnet, canvas, or banners; piles of rock or cliff faces; or high walls or fences are merely a few items that come to mind as possibilities for side masking. And then there are the all too numerous occasions when nothing of the sort can be found and you must fall back on the hanging of black legs, which obviously detract from the total reality of the setting.

Overhead masking is a greater problem because there are much fewer possibilities. With the exception of black borders (from the aspect of reality, a last resort, but frequently used) the most useful of the devices mentioned in the last chapter may be fragmented bits of reality suspended above the stage. Occasionally architectural devices such as roofs or the under sides of bridges or catwalks may be used, but the most common method after black borders is the use of some form of foliage—usually a cut-out, painted foliage border. It is highly questionable as to how realistic these actually appear. This leads us to the next problem—that of re-creating natural forms.

*Duplication of Natural Forms*

It is usually inadvisable to use real natural objects (leaves, trees, stumps, rocks, etc.) on-stage except in limited quantities. Leaves wither and die quickly, trees and stumps are heavy (and may contain termites or other un-desirable characters), and rocks are also very heavy. Lightweight substitutes can be made that, carefully designed and executed, may con-vey a reasonably realistic illusion of the actual object. Because of the irregularity of natural forms, however, the process can often become involved and time-consuming—particularly in the case of foliage, each leaf of which must be constructed separately, painted, and then se-cured to a stem or vine. One of the important considerations for an exterior setting must be whether the realistic effect is sufficiently im-portant to the play to justify the time and effort required to duplicate, with any degree of effectiveness, natural foliage, earth, rocks, trees, and flowers.

*The Question of Style*

With the possible exception of a small num-ber of plays such as *Tobacco Road, Dead End,* and *Street Scene,* a great many plays requiring an exterior setting could just as effectively, if not more effectively, be presented with sim-plified or stylized scenery. When we move out of the realm of total realism the problems in-volved with exterior settings become greatly lessened. Masking may be achieved through the use of elements that by their texture, color, or form are expressive of the style or mood of the play. Duplication of natural forms may be eliminated or reduced to the minimum, in-volving only those objects essential to the ex-pressiveness of the design or to the action of the play. More imagination is required of the designer and the audience, but this can often lead to more exciting theatrical experiences.

How may exterior settings be removed from the strictly realistic? They may be simplified by using only those objects necessary to the creation of the proper environment for the play (Simplified Realism, as exemplified in Plate 70). Realistic forms may frequently be fragmented and reduced in number to produce a setting

Plate 70. *SIMPLIFIED REALISTIC EXTERIOR: Platforms and levels plus a number of bamboo stalks create the impression of an oriental forest.* Rashomon *designed for the University of Georgia by Raoul Johnson. (Photo by Gates Studio)*

that might be termed Stylized Realism or Fragmentary Realism as exemplified in Plate 76. Exaggeration and distortion of forms, which can be made more decorative through the method of painting, can produce the kind of stylized exterior as seen in Plate 71...a fantasy ballet setting. Additional simplification and stylization may even result in an exterior suggested by a few simple shapes enhanced by carefully designed lighting, as can be seen in

would be well to consider all the possibilities before finally deciding on the style that is to be used.

### SCRIPT GUIDELINES

Many of the same questions we applied to the script when designing an interior are applicable to the play requiring an exterior

Plate 71.  *STYLIZED EXTERIOR: Exaggerated painted elements derived from children's book illustrations create an appropriately foreboding quality for* The Firebird *produced by DePass Dance Theatre. Scenery by the author.*

Plate 70. Lighting may also reduce the need for specific masking by focusing on a central scenic unit isolated against black masking as seen in Plate 71. And there are as many other ways of creating effective exteriors as there are imaginative designers to think them up. The possibilities are endless.

It is certain, in any case, that the realistic approach is only one of many, and, considering the problems inherent in that approach, it

setting. We are still interested in the place, period, mood, and style of the play. In view of the preceding section, we can see that we will want to pay particular attention to the style of the play to determine the possibilities of types of designs other than realistic. We will want to determine the specific setting requirements—those items necessary to the action of the play. We will, perhaps, need to pay less strict attention to the characters in the play

Plate 72. *SIMPLIFIED EXTERIOR: A wooden platform framed with bare branches suggests the exterior location in this setting for* Three Sisters *produced at the Alley Theatre, Houston, and designed by Peter David Gould. (Photo by Jim Caldwell)*

because they may be less likely to directly influence the decor or contents of an exterior setting—except, of course, in the case of a play that requires the house and/or yard of a particular family. We must be careful to note time of day, season, and weather conditions—particularly if there is any change necessary. When seasons change, so does foliage, and this may necessitate the addition or removal of foliage at some time during the play. It occasionally rains or snows during the course of a play, and provision must be made for this effect. In order to avoid having it rain or snow over the entire stage, you will want to design the setting in such a way as to confine the effect to a small portion of the stage—particularly in the case of a rainstorm, which can flood a stage in no time unless such provisions are made. Keep an eye out, also, for any mention in the script of items that might be used for side masking purposes. If no mention is made

of any such items, then you may have to depend on research.

## RESEARCH

Many of the sources mentioned in the preceding chapter will still be useful. Architectural histories, for instance, are still important. In addition, many profusely illustrated travel books of inestimable value to the designer are currently on the market. Illustrated geographical studies of particular countries and regions plus specialized books on trees, flowers, rocks, and land formations may prove important. In several instances, books on gems and jewels have provided sources of inspiration to designers. When researching exteriors in the library, it will pay you to look under these general headings and also under the individual country, state, or region headings to locate source material. And don't forget magazines. Those mentioned previously are still of use, plus *Holiday* and similar travel magazines. Any of these may provide you with valuable information or ideas that can be used to enhance the setting.

### PLANNING THE SETTING

In planning the setting, the designer should be aware that there are three general types of exterior scene: the urban scene, composed primarily of buildings and streets; the "yard" scene, consisting of residences and their surrounding yards or fields; and the scene that takes place in a forest, on a mountain, in a desert, or in some other such locale characterized by strictly natural elements. As might be expected, the more man-made forms used in the setting, the easier it is to design, so that the urban scene is perhaps the least demanding form of exterior setting. In addition, it is possible to depict each of these types of

setting in a variety of styles ranging from the realistic to the almost totally abstract. It has been pointed out earlier that the realistic exterior is the most difficult to create satisfactorily.

All of the above represent a wide range of choices for the designer. The play itself will, obviously, dictate whether the setting is to be urban, "yard," or natural, but the choice of style is up to the designer and the director. There can be no doubt that the choice of style is the foremost decision to be made, for all other developments of the setting are predicated upon this decision. The choice of a realistic style means that realistic means of masking must be devised. Choice of simplified realism or stylization lessens this problem, but necessitates a clear understanding of the particular mode of presentation so that it can be carried through all of the elements of the setting.

Since the masking is one of the principal concerns of the exterior setting, the first step in planning the setting must usually be the development of a floor plan. Those units of

Plate 73. *EXTERIOR ISOLATED AGAINST BLACK: The lighting focus on the central building isolated against the black surround eliminates the need for realistic masking in this setting for* The Night of the Iguana *designed by John Ross for the University of Alabama.*

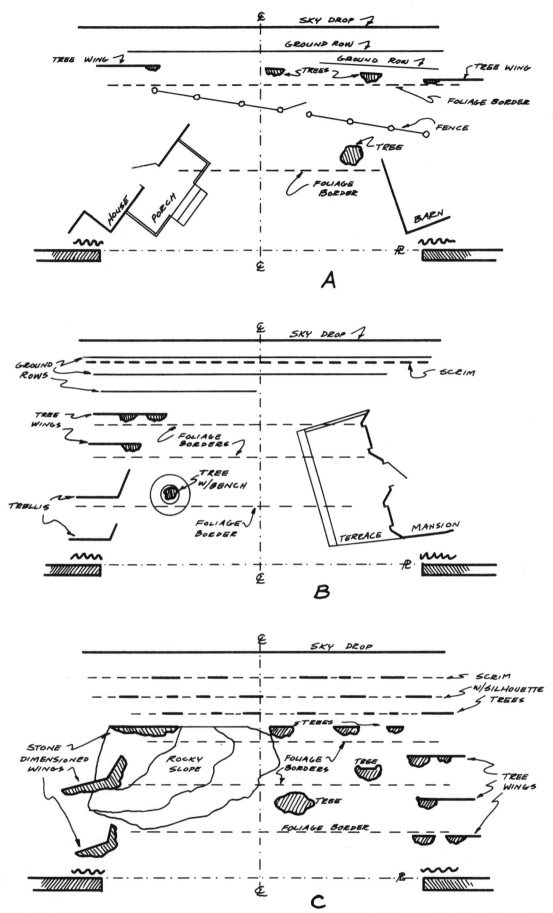

Plate 74.   *SAMPLE FLOOR PLANS FOR REALISTIC EXTERIORS:  (a) farmyard setting; (b) mansion garden setting; (c) forest setting.*

**113**

scenery required by the script must be noted and then arranged in a manner that can best serve the action of the play. In a realistic style of setting, this arrangement may be complicated by the fact that the required units of scenery (particularly the large architectural units) must not only serve the action of the play, but must also be used to mask a portion of the offstage area. This means that buildings are usually placed to one side of the stage or the other in order to serve as masking for that side of the stage. Ordinarily, this will not be a particular handicap in so far as the visual design is concerned, since it usually results in an asymmetrically balanced design, such as the set shown in Plate 68. It does, however, need a designer's careful planning and design of the building unit in order for it to serve both the masking and the action of the play, since the action might work more effectively if the building were in a more central location. In the natural scenes, it is the large natural elements that must be placed at the sides of the stage in order to serve as masking.

In many cases, the scenic elements required by the script will not be sufficient to provide complete masking. It is then that the designer is called upon to devise masking units such as those mentioned in the first section of this chapter. The sightlines of the theatre must be carefully plotted and the various masking elements tested until the offstage areas are effectively concealed. Several floor plans illustrating masking arrangements for realistically designed exterior settings are shown in Plate 74.

The choice of a less realistic mode of presentation results in less emphasis being placed on the exact realism of the masking elements. The edges of the stage can be allowed to fade off into black—achieved either through the use of black masking or by only a suggestion of realistic forms or silhouettes. When it is less important that they serve as masking, the principal setting elements can be moved onstage and assume a more dominant playing position. This release from the multiple duty of masking and acting allows the scenic elements to be better arranged to serve the action of the play.

In the simplified realistic setting, lighting becomes increasingly important in the creation of the exterior atmosphere. Leaf patterns projected onto a wall, or other surface of the setting, can very effectively suggest the presence of trees and foliage. Note the effectiveness of

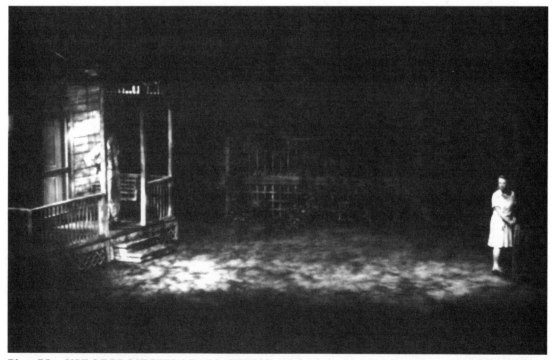

Plate 75.   *USE OF PROJECTED LEAF PATTERNS: Multiple layers of leaf patterns projected from gobos in ellipsoidal lighting instruments help to create the exterior reality in this rather fragmentary setting for* To Kill a Mockingbird *produced by the Gainesville Theatre Alliance, Gainesville, GA. Scenery and lighting by the author.*

device in the setting for *To Kill a Mockingbird* shown in Plate 75. More elaborate projected images can create an even stronger sense of exterior, as may be seen in the setting shown in Plate 76. Simple signed in the manner of the Renaissance (Plate 79) or a suggested Baroque (Plate 80).

Such unity between the masking devices and the dominant scenic elements is an extremely important

Plate 76. *USE OF AN EXTERIOR PROJECTION AS A BACKGROUND: A large-sized image of a forest scene fills in this setting composed of otherwise relatively few scenic elements.* Dido and Aeneas *designed by Richard Mason for the Ensemble Players Guild of Hawaii. (Photo by Francis Haar)*

suggestive devices make the realistic setting more atmospheric, more exciting, and (strangely enough) more convincing than the setting that attempts to depict an exterior completely realistically.

As the style of production moves further from realism, opportunities open to use the setting elements and the masking for more expressive purposes. Although, at first glance, the setting in Plate 77 appears realistic, closer inspection reveals that building details and the signage have been enlarged, simplified, and somewhat distorted to enhance the exaggerated nature of the performance in the modern melodrama for which it was designed. Choice of a style patterned after the settings of a more historical theatrical period may result in an exterior de-

part of any setting, and is frequently much easier to achieve in a stylized setting than in a realistic one.

Although the floor plan, depicting the arrangement of major scenic elements and masking units, is usually the initial step in the design of the exterior, it is important that the designer not lose sight of the appearance of the entire setting from the audience point of view. It is usually wise to make thumbnail sketches, as a record, of each trial floor plan so that an idea can be gained of the visual appearance of each arrangement. Once the final floor plan has been devised, then the pictorial composition becomes the primary concern. At this point, it is important for the designer to remember that there is infinite variety in nature as well as in architectural shape and decor.

Plate 77. *STYLIZED CITY EXTERIOR: Building details, arrangement and decorative signage have been enlarged and distorted in this setting for a modern melodrama entitled* Riverview *which premiered at The Goodman Theatre with scenery designed by Thomas Lynch. (Photo by Liz Lauren)*

Plate 78. *STYLIZED RURAL EXTERIOR: Openwork building frames against realistically painted tree profiles create a clean, fresh quality in this setting for* Second Sons *produced at the Cumberland County Playhouse, TN, with scenery by Leonard Harmon.*

A tree is not just a tree, but it is a specific kind of tree with a definite form and its own type of leaf—a pine tree being vastly different from a weeping willow, for instance. Each of the forms of the various trees can provide varying qualities to a setting, particularly if the peculiarities of the tree are emphasized; and this is true of all the elements of nature. Careful attention should be paid to the choice of elements in order to project the desired atmo-

tion are more often used in exterior settings and should be familiar to the designer.

### CONSTRUCTION TECHNIQUES

The construction techniques more often employed in exterior settings than in interiors are those concerned with irregular objects—rocks, trees, foliage profiles, scenic vista ground rows,

Plate 79. *STYLIZED EXTERIOR DESIGNED AFTER THE STYLE OF THE RENAISSANCE: In this setting for* A Comedy of Errors *produced at the University of Georgia, a perspective vista behind an inner portal (note Shakespeare and his twin as puppeteers controlling the action) together with highly simplified and brightly colored buildings in the Renaissance style set this production into a highly theatricalized outdoor environment. Scenery by the author. (Photo by Gates Studio)*

sphere and mood of the play—these being produced by the line, mass, color, and texture of the elements of the setting and the way in which they interact with one another. In the more stylized designs, the dominant characteristics of the chosen elements can then be emphasized to project more clearly the proper atmosphere. Note the way this was accomplished in the setting shown in Plate 78.

As in the design of any other type of setting, once the design has been completed and approved, the next step is the preparation of construction drawings. Several types of construc-

and similar units. This may be divided into three categories: two-dimensional irregular units, three-dimensional irregular units, and soft scenery units such as backdrops, foliage borders, and cut drops. A brief description of the methods of constructing these units follows.

*Two-Dimensional Irregular Units (Plate 81)*

An irregular two-dimensional unit may be broadly defined as any flat unit that does not conform to a strictly rectangular or otherwise geometric shape. Usually these units, when used for exteriors, take the form of profile

Plate 80.  *A STYLIZED BAROQUE EXTERIOR:  A projected background of simplified tree shapes and projected leaf patterns on the floor combine with projections of outdoor statuary to suggest an exterior locale for this production of* Twelfth Night *at the University of Georgia.  Designed by the author.*

units (units with irregular cut-out edges) designed to simulate trees, foliage, rocks, etc., and used as wings or ground rows for the setting. The settings shown in Plates 67, 69, 75, and 76 utilize these types of units. The irregular outline is cut from ⅛″ plywood, ¼″ plywood, upsom board or, occasionally, ¾″ plywood. The material used depends on the amount of rough treatment the unit must withstand during performance. In most cases, upsom board is sufficiently durable for the purpose. It is also the least expensive and the easiest to cut. The framing members are constructed from 1″ x 3″ lumber or 1″ x 2″ lumber.

Wherever possible, stock flats should be used in the construction, with the cut-out profile being added to the edges of the flats. This is by far the most economical method—in terms of both time and money. There are times, however, when the unit is too irregular in contour to allow the use of stock flats. In such a case the unit must be constructed in its entirety.

In both cases the procedure is basically the same. The cutting of the material (upsom board or plywood) is accomplished first. The cut-out piece is then laid face down, the framing members are cut and laid out to match the contours of the profile, then fastened together with corner blocks and keystones. Here are a few general rules to remember concerning the construction of the frame:

1. Bottom rails should extend the full width of the unit.

2. The longest external and internal framing members should extend through all other internal members.

3. No more than 6″ of free-standing profile should be left unframed.

4. Any edge of the profile that is to be attached to another unit should be framed.

5. The framing members should not extend beyond the profile at any point.

When the profile is to be attached to a standard flat, the outer framing members of

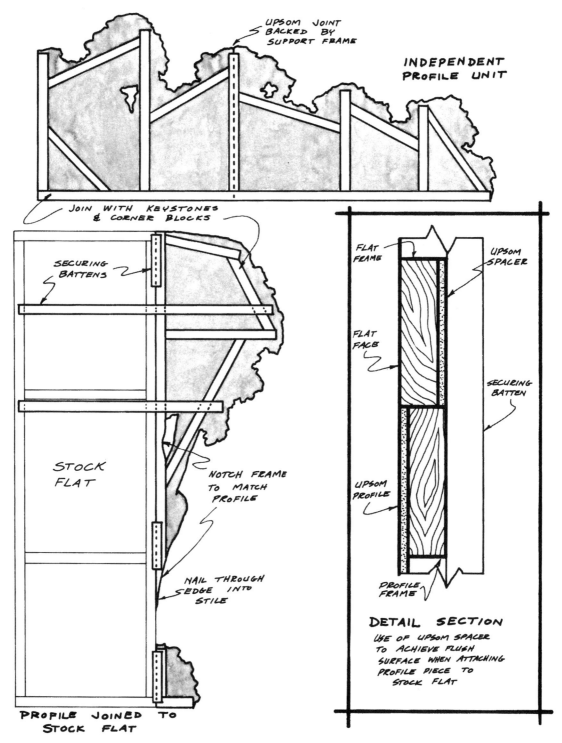

Plate 81. *CONSTRUCTION OF IRREGULAR TWO-DIMENSIONAL UNITS*

the flat to which the profile will be attached must be backed with the same material used for the cutout before battening on the profile piece. This ensures a flush joint on the face. All such joints should be dutchmanned before painting. Often it is a good idea to cover the face of the profile with fabric (e.g., cheesecloth) to more closely match the surface of the flat; or both elements may be covered with a readily available texturing compound to provide a more interesting surface quality.

*Three-Dimensional Irregular Units (Plate 82)*

Rocks, irregular ground, and tree trunks are the most common units of three-dimensional scenery used in exterior settings. The construc-

The principal method employed uses a basic two-dimensional frame cut from appropriate width lumber (usually 1″ x 6″ or 1″ x 12″) and fitted together to form the outline of the

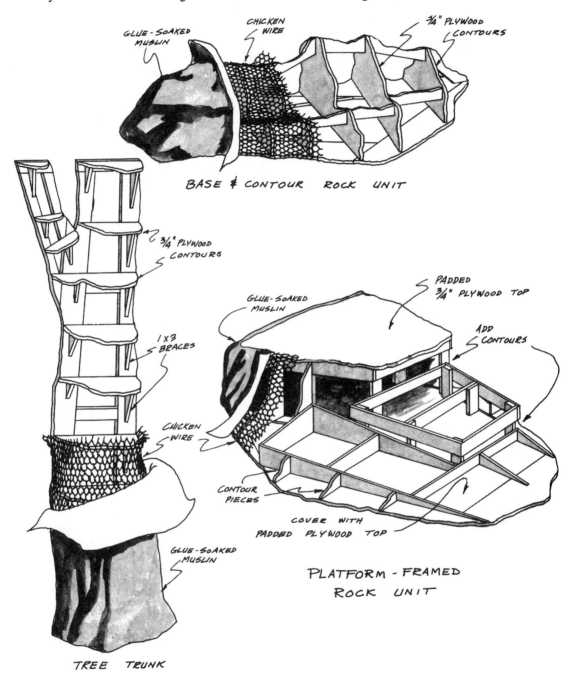

Plate 82. *CONSTRUCTION OF IRREGULAR THREE-DIMENSIONAL UNITS*

tion methods for such units are more or less extemporaneous, since no two such units are alike. However, certain general methods can be adapted to the majority of such scenic elements.

unit. In rock units this frame follows the exact shape of the base of the unit. For trees, the frame provides the basic outline of the trunk. Across the shortest dimension of this frame is attached a series of contour pieces of ¾″ plywood cut to the desired shape of the unit at that point. These contour pieces are stiffened with cross-bracing of 1″ x 2″ lumber or additional ¾″ plywood cut to a contour shape. Any weight-bearing surfaces should be provided with additional reinforcement—enough to ensure adequate support.

Plate 82 shows the unit being covered with 1″ chicken wire or 1/2″ screen wire, shaped to the desired contours. In this more traditional method the skeleton framework is then covered with either papier mache—newspaper and paper towel soaked in wheat paste—or glue-soaked burlap or muslin, which is secured over the frame and allowed to harden. More contemporary solutions involve solid foam cut-outs applied to the framework and then covered with glue-soaked fabric or one of the several hardening pastes and sealers for foam found on today's market. Sawdust, ground cork, foam chips or wood chips added to the final surface paste provide additional texture to the completed unit.

Three-dimensional units designed primarily as playing areas usually require a number of flat, or nearly flat, platform surfaces on which the actors can perform. In this case, each flat or slanting platform area is constructed in the same manner as the rigid platform described in Chapter IV. This method is adapted to the particular slant or shape of the various surfaces. The platform frames are then attached together into the desired arrangement. The exact shape of the base of the unit is formed by attaching base contour pieces of 3/4″ plywood to the bottoms of the supporting members of the platform frames. The irregular edges of the unit are formed by vertical contour pieces set in between the base contour and the platform supports. The platform tops are then cut to the desired shapes from 3/4″ plywood and attached in position. The outside contoured edges are created by any of the means described above; however, the surface upon which the actors trod should be kept free of any materials which might crackle or crack under the feet of the actors walking upon the surface.

*Soft Scenery Units (Plate 83)*

Backdrops, foliage borders, and cut drops, borders, and legs are usually constructed from muslin or cotton duck—muslin being the preferred material for backdrops. All of these units are designed to be attached to a batten at the top, with another batten or pipe being used to hold the bottom in place. All drops are sewn with horizontal face-to-face seams, which, when the drop is hanging, are under enough pressure from the weight of the material and the bottom batten to stretch into a smooth surface. There are two ways in which the top and bottom can be constructed:

1. Top: A 4″ to 6″ hem is sewn, heavy canvas webbing reinforcement is sewn across the back of the hem, and metal grommets are set through the muslin and webbing at 1′ intervals to accommodate tie-lines.

Bottom: a. The bottom may be sewn in a wide hem (4″ to 6″) through which a pipe batten may be inserted, or

b. it may be hemmed, grommets inserted at 1′ intervals, and then tied onto a batten.

2. Top: The top edge of the material is tacked to a wooden batten the full width of the drop, then a second batten is placed on top of the material and screwed to the first, thus sandwiching the material between the two battens.

Bottom: a. The material may be fastened between two battens, as in the top construction, and the battens rounded off, or

b. the material may be wrapped around a batten on the rear of the drop. If this method is used, the bottom of the drop need not be concealed from the view of the audience.

For cut drops, borders, and legs, the top and bottom construction just described may also be used. The face is then painted in the desired manner. After the paint is dry, the material is cut away into the desired shape. The cut portion of the fabric is then supported by gluing 1″ mesh netting across the rear of the cut opening.

Carefully constructed as they may be, none of the units just described—whether they be two-dimensional or three-dimensional—will be entirely convincing until it has received careful painting. There are several painting techniques, in addition to those described in the preceding chapter, that may be used to make these units more convincing.

## PAINTING TECHNIQUES

Many of the techniques mentioned in Chapter IV are useful in painting exterior settings. Two additional methods for achieving textures are particularly useful in these types of settings:

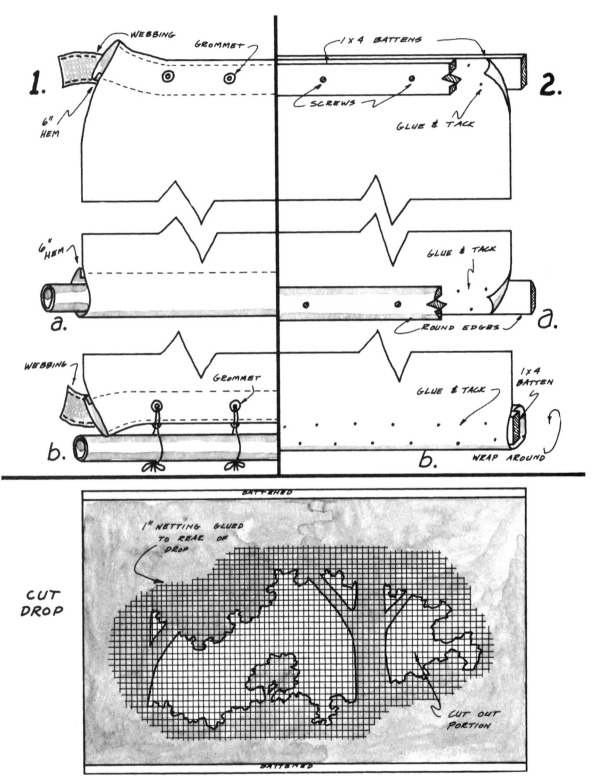

Plate 83. *CONSTRUCTION OF BACKDROPS*

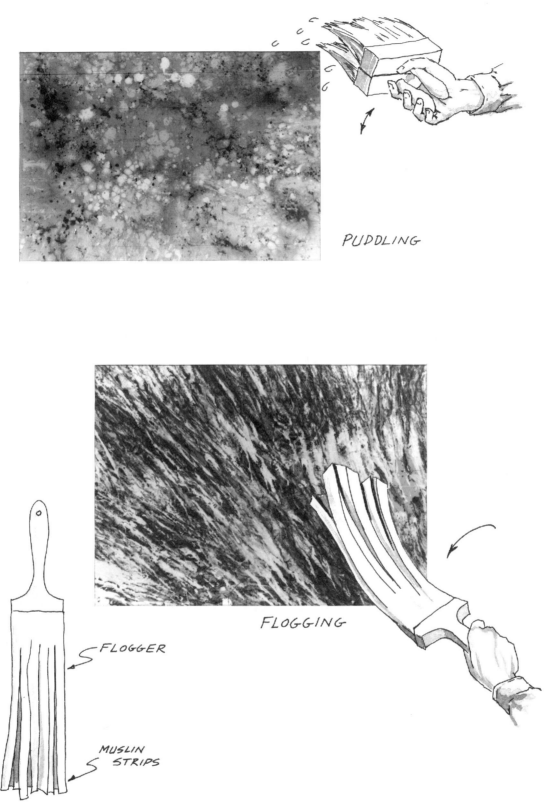

PUDDLING

FLOGGING

FLOGGER

MUSLIN STRIPS

Plate 84. *TEXTURE PAINTING TECHNIQUES FOR EXTERIORS*

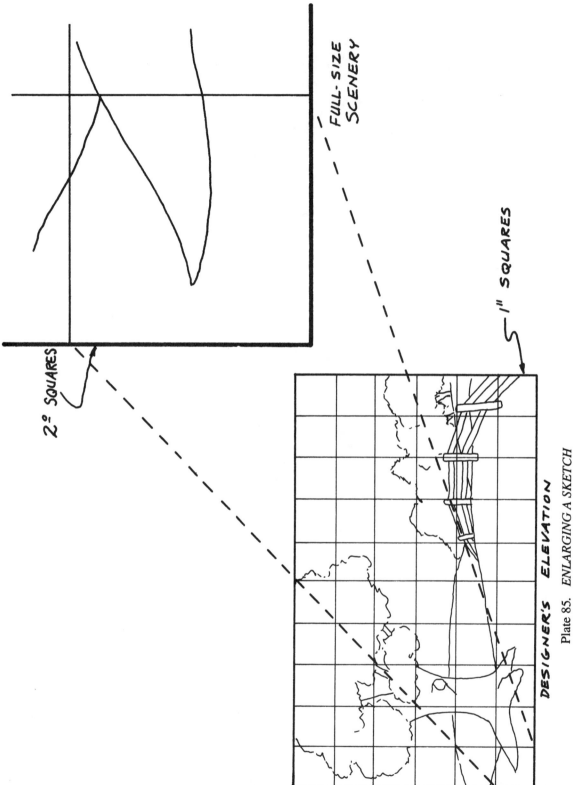

DESIGNER'S ELEVATION

Plate 85.  ENLARGING A SKETCH

*Texturing (Plate 84)*

PUDDLING: The blending of several colors onto a wet surface to give the appearance of great depth. This is particularly useful for the suggestion of foliage, marble, old plaster, and other surfaces that require great richness and depth. The scenery is laid face up on the floor and painted while the base coat is still wet. Two or more brushes charged with different colors are used simultaneously, held at waist height and shaken over the scenery to achieve drops and blended puddles of color. Colors may be added and eliminated as neces-sary to achieve the desired blend and gradation of hues.

FLOGGING: A useful method for simulating certain types of foliage. Strips of cloth (usually muslin or burlap) are attached to a handle, charged with paint, then flogged across the scenery. Variations in the type of material used, the type of stroke, and the direction of the stroke can produce a variety of effects.

*Pictorial and Detail Painting*

Much painting for an exterior setting is of a pictorial nature. As such, there are no hard

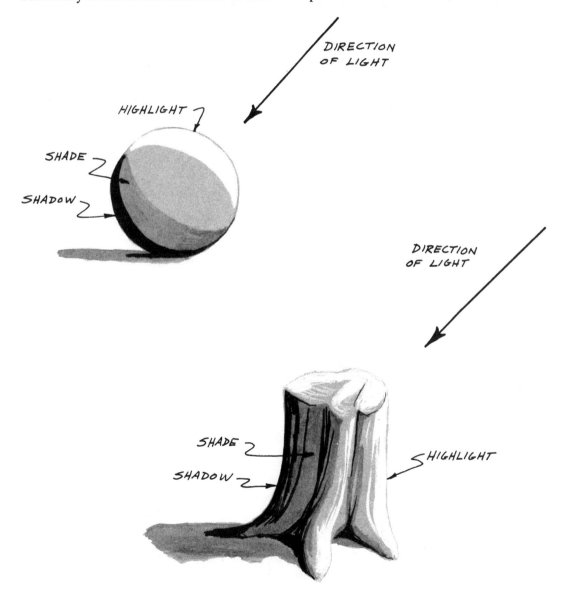

Plate 86. *HIGHLIGHT AND SHADOW: Achieving three-dimensionality through paint.*

FOLIAGE

STONES

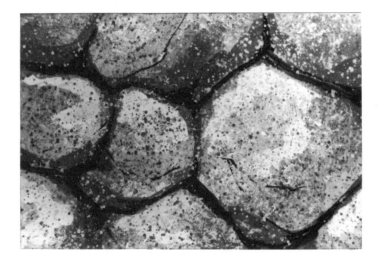

BRICKWORK

Plate 87. *PAINTING TECHNIQUES FOR EXTERIORS*

and fast rules or techniques to be applied. Each painter usually develops his own style and technique for his type of painting. A few hints, however, might be of help.

ENLARGING A SKETCH (Plate 85): In order to transpose a landscape or some other such pictorial or irregular design accurately from a small sketch onto the full-size scenery, rule off the surface to be painted into 2' squares. A snap line is often useful for this job. Rule off the painter's elevation, or sketch, into an equal number of squares, then copy each square as accurately as possible to enlarge the design.

HIGHLIGHT AND SHADOW (Plate 86) : in pictorial painting, three-dimensional objects are delineated and described by highlight and shadow. Those surfaces of an irregularly shaped object that are closest to the source of light appear highlighted, and those areas that recede, or are away from the light, appear shadowed. These effects are achieved by taking the base color(s) of the object and adding white to obtain highlight, and adding black, dark brown, or dark blue in varying degrees to obtain shadow. Any object to be simulated through paint should be carefully studied as to color, texture, and the way in which highlight and shadow fall on the contours of the surface. These, then, should be duplicated as closely as possible in broadened and simplified style.

For exterior settings, three of the most often required painting techniques are those used to duplicate stones, brick, and foliage. There are many ways of achieving effective results in painting these surfaces. As an example, however, I will describe the techniques used to achieve the results shown in Plate 87.

FOLIAGE: This was really a quite simple procedure. The background was puddled in with varying shades and values of green. After that dried, the leaves were roughly detailed in by brush, using a base green plus highlight and shadow green. Other techniques for foliage might incorporate the flogging technique described earlier and also the use of a feather duster, which might be stippled or flogged onto the surface.

ROCKS: The base coat was scumbled on, using several shades of gray—warm and cool. Slightly darker and slightly lighter values of gray were then rag-stippled onto the surface, using a burlap rag. The highlights and shadows were roughly brushed in, then the entire surface was spattered with two of the original shades used in the scumbled base coat. The final touch was to use a small brush charged in dark shadow color to sharpen up the deep shadows and crevices.

BRICKS: The base coat of red-brown was brushed on smoothly, then two heavy burlap rag-stipple coats were applied with varying tones of brick color. The mortar was lined in with a light gray, using a straightedge. The entire surface was lightly spattered with two medium tones of shade value; then the final dark shadow was applied freehand with a small brush.

One final general word about the painting of landscapes before I close this chapter. It is usually wise to keep the colors as light as possible, varying the value of tints and avoiding black shadows. Objects in the far distance are painted much lighter in value and very close to blue-gray in color. As objects move closer to the foreground, their colors become purer and brighter, and their detail becomes sharper and clearer.

Although these painting techniques have been included in this chapter on exterior settings (where they are most often used), it is quite possible, and likely, that they will also be used in the two general types of settings found in the next section: multisetting dramas and musicals.

# SECTION III:
# DESIGNING THE MULTISETTING SHOW

# chapter VI

# DRAMAS

From the beginning of recorded theatre history, playwrights have been unwilling to confine the action of their plays to a single setting. Aeschylus called for multiple settings in several of his plays, although we have no clear record of the means the Greeks used to change the scene. Some historians hypothesize the use of painted panels and *periaktoi* (prism-shaped arrangements of flats) to change the scene in Greek theatre. In medieval times, the various scenes were set up on pageant wagons and trooped in a procession through the town. The Renaissance theatre (which introduced the proscenium arch) provided the first multisetting productions in which the total stage picture was changed—usually in full view of the audience. As a matter of fact, the audiences of that time enjoyed the scene changes so much that plays often became merely vehicles to provide extravagant scene changes. Scene changes then—and for the next several centuries—were accomplished primarily by sliding wings on- and offstage and flying backdrops in and out, with some use of *periaktoi*. Although the mechanisms were crude by our standards, the effects were quite magical—particularly in the dim stage light of the period.

During the latter part of the 19th century, European theatre personnel became dissatisfied with those mechanisms and began experimenting with other means of altering the setting—bringing the turntable idea from Japan, introducing elevators, and experimenting with lighting effects. This trend has continued until the present time when we find ourselves truly in the machine age insofar as scene-changing devices are concerned. For those with the necessary funds, there is a bewildering galaxy of sophisticated mechanical devices that can be incorporated into a theatre to make scene changing literally a push-button operation.

It is perhaps unfortunate that most theatres cannot afford many—if any—of these devices. All too often, scene changes must be accomplished through sweat and ingenuity—the latter replacing the former whenever possible. Fortunately for the designer struggling with inadequate facilities, the trend in recent years has been away from full-stage settings replacing one another in endless succession, as was the ideal during the era of realism. Spot settings, unit settings, settings created through lights, settings changed by the actors, and settings that are altered through one or two minor changes have become the norm for modern multisetting shows. Even these types of settings, however, have not completely alleviated all of the problems of the multisetting production.

## SPECIAL PROBLEMS AND CONSIDERATIONS

Most problems connected with multiset shows are logistical in nature—how many settings, how much scenery, where can it be stored, how can it be moved in the most efficient and speediest manner, how many persons will be required to accomplish the changes, and how long will it take to construct the settings? Most of these should be taken into consideration before the show is finally selected for presentation. Plays with extremely complicated scenic requirements should not be undertaken for production with limited stage facilities without full awareness that the necessarily reduced settings may not provide much visual support for the actors. It is trite but true that a simpler production well presented is far more desirable than an elaborate production with a slap-dash, half-finished appearance.

It is obvious that the more individual settings required in a play, the more time required to construct and paint the show, and the more space required for offstage storage of scenic units. Fully-changing settings will require more stagehands, and more space for personnel backstage. All of this requires the designer to carefully scrutinize the physical needs of the play together with the space and equipment available in order to achieve the most efficient and effective design possible.

It is extremely important that scene shifts be accomplished with great speed—particularly shifts which occur during scene breaks where there is no intermission. The trend in contemporary theatre is to plan scene changes which occur in full view of the audience (*a-vista*), requiring careful planning to provide an interesting spectacle for the audience as well as rapid and effective alterations in the stage picture. Rare these days is the setting which is changed behind a closed curtain while the audience waits, impatiently, in darkness or semi-darkness.

*A-Vista* scene changes must be carefully planned and executed, since the performers themselves often execute part, if not all, of the scene changes. This requires that the designer and director discuss thoroughly the scheme and timing of the scene changes, and the changes themselves must be as carefully choreographed and rehearsed as any other part of the play. While difficult, the results can be extremely effective and exciting—as may be seen in productions of *Les Miserables* and *Sweeney Todd: The Demon Barber of Fleet Street*.

Aesthetically, a multi-setting show presents a problem with regard to unity of design. It is necessary to maintain a consistent style and point-of-view through a series of settings which may range from a Western saloon to an ocean liner. The designer must make a firm commitment to the total production concept and maintain this concept throughout each of the individual settings by means of consistent use of design elements and style—this in addition to planning the method of shifting each setting. As always, the script is the starting point in achieving this goal.

## SCRIPT GUIDELINES

The script will provide information to help the designer make a decision as to the best method of presentation. Again, this information may be acquired by answering several specific questions:

*How many separate settings are required in the play?* This is basic to an intelligent appraisal of the magnitude of the job.

*How many times is each setting used?* A play requiring three settings may also require that each setting be used several times, alternating from one setting to another and back again, so that there may be as many as seven or eight scene changes with only the three settings.

*What are the physical requirements of each setting?* This includes such things as doors, windows, furniture, space for necessary action, number of actors who use the setting, and any special physical requirements such as were mentioned in Chapter IV. Settings with minimal requirements used by only one or two actors may well be designed as small "spot" settings.

*What is the sequence of the use of the settings?* It is at this point that the major trouble spots will show up. The most difficult scene changes are those in which one large complex setting must rapidly be changed to another large complex setting. Determining the sequence of the settings will tell you how often this occurs in the show. It is often possible that a large setting will be followed by a setting that can be small enough to be played "in one" (see Chapter II), or set within the large setting, which can then be changed behind or around the small setting during that scene.

*Are there any times when two settings must be used simultaneously?* Frequently a play will require that action be seen in two separate rooms at the same time—showing both ends of a telephone conversation, for instance. Along the same lines, it sometimes is necessary for an actor to walk directly from one room into another with no pause to allow for any sort of scene shift.

In consultation with the director, the designer must evaluate the effect the style and form of the play might have on the setting. For instance, how necessary are completely realistic settings to the play? Is it possible, or even preferable, to suggest scenes with small set pieces and furniture? Should there be individual settings for each scene, or should the scenes be played on a more permanent type of structure with only minor changes to indicate the various locales? How necessary is a total visual environment to the effectiveness of the play? An answer to this question will determine the basic approach to the setting—the choice of a type of setting most appropriate to this particular play.

## TYPES OF SETTINGS

Roughly four types of settings are most often seen today in multisetting productions: the *permanent*, or "formal," setting; the *simultaneous* setting; the *unit* setting; and the *fully shifting* setting.

*Permanent, or Formal, Scenery*

The permanent setting remains constant throughout the play, presenting multiple acting areas upon which all of the scenes of the play occur without any major change in the setting except through lighting, costumes, or set props. This type of setting is usually characterized by an arrangement of steps, ramps, and platforms that may or may not be combined with other scenic elements. The purpose is to present a setting suggesting the style and atmosphere of the play, providing a variety of acting levels and areas, but not re-creating any particular place. A setting of this nature is particularly useful for plays that require a multitude of assorted locales with little emphasis on actual

few set pieces or props. Three examples of this can be seen in Plates 88, 89 and 90, while a modern version of a permanent setting is shown in Plate 91.

In planning a setting using a variety of levels, it is important to provide at least two means of access to each level—from either a lower level, a higher level, or from offstage. This is particularly true for a production that requires a large number of differing scenes or a large number of actors. In addition, it is important that the levels provide adequate playing space, and that steps and ramps not be so high or steep as to make movement difficult for the actors. Ideally, the most important playing levels should be as near center stage as possible.

Small, easily movable decorative pieces such

Plate 88. *PERMANENT SETTING WITH GENERALIZED PERIOD DECOR: Painted texture and pylon shapes suggest a general historical period in this setting for* Troilus and Cressida *at the University of Georgia. Scenery by the author. (Photo by Gates Studio)*

place – as in Shakespeare, for example. Most permanent settings today suggest the general period of the play by providing a generalized playing space which can take on different appearances through changes of lighting and the adding or deleting of a

as banners, tapestries, and heraldry, combined with necessary furniture units, serve to indicate changes of locale. These should be as decorative as possible in keeping with the style of the production. (One rule of thumb is that the

Plate 89. *PERMANENT SETTING WITH GENERALIZED PERIOD DECOR: Elegant early 18th-century ornament supplemented with multiple projected images create a stylish permanent setting for* Twelfth Night, *produced by the University of Georgia with scene design by the author.*

Plate 90. *PERMANENT SETTING IN A CONSTRUCTIVIST STYLE: The visible structure of the rear surround and the upper level combined with the irregular appearance of the planked floor creates a rough-hewn period quality in this setting for* The Taming of the Shrew *at the University of Western Kentucky. Design and sketch by Tom Tutino.*

smaller and fewer the scenic units used in a scene, the more decorative each must be.) The setting shown in Plate 88 uses such elements to change locale for various scenes. Lighting also aids in changing the locale, highlighting different areas at various times and in varying ways and suggesting a

interior, as can be seen in Plates 96 and 97.

Many plays require a simultaneous setting. *The Miracle Worker*, *Death of a Salesman*, and *The Diary of Anne Frank* call for this type of setting. Many other plays would work quite well within the framework of a simultaneous setting, which speeds

Plate 91. *PERMANENT SETTING USING CONTEMPORARY MOTIFS: Materials and elements suggesting a modern factory-like environment shape this setting for* The Good Person of Setzuan *produced by The Goodman Theatre, Chicago, with scenery by Loy Arcenas. (Photo by Liz Lauren)*

place or period. Plates 89 and 92 show the use of projections to augment and alter a permanent setting. Such effects help to achieve a sense of the locale of each scene without breaking the rapid flow of the scenes of the play—one of the particular advantages of the permanent setting.

*Simultaneous Setting*

The simultaneous setting is similar to the permanent setting in that the setting rarely changes; however, the setting is more clearly representative of the locales in the play. Usually the locales represented are fewer in number than those required in plays for which the permanent setting is used. Frequently the interior and exterior of a building are depicted, as in the settings in Plates 93, 94, 95 and 98. Other settings may show several rooms within a single

up the flow of a play by allowing the action to move rapidly from one area to another, depending on lighting to shift the focus of attention.

One disadvantage of the simultaneous setting is that it usually requires more than the average amount of stage space in order to provide adequate acting space within each individualized area. However, careful utilization of space will sometimes make it possible to squeeze a setting of this sort onto a very small stage.

You will, no doubt, have noted that most of these settings make use of varied or multiple levels—often used as a full second story. This helps to create a visual separation of the various playing areas, and also helps to conserve stage space by playing one scene directly over another. The various areas and levels must be carefully planned and constructed to

Plate 92. *PROJECTED IMAGES USED WITH A PERMANENT SETTING: A highly stylized permanent setting was supplemented with projected period images in this very propagandistic docudrama. A production of* Indians *at the University of Hawaii. Designed by Richard Mason. (Photo by Francis Haar)*

Plate 93. *INTERIOR-EXTERIOR SIMULTANEOUS SETTING: Very simplified and suggested scenic elements and set properties are the foundation of this setting for* All the Way Home, *Broadway production at the Belasco Theatre, NYC. Scenery design is by David Hays.*

Plate 94. *INTERIOR-EXTERIOR SIMULTANEOUS SETTING: Two interior rooms plus a porch and a generalized interview area are presented in a very modern, northern- California style setting for* The Shadow Box *produced by the Alliance Theatre, Atlanta, with scenery by the author.*

Plate 95. *INTERIOR-EXTERIOR SIMULTANEOUS SETTING: Cut-away ceilings plus varied roof and exterior elements add visual interest to this setting for one of Tennessee William's most famous plays. A production of* A Streetcar Named Desire *at the University of Minnesota-Duluth. Scenery by Richard Durst.*

Plate 96. *INTERIOR SIMULTANEOUS SETTING: Glimpses of exterior roof and house foundations add a sense of period and architectural character to this simultaneous setting for* The Art of Dining. *Design and sketch by Richard Durst for the University of Minnesota-Duluth.*

Plate 97. *INTERIOR SIMULTANEOUS SETTING: Multiple levels help differentiate the various areas of this attic room while projected images reinforce the historical reality of* The Diary of Anne Frank. *Designed by Leonard Harmon for Cumberland County Playhouse, TN.*

allow necessary access to each, as well as to present a visually logical arrangement to the audience—particularly in cases in which the various areas are different rooms of a single building. Some indication of the shape and style of the exterior of the building will often help to unify the several areas. The distinctive roof elements plus the shape and architectural features added to the base of the setting illustrated in Plate 96 indicate much about the period and architectural style of the building as well as suggesting the organization of the rooms. In the setting for *A Streetcar Named Desire* illustrated in Plate 95, the fully realized exterior with its varied roof elements and the cut-away ceilings clarify the locale and the building layout, in addition to adding great visual interest to the setting. The surround of the setting is also very important to the overall effect. Even the simplest indication of elements surrounding the setting can provide a strong atmosphere for the setting. Note the effect achieved by the planking background in Plate 93 and the very different feeling created by the collage background used in the setting in Plate 97.

*Unit Setting*

A unit setting employs several basic scenic ele-ments, which usually remain onstage during the entire production, but are turned, moved about, and combined with a variety of other scenic elements to alter the appearance of the setting. There are several varieties of this form of setting. One of the more popular incorporates a permanent façade contain-ing a series of openings or arches, which are filled with various plugs to represent the various scenes in the play, or, for some scenes, may be left clear to reveal a background scene. In plate 99, permanent doorways and balconies on either side provide for varied acting areas while the central archway frames different elements used to alter the locale for each scene.

Another variation makes use of a permanent struc-ture of platforms and surrounding masking struc-ture. Changes are made by set pieces that fly, roll, or are carried on to alter the appearance of the setting. Differences between this form of setting and the permanent setting mentioned earlier lie in the size and complexity of the set pieces used to alter the appearance of the permanent structure. Plate 100 provides an example of this form of unit setting.

Unit settings also may be composed of a semi-permanent structures remaining onstage through-out the play, but altering shape or position to

Plate 98. *FRAGMENTED INTERIOR-EXTERIOR SIMULTANEOUS SETTING: The inside and outside of a rural cafe are depicted with an almost collage-like arrangement of scenic elements. An additional element in this setting is the use of a turntable which allows the exterior portion of the setting to be revolved to a more dominant position onstage. A setting for* The Ballad of the Sad Cafe *produced at Samford University with scenery by Eric Olson. (Photo by Eric Olson)*

Plate 99. *PERMANENT STRUCTURE UNIT SETTING: Different scenic units filling the central arch combined with a variety of set pieces and furniture create both exterior and interior scenes in this setting for* Don Giovanni *at the University of Western Kentucky. Design and sketch by Tom Tutino.*

suggest locale changes. Plate 101 shows a platform setting, the central portion of which is placed on a turntable and, by revolving to various positions, provides altered aspects for different scenes. The setting in Plate 102 shows another possibility, where the ramped platform structure remains basically the same throughout (except for stage left, which changes position on the teeter-totter principal); however, the draped backcloth is raised and lowered into different configurations for various scenes. A few additional set pieces roll or fly onstage.

One additional variation, on the unit setting, involves the use of several small units that can turn, move, or alter the visual relationships to provide a

Plate 100. *UNIT SETTING WITH MOBILE UNITS IN FRONT OF A PERMANENT BACKGROUND: The skeletal form and the cording used in the movable units work well with the cording used for background trees to provide a unified appearance for all the settings in this production of* The Seagull *produced at the University of Alabama with scenery by John Ross.*

variety of settings for a play. In the production shown in Plate 103 the principal elements are free-standing profile units which move about the stage and are combined with one another to form various settings in an interesting, yet simplified, manner. The key to this type of unit setting is the flexible use of scenic units. Wagons designed in a three-dimensional architectural form are also quite adaptable for this purpose. Combinations of steps, playing levels, columns, arches, alcoves, or similar three-dimensional elements on a wagon may be coordinated very effectively with a few other scenic pieces to form all the setting necessary for a multiplicity of scenes.

Wagons so designed take on a variety of appearances when viewed from various angles and alter units to provide great variety in the settings.

The advantages of a unit setting may be easily

Plate 101. *REVOLVING PLATFORM UNIT SETTING: As the central unit revolves, the sculptural levels meet up with the surrounding structure in a variety of different configurations to provide for different acting areas, movement patterns, and visual compositions.* The Duchess of Malfi, *produced at the University of Iowa with scene design by A.S. Gillette.*

the stage picture quite considerably merely by turning or moving to another position on-stage (see Plate 106). *Periaktoi* (see Plate 104) are also quite useful in this type of setting and may also be combined with the wagon units and other scenic seen. Because of the use and reuse of scenic units, the total production design is kept unified; the changes can be made very quickly; and there is usually a minimum of scenery to be stored off-stage. This last advantage makes the unit setting a good choice for those stages with limited offstage storage area. A designer who must design for a stage with limited facilities and storage area should give the unit setting strong consideration when called upon to design a multisetting production.

*Fully Shifting Settings*

Realistic plays requiring several settings sometimes necessitate the use of settings that change completely for each scene with few, if any, scenic units being used in more than one setting. Complete scenic changes of this sort require more storage space, more manpower, and, frequently, more sophisticated stage machinery than do any of the other types of settings mentioned. Often all of the possible methods of shifting scenery must be called into play.

### SHIFTING METHODS

The three principal ways of shifting settings are: manually; by flying; or by rolling.

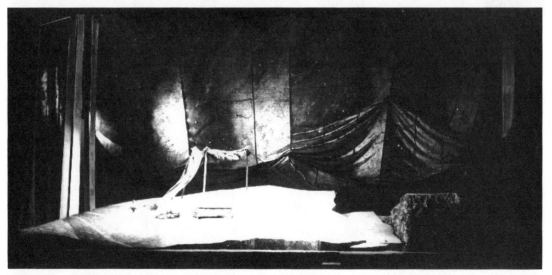

Plate 102. *SEMI-PERMANENT STRUCTURE UNIT SETTING: In the upper photo, the stage right platform unit rolled into position through tracking cut into the "hillside" unit, picking up a cloth wing as it did so to create the swagged roof. The setting for the Broadway production of* Gideon *designed by David Hays.*

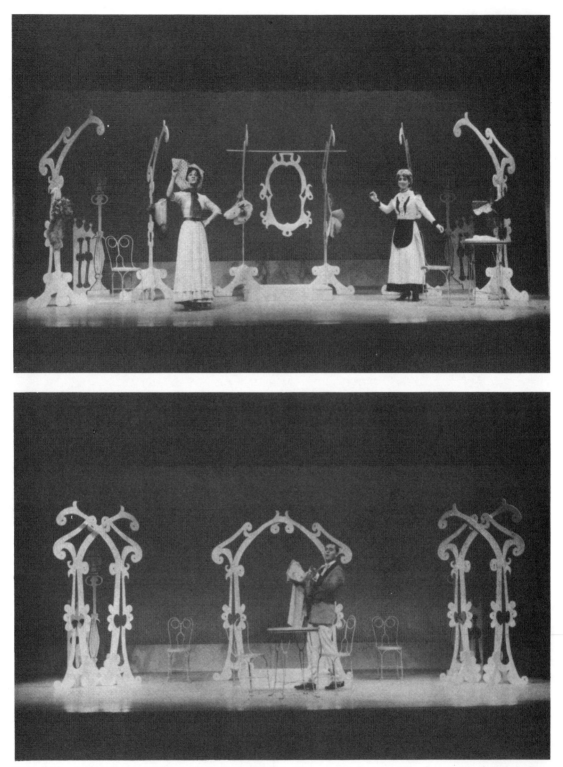

Plate 103. *MOVABLE ELEMENTS UNIT SETTING: The careful design of the decorative detail on these units allow for a wide variety of combinations in this very simple but charming setting for* Earnest in Love *designed by William Wolak for St. Mary's College. (Photo by Bigler)*

Plate 104. *PERIAKTOI IN USE: As shown here, a series of revolving periaktoi offer interesting possibilities for comic business. Part of a setting for* The Imaginary Invalid *produced at the University of Iowa with scenery by Anthony R. Collins.*

*Manual Shifting*

Manual shifting involves the use of a large number of stagehands who pick up and carry the scenery on- and off stage. This is the oldest and slowest method of shifting scenery, requiring light scenery and a multitude of stagehands to reach any degree of efficiency. In addition, the stagehands must be well drilled in their particular jobs, knowing exactly what they are to do at each given moment of the change. Plate 105 shows several methods of handling scenery applicable to manual shifting and also to the handling of scenery at any time – in the shop or onstage.

*Flying Scenery*

Flying systems already have been discussed in some detail. These provide very efficient means for shifting scenery. The use of flying equipment, however, does require certain precautions.

1. Make sure that all parts of the flying system are in good condition – no worn ropes, cables, sandbags, etc.

2. Keep people from under the fly gallery or loading ramp while the weighting is in progress.

3. Bolt all flying hardware to the scenery to be flown.

4. On heavy pieces of scenery, attach the flying lines to the bottom framing member of the unit.

5. Make sure the scenery is counterweighted as well as possible – one man should be able to operate a single unit – and be sure the flymen are thoroughly trained in the operation of the system.

The procedure for flying a piece of scenery is as follows:

1. Determine the proper batten or set of lines to be used and lower to the stage floor.

2. Lay the scenic unit face down on the stage floor with the upper edge of the unit below the batten on which it is to be flown. Make sure it is properly positioned in terms of right, center or left stage.

3. Attach the lines from the line-set to the

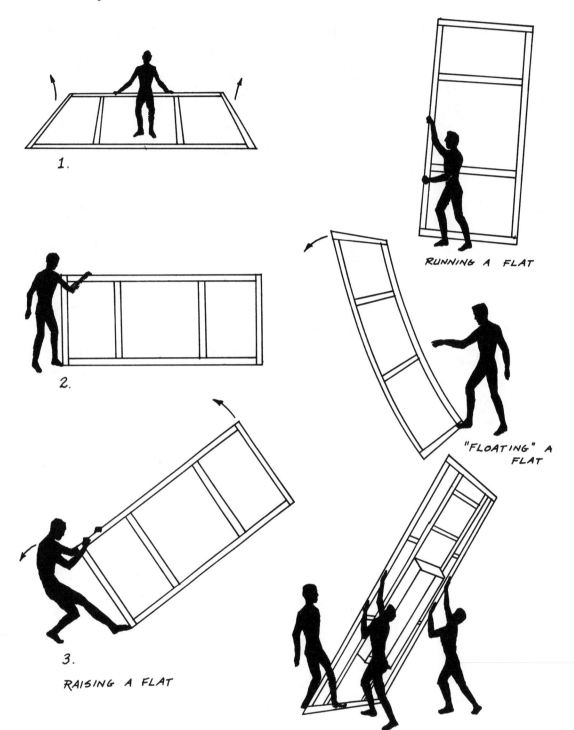

1.

2.

3.

RAISING A FLAT

RUNNING A FLAT

"FLOATING" A FLAT

WALKING A HEAVY FLAT UP OR DOWN

Plate 105. *HANDLING FLATS*

scenic unit, or run lines from the unit to the batten if you are using a counterweight system.

4. Counterweight the lines. Remember that the arbor will be weight heavy as long as the scenery is on the floor. Be careful in raising off the floor and then, when the scenery is fully raised, check to be sure that true balance of weight has been achieved—that the scenery "floats" without moving up or

down when the operating line is released.

    5. Raise the unit to playing position, adjust the trim and mark the operating line for both playing trim and storage trim.

    6. Raise the unit to its storage position and then repeat the process with all other flying units. (In the case of the hemp flying system, the unit will have to be manhandled up to its storage position before the sandbag weights can be attached to the lines.)

Always check the clearance between your flying units to be sure they will not snag or tangle during the operation. It may be necessary to make minor adjustments in the position of units to eliminates snagging problems. Check all of this out *before* rehearsal with the cast.

Theatres with limited fly space may still not be completely hindered from flying. Small scenic units such as cut-out windows, foliage units, and archway tops may be flown in a limited space. In addition, use of backdrops that may be tripped (flown in a space less than full height) or rolled can further open up the flown scenery possibilities—even in small, cramped theatres. (See Chapter VII for a more detailed discussion of various forms of backdrops.)

*Rolling Scenery*

Attaching wheels to scenery so that it may be rolled on- and offstage is the third basic method of shifting scenery. This may be accomplished in a number of ways. Perhaps the most common is the use of wagons (rolling platforms). These may range in size from the large slip-stage, which is a full-stage-sized wagon designed to transport a complete setting, to a very small wagon only large enough to carry a single unit such as a counter or fireplace. Wagons may be used with rolling scenery in a variety of ways, several of which are illustrated in Plate 106. Smaller wagons may be combined with flown scenery, manually shifted scenery, other wagons, or with permanent units in order to form settings. The only limit to the use of wagons is the size of the offstage storage area. Unless the wagons are to remain onstage at all times and simply change position to alter the settings (as in the unit settings), there must be offstage storage area sufficient to store them and still allow room for the passage of actors and backstage personnel. Use of a slip-stage, for instance, requires offstage storage equal in size to the onstage area, at least.

Another method of rolling scenery is by revolv-ing it around a fixed pivot point—full-stage turntables being an example of this method. Several uses of revolves and variations thereof are illustrated in Plate 107. Use of a full-stage turntable to change settings requires a stage with a depth equal to, or greater than, the width of the proscenium opening; however, multiple smaller turntables, turntables with irregular profiles (as opposed to circular), or units with off-center pivot points can provide equally useful methods of effecting scenic changes. One particularly interesting use of a turntable is to design a permanent "sculptural" scenic unit which will then take on different appearances as various sides of the unit are presented to the audience (see Plate 101).

The tip jack, the lift jack, and the outrigger wagon are other devices for rolling scenery. They are used more often to shift smaller scenic units than to move complete settings—being useful for shifting units of flat scenery and such scenic units as alcoves, bay windows or fireplaces. These devices are shown in Plate 115.

It is important to remember that, in designing scenery for any form of rolling platform (wagons, slipstages, turntables, etc.), the scenery must be fully self-supporting with greater internal bracing than in a stationary setting in order to withstand the forces exerted when the units begin to be moved on- or offstage.

A good understanding of the advantages and limitations of each of these methods of shifting scenery is necessary before the designer is fully prepared to begin planning the setting.

PLANNING THE SETTING

The first step in the process is to make a definite decision regarding the style of the show and the basic type of setting to be used. This decision must be based not only upon the demands of the play and the desires of the director, but also on the advantages and limitations of the stage onto which the setting must be placed. It is foolish to attempt to design the five locales for Cyrano de Bergerac as individual, fully shifting settings if your theatre has no fly space, little depth, and little wing space. You would be wiser to develop some form of unit setting or, conceivably, some form of permanent setting. As your fly space and offstage storage space increase, the possible methods of changing the scenery increase. It is important not to ignore the capabilities of your theatre when you reach the decision regarding style and type of setting to be used.

The next step is to develop the floor plan(s). For permanent and simultaneous settings the requirements of adequate playing space in each not be ignored, and it is wise to make quick perspective sketches of the setting as you go along, but in the long run the feasibility of

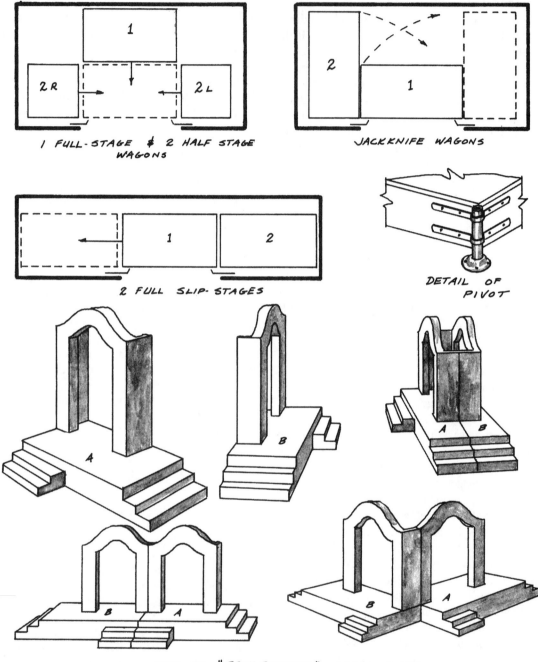

Plate 106. *THE USE OF WAGONS*

individual area or level, and numerous means of access to each area or level, necessitate careful plotting on the floor plan. Obviously, the visual appearance of the arrangement can-

platform and stair arrangement, as determined by the floor plan, will be the deciding factor as to the visual appearance of the setting. This is not necessarily a limiting factor, since there

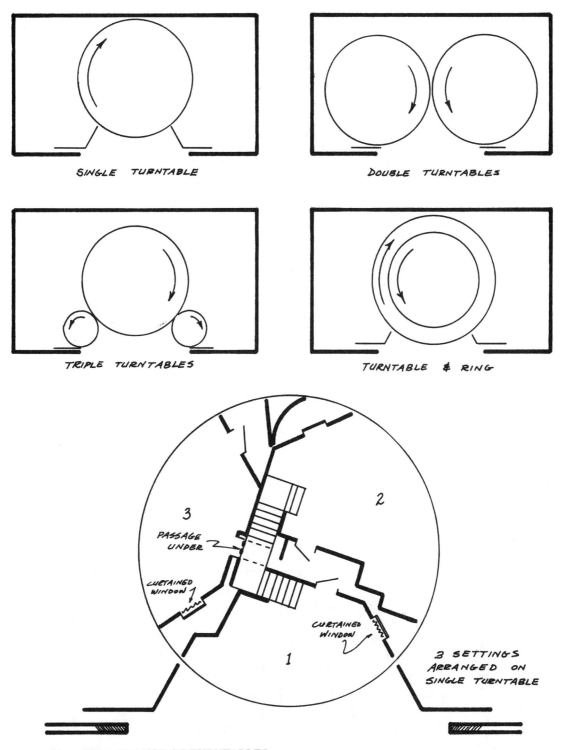

SINGLE TURNTABLE

DOUBLE TURNTABLES

TRIPLE TURNTABLES

TURNTABLE & RING

3

2

PASSAGE UNDER

CURTAINED WINDOW

CURTAINED WINDOW

1

3 SETTINGS ARRANGED ON SINGLE TURNTABLE

Plate 107. *THE USE OF TURNTABLES*

are endless possibilities of arrangement, and it is necessary only to persevere until floor-plan practicality and good visual composition come together into a workable setting of pleasing appearance.

Plates 108 and 109 show preliminary sketches and floor plans for two different types of permanent settings.

The floor plan for unit settings and fully

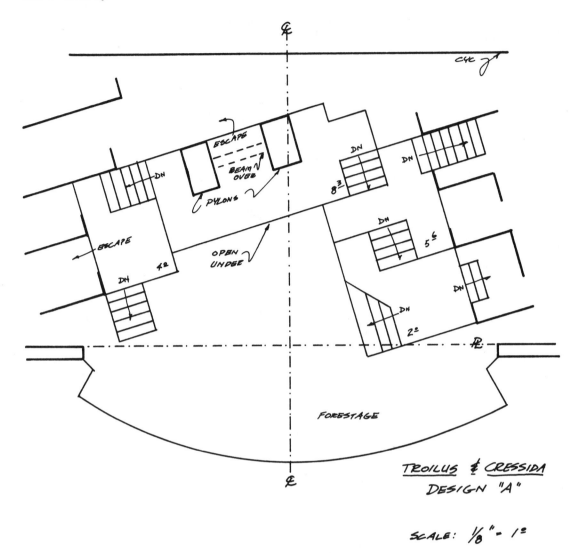

Plate 108. *DESIGN SKETCH FOR A PERMANENT SETTING: A preliminary sketch for* Troilus and Cressida. *Compare this with the finished setting shown in* Plate 88.

shifting settings is more involved. It must show the position of each setting onstage but, in addition, it must show how and where each scenic unit will be stored when offstage. The position of flying units must be carefully determined and plotted into a hanging chart that will show exactly which set of lines will be used for each piece to be flown. It will probably

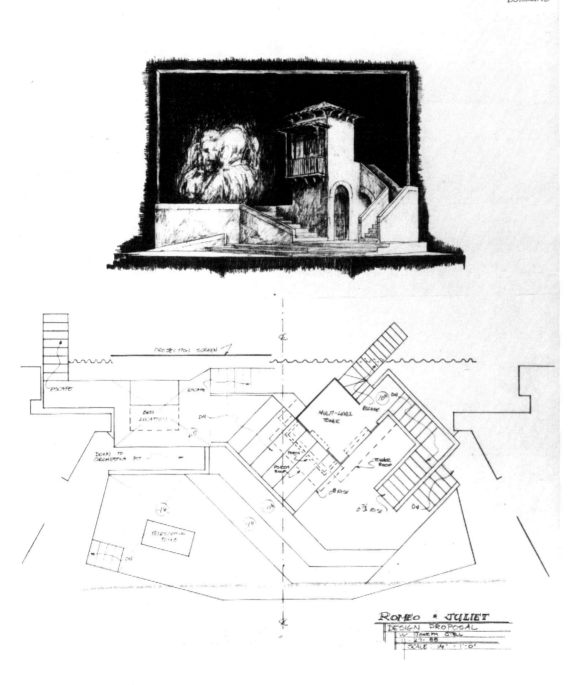

**Plate 109.** *DESIGN SKETCH FOR A PERMANENT SETTING: Preliminary sketch and floor plan for a production of* Romeo and Juliet.

be necessary to draw a floor plan showing not only the onstage area, but also all wing space and other possible storage space. The size and shape of each scenic piece should be tested both onstage and offstage to determine whether there is adequate storage area for each piece. It is probably a good idea to cut a scaled plan view of each unit out of paper and then move the paper pieces around to determine if they can be stored adequately and still leave space

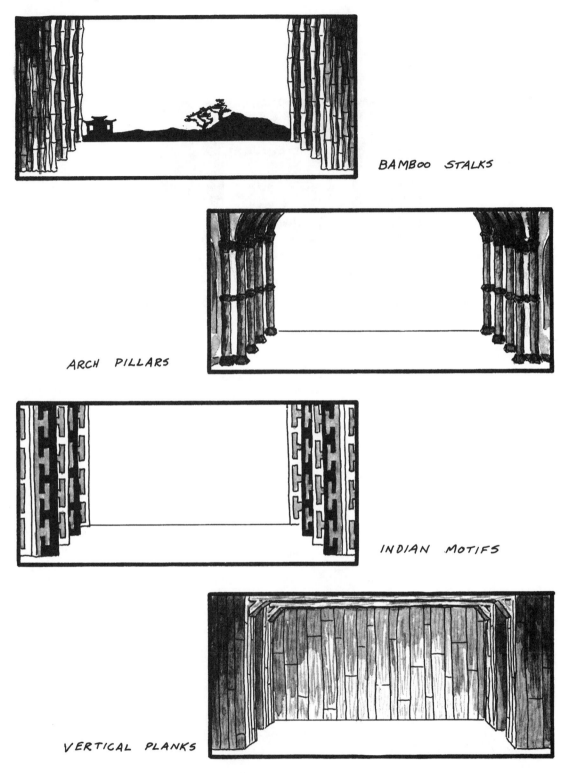

BAMBOO STALKS

ARCH PILLARS

INDIAN MOTIFS

VERTICAL PLANKS

Plate 110. *POSSIBLE MASKING DESIGNS FOR MULTISETTING SHOWS: The scale of the ornament in these sketches has been exaggerated for clarity and would need to be scaled down to match the scale of the stage and the setting.*

for the actors and technicians.

Masking should be worked out at this time. If there is a great deal of movement of scenery on- and offstage, the masking must be so planned as to allow this movement. It must be capable of being moved out of the path of the scenic units, or there should be large enough paths through the masking to allow the passage of the scenic units.

During this time, of course, the specific means for shifting each piece of scenery must be determined—will it roll, fly, or be carried on and off? How many units will be needed to comprise each individual setting? By using what we have learned from the script regarding the necessary size for each setting, we can determine just how large each setting must be. Often a single small unit will serve for a scene, saving precious moments of shifting time. It might be a wise idea to provide a black curtain midway up- and downstage, which can serve as backing for such small "spot" settings. In this way a larger setting could be changed behind the curtain while a scene is in progress downstage.

All of the component parts of the various settings must be as carefully thought out and fitted together as the pieces of a jigsaw puzzle or a complicated piece of machinery. The floor plan is the means for setting down all of these calculations on paper—both during the planning process and as a final record of the resulting design. One large plan showing all of the individual settings onstage and also in their storage position may be the clearest method of depicting the final scheme, or it may be clearer to draw separate floor plans for each of the individual settings. In either case, it is important that the offstage storage space be as carefully planned as the onstage arrangement.

Although the method for changing the settings is a major concern in the design of a multi-setting show, the designer must also be concerned with the unity of the visual elements in the production—how the appearance of each setting (however different from other settings) fits into the overall scheme/ style/concept of the production. Obviously, this must be a concern throughout the entire planning process, even while developing specific floor plans and devices for shifting the settings. The arrangement of the scenery and type of scenic elements used greatly influence the visual appearance. Now is the time, however, for the designer to consider the problem of achieving unity of appearance throughout all of the individual settings and also to be sure that each of the settings presents a pleasing composition within itself.

There are several methods of achieving unity throughout the settings without sacrificing the essential individuality of each scene. All of the methods rely on the principle of repetition—use and reuse of one or more elements throughout all of the settings. This element may be a particular method of presentation—a style of painting (cartoon, sketchlike, à la Mondrian, etc.), a specific use of unusual materials, or a special way of constructing the scenic units (cut-out frames, transparent walls, or cut-down scenery). Repetition of a particular line or mass throughout the settings may provide unity, as may the repetition of a particular color or group of colors, or the repetition of a texture. A major unifying device can be the masking for the setting— the scenic elements along the sides and rear of the stage. Masking may provide a constant defining surround for all of the individual settings of the play. The masking may make a statement about the style, period, or locale of the play, or simply provide a constant framework within which the various scenes are presented. Some examples of such masking are shown in Plate 110. The masking may also make use of textural elements (shiny fabrics, heavily textured fabrics, flats with implied textures such as brick, stone, or concrete) which coordinate with the specific settings for the play. Because the elements portrayed in the masking remain constant throughout the production, they provide for each individual scene a visual tie-in with the remainder of the scenes in the production and work as a tremendous unifying factor throughout the production. The masking for a multi-setting production should be a major design consideration—*not* be a last-minute decision to simply use black draperies as any easy way to conceal the offstage areas.

Once the overall style and scheme have been decided upon, then attention may be turned to the individual settings. Each setting should be considered as a separate unit in terms of the principles and elements of composition, so that the stage picture is always well arranged for each scene. Line, mass, color, balance, unity, and all the other factors should be carefully applied to each setting, without losing the overall unity of the production. It is very helpful to develop the design in model form in order to determine the exact appearance of each setting as well as the appearance of the overall production. The model can also be used to test methods of shifting and storage space. The more complicated the production scheme, the more the model will aid in determining the

Plate 111. *PERMANENT PORTAL UNIT SETTING FOR A CHILDREN'S SHOW: A series of permanent tent portals create the circus setting for this production of* Cinderella *in which sliding curtains, flown lights, and small set pieces are used to establish the different locales. Produced at Cumberland County Playhouse, TN, with scenery by Leonard Harmon.*

effectiveness of the design scheme. It will also provide definite information necessary to the planning of shifts—a process that must be accomplished before the first technical rehearsal.

## Planning The Shifts

The first step in planning the actual shifts is to determine all of the operations necessary to accomplish the change. This will include such things as removing stage braces, separating units, raising flying units, rolling units offstage, carrying units offstage, and removing furniture and properties; then reversing the procedure to move the next setting into position. Each separate action of this sort should be listed for each change, and the number of persons required to handle each operation should be determined.

Final determination of specific storage spaces for each piece of scenery and furniture must be made at this time. Every unit must have a definite assigned location in which it stores, which may vary before and after its appearance onstage. It should be remembered, however, that if a scenic unit's storage position after use is different from that before use, then it must be reset before each performance. Notes must be made of any circumstances of this sort. Full-stage floor plans showing both onstage positions and offstage storage of all scenic units, and changes in those storage positions, are absolutely indispensable at this point.

A scene change is made in a series of moves, each of which contains a number of separate actions. The general sequence of moves, the number of moves, and the specific actions to be accomplished in each move must be carefully listed and each action assigned to a particular crew member. Plate 112 illustrates a master shift assignment chart detailing this information. The number of moves included in a shift determines the length of a change to a great extent—the more moves included, the longer the change. Adding men to the shift crew so that more actions may be accomplished simultaneously can decrease the number of moves necessary. The quickest scene change is accomplished when each member of the shift crew has only one thing to do during the change. When all members of the crew have accomplished their jobs (simultaneously), the change is completed. Ordinarily, the fewer people used in a shift, the more moves necessary and the longer the change; and vice versa.

It is important that each member of the crew know exactly what he is to do and that he be rehearsed in that procedure. Each member of the crew should be given a card listing, in order, his particular duties for each shift. An example of such a card is shown in Plate 112. When each member of the crew has accomplished the duties listed on his card, the change should be completed. Scenery-shifting efficiency is achieved by rehearsing the change and timing the procedure. Complicated changes may need to be rehearsed over and over again until each member of the crew does his assignment virtually automatically—quickly and carefully, but without haste.

The general sequence for a scene change is as follows:

1. Move all furniture and set props down-stage center, near the curtain.
2. Remove all backings and flying units.
3. Strike the main set pieces.
4. Strike the furniture and set props.
5. Bring on the furniture and set props for the next setting.
6. Bring on and set up all of the main set pieces.
7. Bring on and set up all backings.
8. Lower in the flying units.
9. Place the furniture and set props into position.

It is quite possible that several of these operations could occur simultaneously, so long as one did not get in the way of another and cause a traffic jam. Definite traffic patterns should be developed to facilitate the change and eliminate the possibility of a jam-up or a collision. If the change is carefully planned, adequate personnel is provided and trained, and the movement and storage of the scenery are carefully organized, the changes can be made quickly and efficiently.

## Construction Techniques

The construction techniques surveyed in this section will be those associated with the shifting of scenery: wagons, turntables, tip jacks, lift jacks, outrigger wagons, and securing devices. There are other quite complex ways of construction these units than the methods to be described, but those included are more than adequate for ordinary use.

### Wagons (Plate 113)

Wagons can be constructed quite easily by

| TINY ALICE | SHIFT FROM LIBRARY TO SITTING ROOM — I-2 TO I-3 & II-1 TO II-2 | | |
|---|---|---|---|
| CREW | MOVE #1 | MOVE #2 | MOVE #3 |
| CARTER (FLY) | LOWER SET | LOWER TRAVELER | |
| COX (FLY) | | | LOWER LEGS |
| OLMSTED (CREW CHIEF) | RELEASE ROPE TIE | OPEN WINDOW WALL (W/DUNCAN) | OPEN WINDOW SEAT |
| RAMIREZ | GUIDE SET - SCREW DOWN — (W/WHITE) | | SET BRACE #1 |
| RAGLAND | | OPEN DOOR WALL (W/KERLEY) | |
| WHITE | GUIDE SET - SCREW DOWN — (W/RAMIREZ) | | SET BRACE #3 |
| DUNCAN | RELEASE WING NUT | OPEN WINDOW WALL (W/OLMSTED) | SET BRACE #4 |
| KERLEY | | OPEN DOOR WALL (W/RAGLAND) | SET BRACE #2 |
| McCUE (PROPS) | STRIKE D.R. CHAIRS TO U.R. PLATFORM | | SET CHAIR D.R. |
| BAILEY (PROPS) | STRIKE D.C. CHAIR TO U.L. PLATFORM | | SET CHAIR D.C. |
| POOLE (PROPS) | STRIKE D.R. TABLE TO U.R. PLATFORM | | SET OTTOMAN D.L. |

*NOTE: KERLEY, RAMIREZ, WHITE & DUNCAN BRING ON STAGE BRACES

MASTER SHIFT ASSIGNMENT SHEET

```
DUNCAN                    Shift Assignment #2

    Shift from Library to Sitting Room
      I-2 to I-3  and  II-1 to II-2

Enter with stage brace #4
  1.  Release wing nut (replace on bolt)

  2.  Open window wall to marks (w/Olmsted)

  3.  Set brace #4.
```

INDIVIDUAL SHIFT CARD

Plate 112. *MASTER SHIFT ASSIGNMENT CHART AND INDIVIDUAL CREW MEMBER ASSIGNMENT CARD*

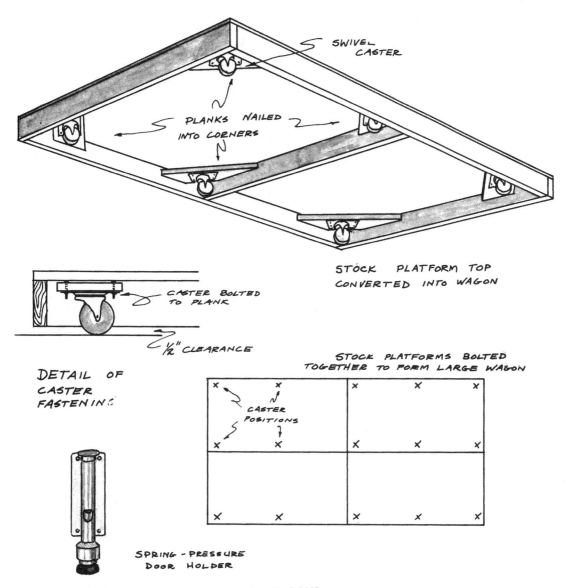

SWIVEL CASTER

PLANKS NAILED INTO CORNERS

STOCK PLATFORM TOP CONVERTED INTO WAGON

CASTER BOLTED TO PLANK

½" CLEARANCE

DETAIL OF CASTER FASTENING

STOCK PLATFORMS BOLTED TOGETHER TO FORM LARGE WAGON

CASTER POSITIONS

SPRING - PRESSURE DOOR HOLDER

Plate 113. *THE CONSTRUCTION OF WAGONS*

taking rigid platform tops and adding rubber-tired casters. If you have a supply of stock platform tops, you can easily convert them into wagons in this manner—either as a single unit or bolted together to form a large-sized wagon. The casters should be large enough or blocked up enough to allow ½" clearance between the edge of the platform and the floor to prevent possible binding on uneven floors. The caster tires should be at least 2½" to 4" in diameter and should be either solid rubber or rubber-covered to reduce the noise factor. Casters should be attached at any point at which you would ordinarily attach a leg to the platform—rarely more than 4' apart at any point—and

should be fastened securely to the platform.

*Turntables (Plate 114)*

The construction of a turntable should be done in such a way as to allow the unit to be disassembled for easy storage. Standard platform tops can be bolted together and rounded out with partial arc units to form a circle. This is perhaps the most efficient and economical method of construction. The casters used should be fixed so that they will not swivel and should be attached so that the tire is perpendicular to a radius drawn at the point of attachment. When all casters are fastened in this manner, the only possible movement will

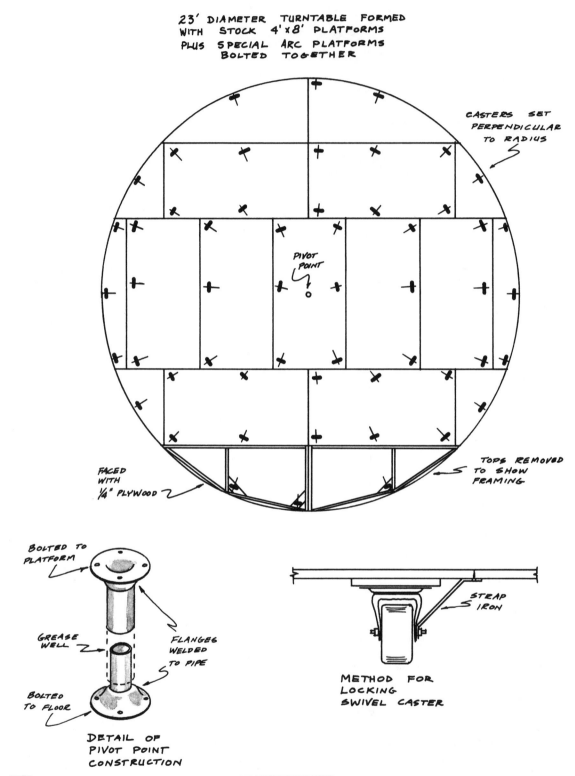

23' DIAMETER TURNTABLE FORMED
WITH STOCK 4'x8' PLATFORMS
PLUS SPECIAL ARC PLATFORMS
BOLTED TOGETHER

CASTERS SET
PERPENDICULAR
TO RADIUS

PIVOT POINT

TOPS REMOVED
TO SHOW
FRAMING

FACED
WITH
1/4" PLYWOOD

BOLTED TO
PLATFORM

GREASE
WELL

FLANGES
WELDED
TO PIPE

BOLTED
TO FLOOR

DETAIL OF
PIVOT POINT
CONSTRUCTION

STRAP
IRON

METHOD FOR
LOCKING
SWIVEL CASTER

Plate 114.  *THE CONSTRUCTION OF TURNTABLES*

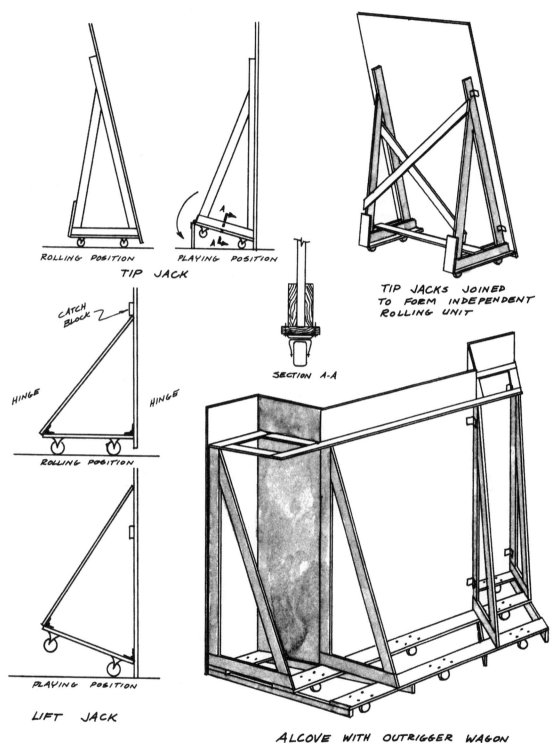

ROLLING POSITION    PLAYING POSITION

TIP JACK

CATCH BLOCK

HINGE                HINGE

ROLLING POSITION

SECTION A-A

TIP JACKS JOINED
TO FORM INDEPENDENT
ROLLING UNIT

PLAYING POSITION

LIFT JACK

ALCOVE WITH OUTRIGGER WAGON

Plate 115.  *THE CONSTRUCTION OF TIP JACKS, LIFT JACKS, AND OUTRIGGER WAGONS*

be circular. The fixed pivot point can be simply accomplished through the use of two pipes of different diameters. The interior pipe should be well greased to allow free movement, and both pipes should be securely bolted in position.

### Tip Jacks (Plate 115)

The tip jack is constructed very much like the ordinary stage jack, with two exceptions: (1) the angle between the base of the frame and the upright is more acute than 90°—usually 75° to 80°; (2) the base of the jack must be widened sufficiently to permit the attachment of casters—accomplished by the addition of 1 x 4 across the base, securely attached and braced to provide firm support. The flipper batten should be long enough to raise the scenery to an exactly perpendicular position. Usually attached in pairs, tip jacks will support the scenery as well as permit it to be easily rolled.

### Lift Jack (Plate 115)

The lift jack is a much simpler device that provides no support for the scenery in its playing position, but will allow the unit to be rolled only. It is easily constructed of 1 x 4 lumber and hinges. The hinge attaching the jack to the flat should be low enough to allow ½" to 1" of the caster to extend below the base of the scenery when in the lifted position.

### Outrigger Wagon (Plate 115)

The outrigger is a structure that allows casters to be attached to the outside of a unit of scenery, providing support and bracing as well as a means for rolling. The construction of this type of wagon must be adapted to each individual unit. Several general instructions, however, should be followed:

1. The base should be flat enough and wide enough to permit a minimum of three casters to be attached in such a way as to surround the unit. Obviously, large units will require more casters than small units.

2. The uprights attached to the unit should extend at least two thirds of the way up the unit.

3. There should be sufficient diagonal bracing to maintain the unit in an upright position.

### Securing Devices

Moving scenery—wagons in particular—must usually be secured to the floor to prevent accidental motion during the action of the play. Rigid footirons and hinged footirons fastened either with a stage screw or by dropping an L-shaped metal rod into a predrilled hole in the floor are the most common methods of securing the scenery. Another extremely useful method is to equip the wagons with spring-pressure type doorstop, as is shown in Plate 113. This device is quicker and easier to operate than the others mentioned, but holds less securely.

These, then, are some of the most common units used in multisetting shows as means of easily moving scenery about a stage. They are useful for the types of settings described in this chapter, and they serve equally well for settings for musicals, which will be briefly described in the next chapter.

# chapter VII

# MUSICALS AND CHILDREN'S PLAYS

In this chapter, I have grouped together musicals and plays for children. Although there are obvious differences between the two types of production, there are many more similarities: both usually demand a lighter and more fanciful design treatment than do dramas; both types usually require more than one setting; frequently, the children's play incorporates music and dance, just as does the musical; and stage effects and illusions are often found in both.

The musical is generally considered to be America's principal innovation and contribution to world theatre. Evolving out of operettas of Victor Herbert, Rudolph Friml, and Sigmund Romberg, and early musical shows by George M. Cohan, Jerome Kern, and George Gershwin, the musical combines drama, music, and dance into a fully integrated production. Whereas the early musicals were aptly named "musical comedies," since they were most often romantic and comical, productions such as *West Side Story, Fiddler on the Roof, Follies,* and *Sunset Boulevard* have turned the musical away from the strictly "comic" image. Because of their strong audience appeal and drawing power, musicals are extremely popular with all types of producing groups—the annual class or school play quite often being a musical today.

Plays for children have been a tradition in England for many years, and have greatly increased in popularity in this country. Many producing companies present a children's play annually and, in the larger metropolitan areas, there are many producing organizations devoted entirely to the presentation of plays for children. The audience for these plays is endless—many people being willing to bring their children to the theatre when they would not otherwise attend themselves. Many organizations have found that producing a children's show is as rewarding (if not more so), financially and artistically, as producing adult theatre.

As a designer, I have found that designing a musical or a children's play can be a refreshing and most enjoyable change, since these shows may allow much freer rein to the imagination. Each of these

types, however, has its own special problems and considerations, even though many of the design requirements are quite similar.

SPECIAL PROBLEMS AND CONSIDERATIONS

*Musicals*

The majority of musicals employ many scenes, which are often set in a wide variety of locales. Frequently, musicals require as many as ten to fifteen settings, which may be used in as many as twenty scenes. This multiplicity of settings and the frquency of changes multiplies the problems mentioned in the previous chapter, although the same general requirments apply. Speed of shifting, careful planning of offstage storage of scenery, and the maintenance of a unified design concept throughout all the settings are still the principal problems the designer must face.

Rapid transitions between scenes is a prime requisite in designing musicals. The average musical runs between 2-1/2 to three hours—which is a long evening of theatre—and this should not be made longer by unnecessarily extended scene changes. Time, however, is only one factor—continuity of action is frequently more important. Although early musicals such as *South Pacific* or *Pajama Game* provided small downstage scenes in between full-stage settings to cover and allow change time, musicals such as *Cabaret* or *Les Miserables* require a more "cinematic" approach with one setting flowing into another in full view of the audience. This requires great ingenuity on the part of the designer and, often, a more frequent use of unit-type settings.

The designer of a musical does have one particular advantage over the designer of a drama, however, and this comes from the nature of the production. A musical is a stylized production—no matter how dramatic the story line may be. The very fact that characters break into song and, frequently, dance from time to time takes it out of the realm of "reality," since spontaneous orchestrated song is not an ordinary day-to-day occurrence. When the audience accepts this conventionalized approach to life (which they do, with great pleasure), they are also ready to accept a more stylized approach to the scenic environment—which makes the designer's task considerably easier and, to my mind, a great deal more enjoyable. Settings for musicals thus can be—and usually are—removed from reality through the use of very fanciful and/or suggestive settings, stripped down and fragmentary settings—even settings that may consist entirely of a small set piece and a pool of light.

Stylized approach to design also aids in achieving visual unity throughout the production. Whether the stylization takes the form of fanciful decor or a particular painting or construction technique, it becomes easier to conceive individual settings which conform to that overall design approach. It is a relatively simple task to achieve unity in a production that employs such stylization as that exhibited in Plates 119 and 123.

Musicals make peculiar spatial demands upon the designer. The incorporation of dances into the production frequently requires predominantly clear floor space for the use of the dancers, which severely limits the possible locations of scenic units for those scenes in which dances occur. At the same time, there are often two- or three-character scenes that require fairly intimate surroundings in order to be fully effective. There are even times when a full-scale dance number and an intimate two-character scene occur within the same setting, which may require the presence of a secluded nook in an otherwise open stage area. The problem here will be to integrate the two types of areas into a well-composed stage picture.

Perhaps more than any other type of production (except, possibly, opera), the musical lends itself to spectacle and decorative design. This, of course, does not mean spectacle or decoration merely for its own sake. A musical setting must serve as a proper environment for the production, in keeping with the overall style and mood; however, many musicals include scenes in which twenty to forty singers, dancers, and cast members are grouped onstage in a grand "production" number, dressed in bright costumes and presenting an enormous spectacle in themselves alone. It is only fitting that the scenery for such a scene also should be bright and decorative, so that the entire scene will be a "feast for the eyes." Oppor-

tunities such as these are all too rare in modern theatre.

*Children's Plays*

Many of the same things that have been said about the musical also apply to the play for children. These plays are often fantasy and call for a similar fanciful approach to the scenery. Although there are usually fewer scenes in a children's play, the need for rapid scene changes still exists because of the limited attention span of the audience. Frequently scene changes may be planned to occur in view of the audience in order to keep the attention of the children directed to the stage and to prevent their becoming restive during a change. Unity of style and period is also extremely important in designs for these shows, just as in any other type of production.

Many of the requirements of settings for children's theatre are related to the nature of the child audience. Extremely simplified settings that require a great deal of "filling in" of details in the minds of the audience are less effective with a child audience than with an adult audience. Children are more likely to take the setting literally, so that a single tree used to represent a forest may to them be only a single tree onstage and, as a result, disappointing. This suggests that the settings for children's theatre should more closely depict the locale they represent or, to put it another way, should provide more details of that locale than might be necessary for an adult audience. This does not mean, however, that all settings must be realistic. Far from it. Children are inundated with stylized and cartooned representations of place in comic books, fairy tale books, and cartoons on television and in the movies; and they readily accept these departures from reality. They will just as readily accept similar departures from reality in stage settings; however, the settings should bear some relation to the place depicted. If the scene calls for a castle, then the setting should, in some way, shape, or form resemble a castle, although it may more likely be a "Walt Disney" castle than one of the cold, dark, and dank castles of reality.

This brings us to another point. Through their familiarity with story books and cartoon features, children have very often formed preconceived notions about various places. The palace or castle is grand and bright and cheerful; a forest may be dark and mysterious; and a peasant's cottage is usually warm, friendly, and comfortable. It is wise to take such pre-conceived ideas into account when designing settings, for the children may register disappointment or rejection if the place depicted on-stage does not live up to their ideas. I know of one instance in which a child audience was extremely disappointed with an actress portraying Cinderella because she was a dark brunette, whereas the children envisioned Cinderella as a blonde. Irrational as it may seem to us, this is an important factor that must be taken into account.

One other item that bears mentioning is the frequency with which special effects and illusions appear in children's plays. Magic abounds in these plays, and it frequently calls for all the ingenuity and technical know-how a designer possesses to provide the effects called for by the playwright or director.

SCRIPT GUIDELINES

*Musical*

In addition to determining general plot, style, and mood, the designer, when reading the script of a musical, must pay close attention to the number and sequence of the settings and the specific action that occurs in each of the settings. As mentioned earlier, traditional musicals were written with small "in-one" scenes between the large settings to allow for scenery shifting during the small scene. More recent musicals do not provide such luxury, requiring settings that evolve directly into other settings—frequently while song or action continues to occur onstage, or even as a part of that song or action. The designer must know where large scenes fall and whether the libretto allows for any offstage shifting of scenery. The arrangement of scenes often dictates the particular style of scenery and shifting methods to be employed. For example, musicals written when the drop-and-wing type of settings were most common are often difficult to design in any other manner. On the other hand, more contemporary musicals frequently require imaginative combinations of unit settings, revolving, rolling, and flying scenery to achieve the necessary fluidity of scene changes.

The action taking place in each scene will also make certain demands on the setting for that scene. As mentioned earlier, large chorus numbers and dance sequences require a great deal of space—usually flat floor space. On the

other hand, there will also be intimate scenes that must be effectively staged and will require more enclosed surroundings. When the two types of action must occur in the same setting, the problems increase. In *West Side Story,* "America," a dance-chorus number, and "Tonight," a love duet, occur in the same setting. The requirements of the two scenes are usually met by providing a fire-escape balcony area for the love duet, while the remainder of the setting portrays an open alley useful for the dance number.

It is a wise idea for the designer to make up a careful plot of the sequence of the scenes, indicating for each scene the number of characters involved in the scene, the length of the scene, and the specific action and spatial requirements of the scene. This type of plot is invaluable in planning the shifting arrangements of the setting. A sample plot of this sort is shown in Plate 116.

*Children's Plays*

The principal item of which a designer should be especially aware in children's plays, over and above those elements contained in other types of plays, is the inclusion of magical effects. It is important to make note of these early in the design process, since it is frequently necessary to incorporate into the setting itself the mechanisms necessary to accomplish the effects. Walls may need to be constructed of scrim to accomplish mysterious appearances, or secret panels may need to be built into various portions of the setting. *Simple Simon* by Aurand Harris requires that a tree be seen growing onstage, and the mechanism for this effect must be carefully planned in the setting itself, as well as provision for concealing the tree until such time as it appears. Few special effects required in children's plays are such that they can be left until after the setting has been designed. More often they must be incorporated directly into the scenic units.

In both musicals and children's plays, the style of the production is less often dictated by the script than in other types of productions. Characterizations and actual locale become somewhat less clearly defined than in dramas, and the effectiveness of the production is usually less reliant on a clear presentation of these elements. More importance is placed on the story line and on the music and dance. When this is the case, the setting needs to be less descriptive and can become more decora-

# CAMELOT

| SCENE | SETTING | REQUIREMENTS | CHARACTERS | ACTION/SONG |
|---|---|---|---|---|
| I-1 | A Hilltop near Camelot. A long time ago. | A large tree with great branches reaching high and out of sight, and a small hillock beyond | 3 + chorus | Arthur falls from tree<br>"I Wonder What the King is Doing Tonight"<br>"The Simple Joys of Maidenhood"<br>"Camelot" |
| I-2 | Near Camelot. Immediately following | "Visions" appear behind Merlyn | 3 | "Follow Me" |
| I-3 | Arthur's Study. 5 years later | Window? | 2 | Guenevere works on tapestry |
| I-4 | A countryside near Camelot. A few months later | | 3 | "C'est Moi"<br>Arthur dragged on by Squire |
| I-5 | A Garden near the Castle. Immediately following | Lush with the green of Spring. Fountains playing among the trees | 4 + chorus | "The Lusty Month of May" (song and dance) |
| I-6 | A Terrace of the Castle. 2 weeks later | Entrance to a castle room. Table w/decanter of port, 3 glasses and backgammon | 5 | "How to Handle a Woman" |
| I-7 | The Tents outside the Jousting Field. The following day | | 5 | "Then You May Take Me to the Fair" |
| I-8 | The Jousting Field | A grandstand in the rear w/royal box | Full cast | "The Jousts" (offstage—watched by cast) |
| I-9 | The Terrace. Early evening of the same day | bench | 4 | "Before I Gaze at You Again" |
| I-10 | A Corridor in the Castle. Immediately following | Combine with I-11?? | Chorus | Knights parade to Grand Hall with banners |
| I-11 | The Grand Hall. Immediately following | 2 thrones dominate scene. Balcony surrounding hall | Full cast | The Investiture |
| II-1 | The Main Terrace of the Castle. A few years later | Flower-covered walls w/view of distant fields. Table & bench | 5 | "If Ever I Would Leave You"<br>"The Seven Deadly Virtues" |
| II-2 | The Terrace of the Castle. A month later | | 3 | "What Do Simple Folk Do" |
| II-3 | A Forest near Camelot. The following day | Shrouded and obscure—played before a transparent curtain | 2 | Lead-in to next scene--combine?? |
| II-4 | The Forest of Morgan Le Fey. Immediately following (combine??) | A labyrinth of tanglewood | 4 + dancers | "The Persuasion" (a Choreographic pantomime by Morgan Le Fey's demons) |
| II-5 | A Corridor to the Queen's Bedchamber. Later that night | | 5 + extras | A crossover/cover scene<br>"Fie on Goodness!"?? |
| II-6 | The Queen's Bedchamber. Immediately following | Large beautiful room. Window. Dressing table. Bed?? | 3 + extras | "I Loved You Once in Silence"<br>Mordred & knights burst in on Lance & Guen. He escapes |
| II-7 | Camelot | 2 towers & "endless blue" | Full cast | "Guenevere" (rescued from burning) |
| II-8 | A Battlefield outside Joyous Gard. A week later | Tents can be seen in distance. One large tent downstage | 5 | "Camelot" (Reprise) |

Plate 116. *SCENE SEQUENCE PLOT FOR A MUSICAL*

Plate 117. *DROP-AND-WING TYPE OF MUSICAL SETTING: Although supplemented with a few set pieces, it is easy to see that the primary visual elements in these settings are the painted backdrops. A production of* Brigadoon *at the University of Iowa with scenery by A.S. Gillette.*

tive and suggestive. This opens the door to fanciful approaches to designing the setting, with the final decision as to style more often resting with the director and the designer than with the playwright. Consequently, research for these shows frequently takes the form of seeking an appropriate style rather than searching for historical accuracy.

### RESEARCH

Although the designer, in his research, still seeks to learn the principal characteristics of the locale he will be called upon to design, he may prefer to look at secondary sources (other artists' interpretations of the locale or period) rather than going to primary sources (the actual locale, photographs of it, or contemporary artists' paintings or drawings). In this type of research, the designer will find most useful those artists who apply their own interpretation of

the subject matter rather than those who report it as accurately as they are able. The cartoons and illustrations of Cruikshank, Dürer, Daumier, Toulouse-Lautrec, and, more recently, N.C. Wyeth and Osbert Lancaster; the drawings and paintings of such artists as Van Gogh, Seurat, Picasso, Roualt, Klee, Mondrian, Miró, Pollock, and Andrew Wyeth; and the sculpture and architecture of Calder, Brancusi, Henry Moore, Frank Lloyd Wright, Nervi and Gaudi may all provide inspiration for a style or method of mounting the production.

Another source that I have found very valuable are the illustrations in children's books. In the past few years, many beautifully illustrated books for children have appeared on the market. One particularly inspiring illustrator is Errol LeCain, with such books as *Cinderella* and *The Little Glass Slipper*, *Thorn Rose* (Puffin Books), and *The Twelve Dancing Princesses* (Viking Press). His wonderful, inventive interpretations of the costumes and decor of various historic periods could convert to extremely beautiful and creative stage designs with little difficulty. Such illustrative work can be a constant source of inspiration to a designer, providing him with a rich cavalcade of ideas on styles and techniques particularly adaptable to musicals and children's theatre.

PLANNING THE SETTING

The steps in planning the scenery for a musical or a children's play are virtually the same as for any other multisetting production. The first decisions to be made regard the style of the production and shifting the scenery. Particularly with musicals, the style established in the script will largely dictate the style of the production. Older, more traditional musicals, such as *South Pacific* or *Brigadoon,* usually require some variation of drop-and-wing setting, while more contemporary shows, such as *Man of La Mancha, A Chorus Line*, or *Into the Woods* call for a semi-permanent or unit setting.

*The Drop-and-Wing Setting*

This is a series of decorative wings which mask the edges of the stage coupled with a number of painted backdrops hung at strategic intervals up- and downstage. The backdrops serve as primary scenic elements for the various scenes, being supplemented with additional scenic units that are rolled, carried, or flown in. Plate 117 shows a scene from a production designed in that form. Frequently, small scenes or songs will be played downstage "in one" with only a painted backdrop or traveler serving as a background, while a large setting is prepared upstage. Plate 118 illustrates such a scene.

A variation on this setting may place more emphasis on the scenic units set in front of the backdrop. In some shows—such as *Oklahoma!*, for example—a single painted backdrop may be used for all the settings in a production. Also, multiple use may be made of a single set piece either by making it double-sided and revolving it for another setting, or by shifting it from one side of the stage to the other and combining it with different set pieces. Different settings required for that same show could be on the reverse side of a scenic unit placed on the opposite side of the stage from other units. In this manner, scenic units may be utilized for more than

one setting and reduce the necessary storage space and scene shifting.

Curtains may add to the flexibility of scene shifting. Neutral curtains (preferably black, brown or gray) hung at intervals up- and downstage serve very well as backings for small spot settings. When opened, tableau or brail curtains used in this way also provide a decorative framework for the full-stage settings (see Plate 120). The tab curtain provides additional flexibility—each side may be opened individually to reveal a small setting.

Stages which have little or no fly space and equipment do not allow the standard methods of using painted drops; however there are several alternative solutions. Drops may be brought on- and offstage by means of drapery tracks. The old-fashioned roll drop (one of several solutions illustrated on Plate 131) is still a particularly effective means of revealing a painted background.

*Semi-Permanent and Unit Settings*

It is frequently desirable for scenic units in a musical to be utilized for as many different settings as possible. The unit settings described in Chapter VI could prove to be particularly useful for musicals, although the multiplicity of settings may require more imagination and ingenuity in the designing of the individual units used. The more you can reuse units, the less you will need to store offstage.

Scenic units that can revolve, roll around to different positions and combine with other units, and contain built-in devices for changing the units' appearance quickly—painted window shades, folding or reversible panels, pieces that flip up or out— are methods by which the practical demands of a musical can be met economically and efficiently. This is especially true when attempting to shoehorn a complicated musical into limited storage space and scene shifting equipment. Plate 123 shows a production of *Once Upon A Mattress* (which uses a minimum of twelve separate settings) produced on a stage with no wing space, little backstage storage, and virtually no fly space. This was accomplished by the use of multi-function scenic units. All of the scenes shown were formed from the same basic scenic units, with the addition of small furniture and connecting units. Plate 124 illustrates those basic units—two of each type were used, although the second unit of each pair was reversed. A roll drop and tableau curtain completed the list of basic scenery used. In this production the changes were rapid

Plate 118. *USE OF A PAINTED "IN ONE" DROP: In this production of* Tintypes *designed by John Ross at the University of Alabama, an "oleo" type of show curtain serves as the "in one" masking.*

(rarely more than 15 to 20 seconds per change, with many changes being effected virtually instantaneously). None of the major scenery was stored offstage—only two special units and several small furniture pieces. Of particular advantage were the movable panel wings that served as masking and also formed an intrinsic part of many of the settings.

A more standard form of unit setting is illustrated in Plate 119. This setting for *The Boy Friend* employs a permanent portal, masking wings, and upstage platform unit with a balustrade and lamp fixtures. The individual scenes were accomplished with scenic units that were added to the permanent units, together with a few changes in furniture. For Act I—the interior of a Riviera girl's school —two flat units in forced perspective and a central arched doorway were added. In Act II—the beachfront—the flats were removed revealing the upstage platform and railing, and two awnings and a beach umbrella cutout were added. For Act III—a beachfront cafe—awnings and cutout were removed, while two additional lampposts and a paper lantern swag were added. A night-time scene, the lamp-

posts and lanterns were illuminated for the first time—adding an element of sparkle to the setting. In this production, as well as in *Once Upon A Mattress*, few set pieces needed to be stored offstage and the changes were accomplished with a minimum of difficulty. A similar approach for a children's show is illustrated in Plate 126.

Various forms of permanent portals, arches, wings, and exterior or interior structures may be employed in a similar manner—as dominant scenic elements into which small set pieces can fill in or reshape the openings or otherwise alter the appearance of the permanent unit to effect the visual changes. The unit setting methods illustrated in Plates 100, 101 and 102 could just as effectively be employed in the design of musicals. Plate 121 shows a design for the musical *Oliver!* using a very complex arrangement of stairs, platforms, arches and dimensional walls, supplemented with flown scenic pieces together with small rolling units emerging from under the permanent platforms to create the different scenes for the production.

Such a large percentage of *The Boy Friend* setting

Plate 119. *PERMANENT PORTAL UNIT SETTING: Small scenic units added to or subtracted from permanent masking units create the scene changes for this production of* The Boy Friend *produced at the University of Georgia with scenery by the author.*

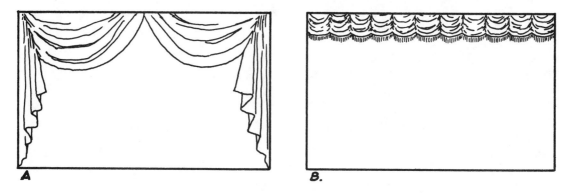

Plate 120. *DECORATIVE FORMS OF STAGE CURTAINS: (a) tableau curtain; (b) brail curtain.*

was permanently in place that it almost qualifies as a semi-permanent setting. Much the same might be said of the setting for *Sweeney Todd: The Demon Barber of Fleet Street* shown in Plate 125; however, the central unit of this setting—a structure housing both Sweeney's barber shop and several rooms of Mrs. Lovett's—revolves and moves around to various portions of the stage to create different scenes in the musical. On the other hand, the setting for *Fiddler on the Roof* illustrated in Plate 125 does utilize a large permanent structure with only minimal changes of furniture and small set pieces being employed for the various scenes. Since all of the scenes were concentrated on this one structure very little offstage storage was required, and few other scenic units needed to be constructed. Aesthetically, it was felt that the massive nature of the principal unit combined with the rough textures of the wood, shingles, and coarse fabrics better expressed the quality of the environment and the inherently serious atmosphere of the show.

In the case described above, the semi-permanent setting was a somewhat unusual choice for the production—very different from most designs which utilize multiple wagons for changing the scenes. However, a number of other musicals, such as *Man of La Mancha*, *A Chorus Line*, *The Robber Bridegroom* and *Quilters* call for some form of permanent or semi-permanent settings. With careful planning on the part of both director and designer, however, more traditional musicals may be staged on similar settings. The production of *Camelot* illustrated in Plate 122 is one such example. Here, the permanent structure was a severely raked platform with a central circle which raised out of the floor to become the round table, and four highly stylized "tree" units. The only other scenic units

employed were three cloth hangings, the large one being used for all interior scenes and trip-rigged so that it took on two different appearances. Gobos placed in ellipsoidal lighting instruments added to the visual variety of the settings. (The contributions which lighting can make to an effective stage setting should never be overlooked—particularly projected patterns and images. More on that in Chapter IV.)

Decisions concerning the design approach for any particular musical are determined in large part by practical production limitations. For instance, the setting for *Once Upon a Mattress* was designed as a result of the stage limitations, which almost prohibited the use of any scenery that had to be stored offstage. Also, because all of the scenes were set within the same castle, the play lent itself very well to the use of architecturally designed scenic units that could be combined and recombined in a variety of ways. The setting for *Camelot*, although produced on a large, fully-equipped stage, was limited by a small budget and a very short time to build the show. Size and type of stage and stage equipment, budget, construction time and personnel are all practical considerations which must be considered when reaching a decision on the type of setting to be created. Beyond that, the setting must meet the needs of the various scenes of the play. The challenge for the designer is to fulfill the practical requirements while at the same time creating a design which is visually attractive and aesthetically appropriate. The design of a musical frequently requires a designer to call upon all the creative resources he or she has available.

The actual planning process of a musical is very similar to that of a multi-setting drama. Once the basic style and type of setting have been determined, then the plotting out of the individual floor plans for

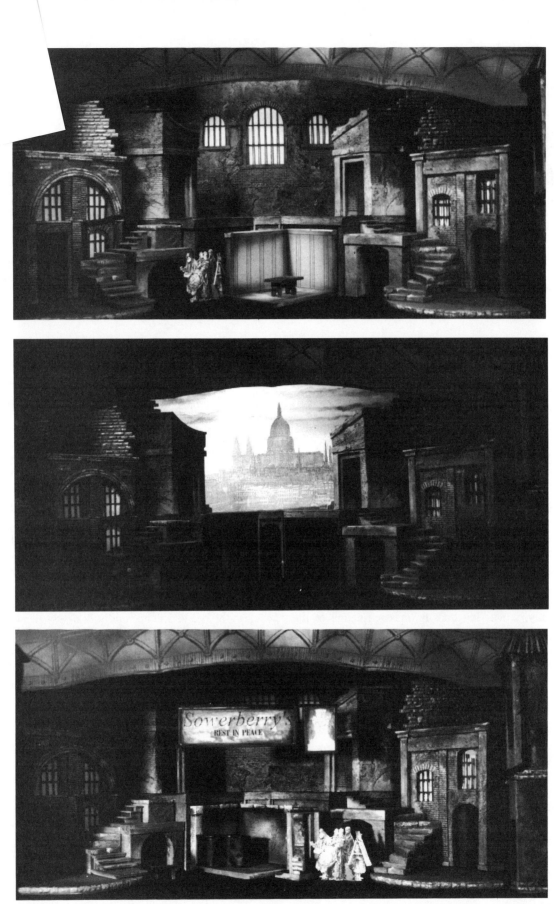

Plate 121. *PERMANENT STRUCTURE UNIT SETTING: This model for a production of* Oliver! *illustrates the use of a very elaborate permanent arrangement of stairs, platforms, arches and wall units, supplemented by smaller flying and rolling elements. Scenery by Eric Olson for Birmingham (AL) Summerfest. (Photo by Eric Olson)*

Plate 122. *PERMANENT STRUC-TURE MUSICAL SETTING: Scenes from a production of* Camelot *in which all the action occurs on a permanent raked stage with lighting and flown curtain pieces providing all the scenic changes: top - preliminary sketch, Guenevere's chamber; center - final rendering, Arthur's chamber; bottom - production photo, execution scene. Designed by the author for the Lakeview Theatre, Morgantown, WV.*

171

Plate 123. *UNIT SETTING USING SEVERAL MOVABLE BASIC SCENIC UNITS: Scenes from* Once Upon a Mattress, *produced at Richmond Professional Institute with scenery by the author, using the multi-function scenic units illustrated in* Plate 124.

172

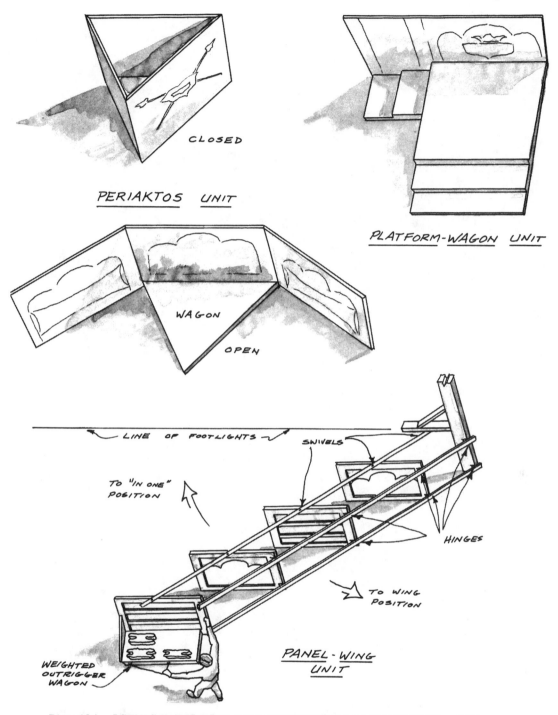

CLOSED

PERIAKTOS UNIT

PLATFORM-WAGON UNIT

WAGON

OPEN

LINE OF FOOTLIGHTS

SWIVELS

TO "IN ONE" POSITION

HINGES

TO WING POSITION

WEIGHTED OUTRIGGER WAGON

PANEL-WING UNIT

Plate 124. *SCENIC UNITS USED FOR* ONCE UPON A MATTRESS (Plate 123)

each setting, the development of the full-stage floor plan showing the storage of each scenic unit, and the detailed designing of each individual unit and scene are the next steps to be accomplished. As always, the overall production style must be carried through each individual setting in order to maintain the unity of the production. The spatial requirements of each scene obviously must be taken into account when designing the floor plan for that particular setting, and sufficient space must be allowed for dances and chorus numbers. Remember, too, that dances frequently require entrances and exits during the course of the

Plate 125. *CENTRAL STRUCTURE MUSICAL SETTINGS:* **Top:** *The large central structure with three permanent levels of acting areas provided all settings for* Fiddler on the Roof *with only minimal changes of furniture and set pieces. The use of multi-raked stage floor had to be approved by the choreographer before the design was completed. Produced at the University of Georgia with scenery by the author.* **Bottom:** *The central unit of this setting revolves around and takes various positions in different scenes in this productin of* Sweeney Todd: The Demon Barber of Fleet Street. *Note also the use of commercial scaffolding to form the permanent surround. Designed by Leonard Harmon for the University of Tennessee.*

dance number, and these types of exit require more space than those through which a person walks. It is well to check with your choreographer and find out if oversized entrances and exits will be needed for any setting. In addition, any time a large number of people must enter or leave a stage simultaneously, a sufficient number of openings should be provided so that a traffic bottleneck is not formed.

The planning of the children's play follows a similar sequence. Usually, fewer settings are required, so the logistics problem is lessened. Frequently more scenery may be used for each individual setting without adding to backstage congestion and storage problems. As pointed out earlier, it is unwise to oversimplify a setting for a children's play, since the child audience usually requires more concrete visual support than does an adult audience, which means that the stage picture must be more complete than for an adult production—fewer details can be left to the imagination.

It is wise to work out the necessary special effects and illusions early in the design process, since many of them may necessitate special types of scenic units—hollow units to hold items that must appear magically, secret panels or scrim walls for other types of appearances, nooks and crannies for the concealment of flash pots and smoke effects, and similar devices. Space must frequently be left overhead to allow for the rigging of objects that must "fly" or "float" mysteriously in midair. (A wise investment for children's shows is a large amount of heavy-duty black fishline.) Objects or characters that must appear out of the ground necessitate the use of traps or the building up of a portion of the stage floor with platforms so that something (someone) may be concealed underneath. Obviously, problems such as these cannot be left until after the main setting is designed. They must be considered as part of the total design requirements and usually must be resolved *before* the setting design is even considered.

One final comment about color and style. For both musicals and children's plays, the color and style can usually be much bolder and freer than for dramatic shows. There are many exciting possibilities for color combinations using vivid tints or shades and intermixtures. Even a limited palette employing only two

Plate 126. *SETTING BASED ON CHILDREN'S BOOK ILLUSTRATIONS: This setting for* The Wizard of Oz *was inspired by a number of illustrated children's books, resulting in a concept featuring flat bright colors and stylized decorative details. All the setting "burst forth" from a bordered illustration in the center stage space framed by a permanent portal unit. Produced at the University of Georgia with designs by the author.*

closely related colors such as blue and green or red and yellow can still offer a wide range of variations when you consider all of the possible tints, shades, and combinations. I have found that tints of colors are often more vivid than the pure colors and by that I mean not the usual soft pastels, but the brilliant colors such as fuchsia, chartreuse, and electric blue. Used in such combinations as pink and orange, blue and green, or violet and red, the final color effect can be quite bright and cheerful. Obviously, such colors must be employed taste-fully and limited primarily to accent areas, or the final effect will be garish and distracting. The setting shown in Plate 123 was designed using the brilliant tints in the heraldry designs, which provided a bright modern comment on the medieval period.

Children react favorably to the use of primary colors in a setting. Bright colors help to catch and hold their attention and are useful in a setting as long as they are not so abundantly employed as to be distracting. The children's setting shown in Plate 111 used primary reds, blues

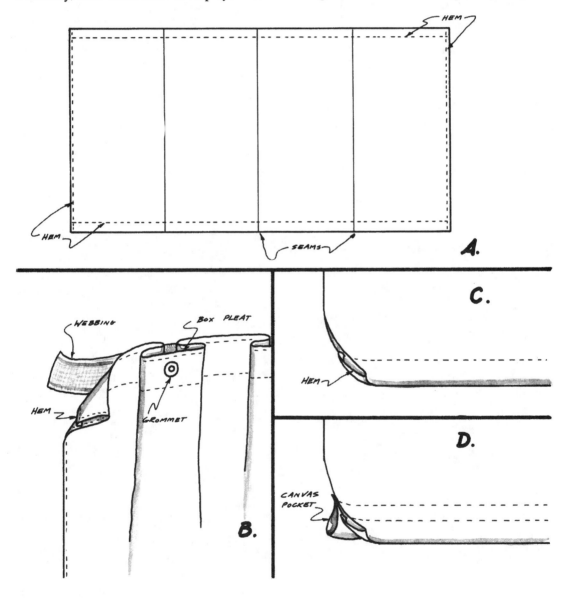

Plate 127. *DRAPERY CONSTRUCTION: (a) panels of material seamed together and hemmed, (b) top construction using box pleats, (c) bottom construction—chain to be inserted into hem, (d) bottom construction—canvas pocket for chain.*

and yellows in the set pieces and costumes, while the setting in Plate 126 was largely painted in bright pastel colors. The portal was painted pastel orange with yellow trim and an assortment of brightly colored flowers. A variety of greens was used for trees and, of course, for Emerald City while, as a contrast, the scene in the wicked witch's castle was in dark purples and violets. In keeping with the cartoonish style of the setting, the colors were all flat painted, and the result was effectively eye catching and attractive.

I should emphasize, however, that when bright colors such as these are used, the designer must plan the color scheme carefully with the costumer to make sure that the final effect of costumes and setting is not discordant. *The most vivid colors and color combinations should normally be reserved for the costumes;* otherwise the attention of the audience will be drawn away from the actors to the setting, which is just the reverse of the desired effect.

CONSTRUCTION TECHNIQUES

A few items of construction and rigging, other than those described in previous chapters, may be useful for musicals and children's shows. These include: drapery construction, drapery rigging, and the rigging of backdrops to either trip or roll.

*Drapery Construction (Plate 127)*

Large panels of draperies are made by joining narrow widths of material with face-to-face vertical seams. There are several reasons for using vertical seams: (1) the weave or decoration of the fabric usually has a better appearance when placed vertically, (2) the seams disappear in the folds of the fabric when it is draped, and (3) there is less strain on vertical seams than on horizontal.

Drapery is usually constructed with a certain percentage of *fullness* sewn in, which means that the drape itself is made wider than the area it is to cover. For instance, if the drape is designed to cover an area 20' wide, it might be constructed 40' wide, or what would be termed 100 percent fullness. This material is then pleated into the desired 20' width, with the additional material providing good rich folds. Usually, the lighter the material, the more fullness is necessary to provide a good appearance. For velour, 50 percent to 75 percent fullness will give a good appearance, whereas

for sateen at least 100 percent fullness is necessary.

The fullness is sewn into the top only. The material is hemmed to the width of the webbing, pleated into the desired fullness, and then sewn to the webbing. The webbing thus holds the pleats in place. Grommets are then inserted at 1' intervals. Occasionally, it is not desirable to sew the fullness permanently into the drape, in which case the top would be constructed in the same manner as the top of the translucent backdrop described in Chapter V. In this manner, the drape could be stretched out to provide a smooth surface, or could be draped by securing the tie-lines closer together.

The bottom of the drapery should provide some means for holding a chain weight to keep the curtain from billowing or floating when operated. The bottom may be sewn with a generous hem (4" to 6" wide) through which the chain may be inserted, or the chain may be run through a separate canvas pocket sewn to the backside of the drapery. No matter which method is used, it is usually a wise idea to attach the chain to the pocket at intervals to prevent its sliding around when the curtain is operated.

*Drapery Rigging*

TRAVELER or "DRAW DRAPE" (Plate 128): This type of curtain operates on a track, which is a mechanical means of controlling the movement of the curtain and may take the form of a hollow metal tube inside of which the *runners,* or *carriers,* travel, or it may be in the form of an I-beam along which the runners travel. The hollow tube is the standard type of track for stage drapery and comes in a variety of sizes and strengths—the heavier and larger the drape, the larger and stronger must be the track. The I-beam track, though not usually as strong as the hollow track, may be curved to provide for the use of a semicircular or irregularly curved curtain. Tracks should be of the best quality your budget will allow, since they must be so constructed as to carry a heavy load, to operate quietly and easily, and to ensure against fouling during the operation of the curtain. The runners are usually equipped with ball-bearing wheels of fiber or rubber construction to ensure quiet operation.

Standard traveler tracks are made in two sections that overlap 2' to 3' in the center of the stage and extend past the edges of the proscenium arch an additional 2' to 4'. This insures against cracks in the curtain either in the center or at the edges of the stage and also provides space offstage in which the curtain may gather when it is opened.

The tie-lines of the curtains are fastened to the runners, which are free to move along the length of the track. The curtain is operated by

The offstage edge of each curtain panel is attached permanently to the offstage end of the track to prevent its flitting onstage with the rest of the curtain and opening up a view of the sides of the stage.

A useful variation for the operation of back-

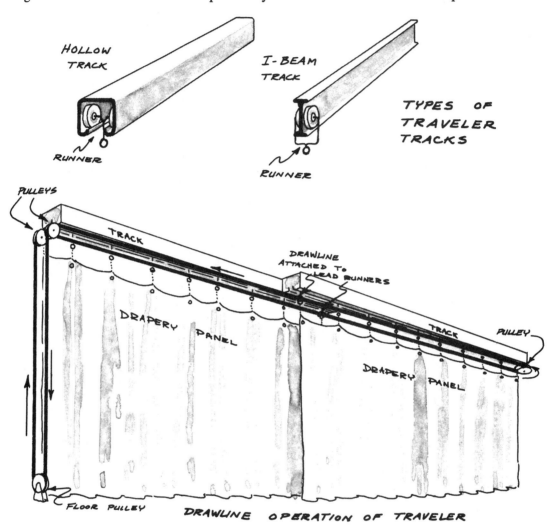

Plate 128. *TRAVELER TRACKS AND RIGGING (track has been drawn oversized in rigging diagram)*

a drawline—a form of endless line running from the floor up and over a pulley at one end of the track, along the track to the other end and around a pulley at that point, back along the track to the first end, over a second pulley, then down to the floor, where it may or may not go around a floor pulley and connect with itself. The drawline is attached only to the onstage runner (*lead* runner) of each curtain panel, and this lead runner pulls or pushes the rest of the runners to open or close the curtain.

drops in a stage without fly space is the *one-way traveler,* which requires a single track extending the full width of the stage. In this instance, the onstage edge of the drop is attached to one lead runner that is then pulled all the way across the stage and back again to open and close the drop. Inclusion of several of these tracks onstage will allow the use of several drops in a single show. For light backdrops on a small stage, lightweight tracks may be acquired from manufacturers of household drapery tracks. These tracks are less expensive than standard stage tracks and provide an economical means of operating backdrops on a limited budget, although they must be handled with a certain amount of care, since they are of less substantial construction and therefore more subject to damage.

offstage end of the batten. When the lines are pulled, the onstage corners of the curtain rise diagonally toward offstage, and a draped opening is achieved. For effective use, the total height of the curtain should exceed the width of one of the panels. In addition, the onstage ring to which the line is attached usually needs

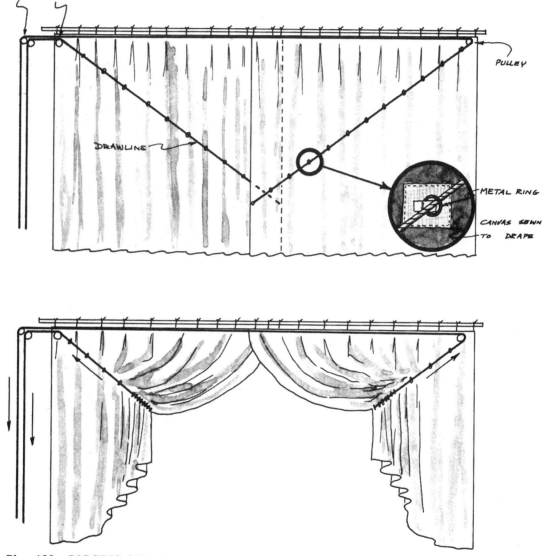

Plate 129. *RIGGING OF A TABLEAU CURTAIN*

TABLEAU CURTAIN or OPERA DRAPE (Plate 129): The tableau curtain, like the traveler, uses two curtain panels hung with a center overlap from a single batten. Each panel is lifted open by a diagonal drawline attached to its onstage edge, about 30″ from the floor, and running diagonally up through rings on the rear of the curtain to a pulley secured to the

to be weighted to assure complete closing. This type of curtain works better when constructed of a lightweight fabric. When heavy fabrics are used, the rings should be attached to a small square of webbing, which is then sewn into position on the rear of the curtain. This prevents the fabric's ripping under the strain of raising and lowering.

The tableau curtain may be used in a variety of ways. It may be opened and closed as a unit. Either side of the panel may be operated individually to provide openings for small settings. In addition, it may be placed on a traveler track and operated either as a traveler or as a tableau curtain, thus increasing the possibilities for use.

BRAIL CURTAIN (Plate 130): This curtain is made in a single panel with a generous

the scenery is pulled up into half the vertical space usually required.

TRIPPING IN THIRDS: Two sets of lines are used in this method also, one set again being attached to the top of the drop. The second set of lines, behind the unit, is attached to a horizontal batten secured to the drop one third of its height from the floor. When both sets of lines are pulled, the drop hangs in one third of the space usually required.

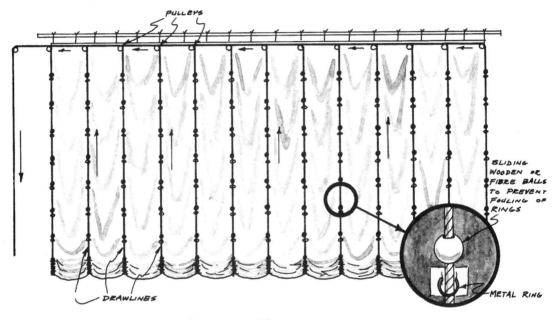

Plate 130. *RIGGING OF THE BRAIL CURTAIN*

amount of fullness from a thin or soft material that drapes well. It is raised by means of a series of vertical drawlines, spaced at equal intervals across the stage, which run from the bottom of the curtain, up through rings on the back of the curtain to pulleys attached to the batten at the top of the curtain, then offstage to a central operating position. The material is usually gathered along the vertical seams to produce a series of soft swags, and the bottom is frequently decorated with fringe.

*Trip-flying Scenery* (Plate 131)

Tripping is a means of flying scenery on a stage whose fly space is limited; but it may be used only with soft or semisoft scenery.

BOTTOM TRIPPING: Two set of lines are used for this method—one set attached to the top of the scenery, and a second set placed behind the scenery and attached to the bottom batten. When both sets of lines are pulled out,

FLAT-BOOK TRIPPING: This method is for use only with small drops, 8' to 12' wide. A horizontal batten is attached to the rear of the drop one half the height of the drop from the floor. The top batten is permanently tied (*dead-tied*) to the ceiling or roof of the stage. A front set of lines runs from each end of the bottom batten up to a set of pulleys just downstage of the drop. A back set of lines runs from the center batten diagonally up to a set of pulleys upstage of the drop at a distance greater than half the height of the drop. When both sets of lines are pulled, the drop folds flat against the ceiling. One disadvantage to this method is that the ceiling space between the two sets of pulleys must be kept clear of other scenery, lights, and equipment.

ROLL DROP or "OLEO" DROP: As in the case of flat-book tripping, the top of the drop is dead-tied to the ceiling or grid. The bottom

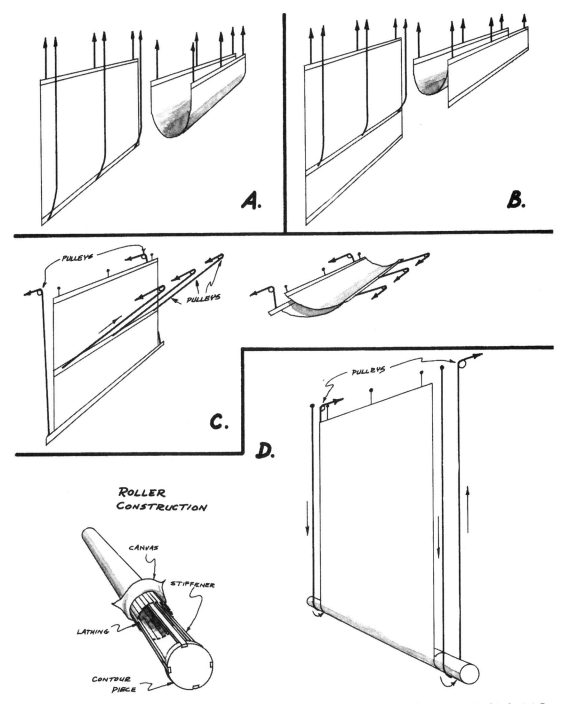

Plate 131. *METHODS OF TRIP-FLYING SCENERY: (a) bottom tripping, (b) tripping in thirds, (c) flat-book tripping, (d) roll drop*

of the drop is wrapped around a drum, or roller, 8" to 12" in diameter, which runs the full width of the drop and extends out on either end 12" to 18". This drum may be constructed by securing together a number of circular contour pieces, attaching 2" wide lath strips around the outside, then covering the whole drum with canvas. A simpler method available for small drops up to 25' or 30' wide is the use of aluminum irrigation pipe, which is quite rigid and comes in 6" to 12" diameters.

Two lift-lines are used, one at either end of the drop. The lines are dead-tied to the grid just downstage of the drop, run down the front of the drop, around the roller, up the back of the drop, over pulleys just upstage of the drop, and then run off to the side of the stage to a central operating position. When the ropes are pulled, the friction of the rope running under the roller causes it to revolve, winding the drop onto the roller as it rises. Where the drum is weak additional lines may need to be added, but, since these would run in front of the visible portion of the drop, they must be disguised by the painting on the roll drop (as were the lines operating the drop shown in Plate 123).

This chapter concludes the section dealing with the more standard methods of designing scenery for the proscenium theatre. The next section will present a brief discussion of less conventional areas of designing, including design practices for non-proscenium stages, design of simplified settings, and the use of new and/or inexpensive design materials.

# SECTION IV:
# SPECIAL DESIGN PROBLEMS AND TECHNIQUES

# chapter VIII

# DESIGNING FOR NON-PROSCENIUM STAGES

In all of the discussions so far we have been primarily concerned with designing for proscenium stages. In recent years, however, theatre practitioners have become dissatisfied with this "picture-frame" type of stage and have experimented with other theatre and stage arrangements. One of the principal goals of this experimentation has been a better actor-audience relationship leading to greater audience involvement in the action of the play. The methods chosen to achieve this greater involvement have been to eliminate the barrier of the proscenium arch and to place the stage closer to the audience area in a variety of relationships.

As we have discovered, the proscenium theatre separates the audience and the stage by means of a proscenium wall into which a viewing hole (proscenium opening) has been cut. The stage and the auditorium constitute two separate and distinct areas, with the proscenium wall and, frequently, an orchestra pit serving as dividers. The audience members tend to become merely spectators viewing the action much as they would a television show – through the picture-frame opening (see Plate 132). Examples of this type of theatre can be seen from both the audience and from an onstage view, as shown in Plate 133.

Directors and designers have worked to break down this picture-frame separation by pushing the action forward through the proscenium opening and into the audience. The orchestra pit has been boarded over and made to serve as a forestage. In some cases, the stage has even been extended over several rows of seats. The setting has been brought out and around the proscenium arch, and even, at times, around the walls of the auditorium itself.

This dissatisfaction with the proscenium type of theatre has led to the construction of non-proscenium theatres, of which there are three basic types: the *open* stage; the *thrust* stage;

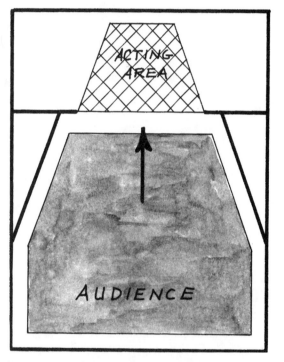

Plate 132. *PROSCENIUM THEATRE STAGE-AUDIENCE RELATIONSHIP*

and the *arena* theatre. We shall discuss each one separately, noting its characteristics and the design problems involved.

### The Open Stage

*Theatre Characteristics.* The open-stage theatre is nearest in form to the proscenium theatre, although it usually dispenses with any form of proscenium opening. By eliminating a formal proscenium opening, the open-stage theatre attempts to combine the acting and audience areas into a single unified space with no visible architectural barrier or separation. This form of stage is no modern creation. As a matter of fact, historical precedent for the open stage may be found in Greek, Roman, Medie-

Plate 133. *STANDARD PROSCENIUM THEATRE: Manitoba Theatre Centre, Winnipeg, Canada; setting for* Summer of the Seventeenth Doll, *designed by Colin Winslow, seen onstage. (Photos by Portigal)*

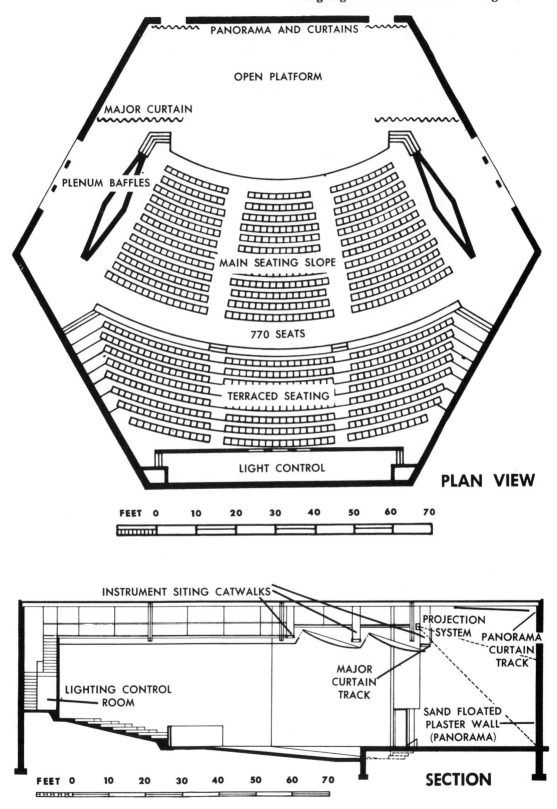

PANORAMA AND CURTAINS

OPEN PLATFORM

MAJOR CURTAIN

PLENUM BAFFLES

MAIN SEATING SLOPE

770 SEATS

TERRACED SEATING

LIGHT CONTROL

**PLAN VIEW**

FEET 0 10 20 30 40 50 60 70

INSTRUMENT SITING CATWALKS

PROJECTION SYSTEM

PANORAMA CURTAIN TRACK

MAJOR CURTAIN TRACK

LIGHTING CONTROL ROOM

SAND FLOATED PLASTER WALL (PANORAMA)

FEET 0 10 20 30 40 50 60 70

**SECTION**

Plate 134. *OPEN-STAGE THEATRE, PLAN AND SECTION: Senior High School, Findlay, Ohio— Perkins & Will, architects and engineers, James Hull Miller, consulting designer.*

Plate 135. *OPEN-STAGE THEATRE, PERSPECTIVE VIEW: Senior High School, Findlay, Ohio—Perkins & Will, architects and engineers, James Hull Miller, consulting designer. (Drawing by Richard Leacroft)*

val, Elizabethan, and Restoration theatres. In recent times, one of the principal proponents of the open stage has been James Hull Miller, who has served as consulting designer for many open-stage installations and has developed a complete theory of stagecraft for this type of stage. Many of Miller's ideas may be found in bulletins distributed by the Hub Electric Company.

In the open-stage theatre, the unity between the audience and acting areas is achieved by several means: (1) extending the wall treat-

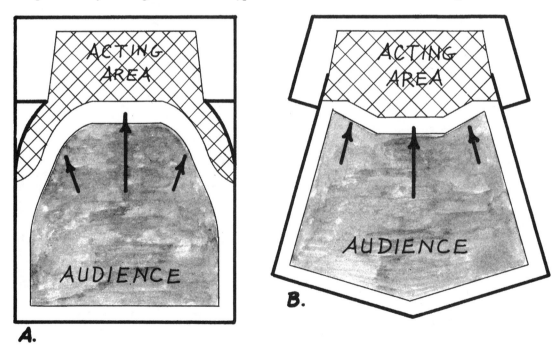

Plate 136. *OPEN-STAGE THEATRE STAGE-AUDIENCE RELATIONSHIPS: (a) open stage with calipers; (b) open stage with slight thrust.*

ment of the audience area around the playing area; (2) extending the stage into the auditorium; and (3) continuing the ceiling treatment of the auditorium over the stage. The rear of the acting area is frequently finished off with a plaster panorama wall. Plate 134 shows a plan and section view of one such theatre; Plate 135 presents an interior of the same theatre.

Although there are a number of possible variations on the stage-audience arrangement, there is still not a great deal of difference from the relationship achieved in a proscenium theatre, except that the proscenium separation is gone (see Plate 136). The audience is usually closer to the stage and, in some cases, tends to surround the stage slightly more than in a proscenium theatre. This may be seen in the theatre shown in Plate 137.

this theatre to compensate for the technical disadvantages of the stage—elimination of the fly loft and equipment and loss of offstage storage area. The answer to this question will probably differ from group to group (and, probably, from director to designer). Certainly, the open stage does present some definite disadvantages to the designer.

*Designing for the Open Stage.* The basic disadvantage of the open stage to the designer is that it tends to limit the possibilities for variety in types of settings. The playing area is usually enclosed by neutral architectural decor, which may or may not be sufficiently neutral to harmonize with all the possible styles of settings. Suggested scenic techniques for this form of stage depend upon centrally located, free-standing settings that create a scenic island in the

Plate 137. *OUTDOOR OPEN-STAGE THEATRE: The stage and seating pavilion at the Oregon Shakespeare Festival. The permanent Elizabethan-style stage façade is supplemented with scenic units for a production of* Othello. *(Photo by Christopher Briscoe)*

As with any change from the accepted norm, the open stage has drawn the fire of many critics. One of the more reasonable criticisms asks the question as to whether the audience-actor relationship is sufficiently improved in

midst of the neutral decor. Complete pictorial delineation is not desirable, the fully realistic scenic elements being confined to the heart of the scenic island. Concealed approaches to and from this island are achieved through the

Plate 138. *OPEN-STAGE SETTING—INTERIOR: Note the fence, tree and backdrop units used to frame the interior setting and help establish the environment in the production of* Strange Bedfellows *at Theatre of Western Springs, IL. Scenery by Nancy Schauer. (Drawing by Richard Leacroft)*

use of neutral masking units – frequently folding screens. In some cases the approaches may be left clear or supplied with set pieces used for the suggestion of environment. Such a setting is seen in Plate 138.

Settings for the open stage are composed of a limited number of scenic elements carefully selected to project the essence of the desired locale. Great reliance must be placed on properties and lighting. The stage is planned to make much use of projected images. The rear plaster panorama wall is designed to be used as a projection surface for an overhead projector, as may be seen in the section view in Plate 134. The effect of such a projection may be seen in Plate 139. It has been found, however, that in many cases this type of projection is impractical, because it tends to be washed out by the acting area lighting.

The principal limitations of the open stage show up during the production of multisetting shows. The elimination of the fly loft and the limited provision for offstage storage space greatly curtail the possible types of settings and shifting methods that may be used. The principal forms of settings that will work in these productions are the permanent setting; the simultaneous setting, such as the one in Plate 140; or a unit setting, such as that illustrated in Plate 141.

Plate 139. *OPEN-STAGE SETTING—INTERIOR WITH PROJECTED BACKGROUND: The interior units in this setting are fragmented so that the projected landscape becomes an even more dominant feature of the design.* The Male Animal *produced by Theatre of Western Springs, IL on the stage of the New Providence, NJ, high school auditorium. Scene design by Dorothy Hattendorf. (Drawing by Richard Leacroft)*

Plate 140. *OPEN-STAGE SIMULTANEOUS SETTING: Steps and platforms help to differentiate the exterior and interior locations in this setting for* The Lovers *designed by James Hull Miller for the Orange Blossom Playhouse, Orlando, FL. (Drawing by Richard Leacroft)*

In both of the latter settings, properties and projected images play a strong role. In all three of the settings, the basic form of the setting remains the same throughout, with the changes occurring in small items such as the properties and lighting. Because the open-stage facility tends to cast all multisetting shows into one of a very few molds, these settings, after a few seasons, can assume a rather monotonous similarity if the designer is not careful. In addition, some plays do not fit comfortably into this sort of design treatment. The theory of using projected images as a major means of altering the settings sounds quite exciting and works well on paper. In actual practice, the projected image is not always so satisfactory—primarily because any degree of brightness in the lighting of the acting area tends to wash out the major portion of the projection

unless there is a wide area of separation between the projection and the acting area.

One designer working on an open stage has quite astutely commented that the main problem with such a stage is that it is neither fish nor fowl. It has not reached the point at which scenery can be entirely suggestive and composed of properties without the necessity for pictorial description, nor does it offer the technical capabilities for achieving a wide variety of types of settings—it cannot work very well without settings, but it limits the types of settings that may be used. For this reason, the open stage has not received the degree of approval that has greeted the thrust stage.

### The Thrust Stage

*Theatre Characteristics.* The thrust stage theatre is so arranged that the audience is

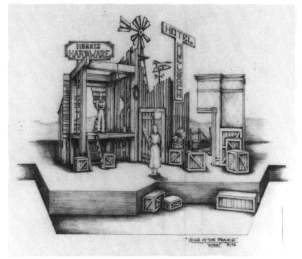

Plate 141. *OPEN STAGE UNIT SETTING: Realistic fragments and varied levels provide visual interest for this setting in which changes of scene are indicated primarily through different arrangements of crates.* Voice of the Prairie, *designed and sketched by Richard Durst for the University of Minnesota-Duluth.*

seated on three sides of the stage area (see Plate 142). The fourth side may be nothing

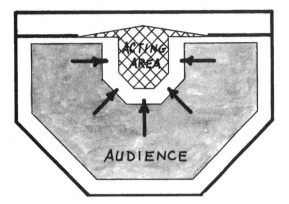

Plate 142. *THRUST-STAGE THEATRE STAGE-AUDIENCE RELATIONSHIP*

more than the wall of the theatre, or it may be designed to provide space and equipment for scenic effects and scenery storage. Although the degree to which the stage thrusts into the audience area varies from theatre to theatre, the audience is usually seated in nearly a 360° fan around the area. This insertion of the stage into the audience requires that the seating be placed on a steeper slope in order to provide adequate visibility for all members of the audience. The theatre shown in Plate 143 is a good example of a thrust theatre with a stage extending deeply into the audience area and the requisite steeply banked rows of seating. As may be observed in the sketch, this theatre also provides space for scenic effects at the rear of the stage.

On a thrust stage, the principal action occurs on the extended portion of the stage, since action taking place at the rear of the stage would be difficult to see from the edges of the seating area. Access to this principal playing area is provided from the rear of the stage and also from vomitories or aisles in the auditorium. Scenery movement is principally from the scenic fourth wall, although small units may be brought in through the vomitories. Except for very small units that may be flown in the grid over the stage, any flying of scenery is usually limited to the rear of the stage where

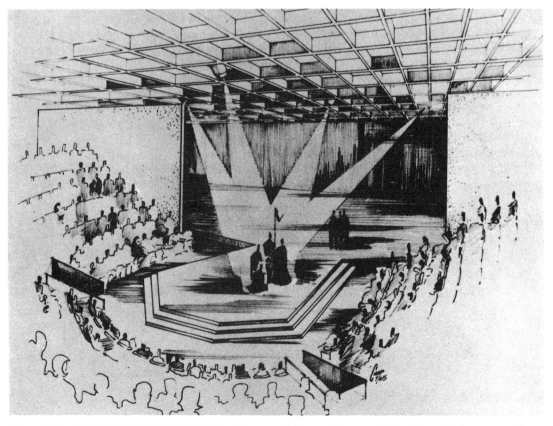

Plate 143. *THRUST-STAGE THEATRE: Theatre Atlanta, Atlanta, GA, Albert Ordway, architect, Vincent Piacentini, theatre consultant. (Drawing by David Chapman)*

standard flying facilities may be situated. Otherwise, scenery movement is limited to units that may be rolled or brought on by hand.

Lighting instruments are primarily situated in the ceiling or grid over the audience and acting area. If a gridwork such as that shown in Plate 143 is provided, the instruments may be moved around to any desirable location. This allows for great flexibility in lighting, which in some ways compensates for the corresponding limitations placed on a setting.

*Designing for the Thrust Stage.* The seating of the audience around three sides of the stage means that the designer must be careful not to block the view of any audience member. This consideration severely restricts the location of any large or tall scenic units, since the only area in which they may be placed without interfering with audience sightlines is along the scenic fourth wall. Steep seating slopes help to relieve this restriction to some degree, but, since in the first few rows the audience will be seated very close to the stage level, it is not a wise idea to use any scenery of a size that would limit to any great degree the view of these audience members. Standard usage of flat scenery is virtually eliminated except for some limited use along the rear of the stage. In addition, any levels on the extended stage must be low enough to allow good visibility.

As we have observed, scenery used on proscenium and open stages is subject to a predominantly one-directional view from the audience. In the thrust theatre, the audience views the scenery from three sides, necessitating scenery so designed as to provide a pleasing composition from many directions. The designer must break away from the "picture frame" type of composition and reorient himself to think in more sculptural terms. Painted and two-dimensional scenery must be discarded in favor of three-dimensional forms selected and arranged to produce usable and expressive shapes and areas. Careful attention must also be given to the execution of each scenic piece, since virtually all sides will be in view, and that view is from closer range than in the proscenium theatre.

Plate 144. *THRUST-STAGE SETTING IN A BIOMORPHICALLY SCULPTURED FORM: The similar shape and form of the levels in this setting for* King Lear *provide a visual unity between the upper and lower units. Scenery by David Chapman for a production at Theatre Atlanta. (Drawing by David Chapman)*

The strongest scenic area on the thrust stage is up-center. Because the height restrictions do not apply here, extremely dominant acting and scenic positions may be obtained through the use of sharply raised levels. Here would be located the grand entrance stairway, the raised dais for the royal throne, the judge's seat, the second-level playing area, or any other feature that needs to emphasize dominance through height as well as a central position. Additional emphasis is given to this area because it is the one portion of the stage that may use a scenic background. The design shown in Plate 144 illustrates the dominant quality of this important up-center area— here achieved primarily through platform height and the massive strength of the visual elements.

Plate 145. *THRUST-STAGE SETTING WITH SIMPLIFIED PLATFORMING AND DRESSING: In this setting for* The Beaux Stratagem *the carefully crafted floor and stair, the asymmetrical portal, and the upper wall of period paintings create a simple but elegant setting for the Restoration comedy. Produced at Studio Arena Theatre with scenery by Leonard Harmon.*

Plate 145 depicts a setting in which the strength of the upstage area is achieved through the use of an asymmetrically arranged stairway, platform and wall decorations, while in Plate 146 the circular up-center unit reinforces the radial design of this setting and also revolves to reveal other portions of the central core of this setting for an unfinished rooftop restaurant.

of the scenery is carried through both areas. This unification of elements is extremely important to a successful setting, which means that the upstage scenic elements must have the same sense of sculptural simplicity as those used on the extended stage area. In addition, although this up-center area may well provide the focal point of the setting, it cannot be considered a background for the action on the stage, since

Plate 146. *THRUST-STAGE SETTING USING RADIAL FOCUS: Both the floor design and suspended ceiling elements radiate out from the central circular core in this setting for* Heavenly Shades of Night Are Falling *produced by the Academy Theatre in Theatre Atlanta. Scenery by the author.*

Although this upstage area provides an opportunity for scenic investiture, the units used here should ordinarily be kept more simplified than those that might be used on a proscenium stage or an open stage. There are several reasons for this. Use of scenery on any other portion of the stage is extremely limited and, since the total design must be unified, the scenic elements used upstage must be in keeping with those that are usable on other areas. Plate 144 provides an excellent example of the unification of elements in the upstage scenic area with those used in the primary acting area. The style, character, and three-dimensionality

a large portion of the audience will be viewing this area from the side rather than from the front. Perfectly flat scenery is therefore virtually ineffective, and backdrops and sky illusions cannot be used with the same effectiveness as they might be on a proscenium or open stage. Many of the audience members will view the actors silhouetted against another portion of the audience or, if they are seated high enough, silhouetted against the stage floor.

Because most thrust-stage theatres have steeply raked seating, audience members have a splendid view of the stage floor; therefore it should be considered a major factor in the overall design concept.

Plate 147. *THRUST STAGE SETTING WITH STRONG EMPHASIS ON FLOOR DECORATION: A variety of outdoor materials and textures and indoor elements such as carpeting provide strong visual emphasis in this setting for* Billy Bishop Goes to War *produced by the Alley Theatre, Houston, in the Arena Neuhaus Stage. Scenery by Robert N. Schmidt. (Photo by Jim Caldwell)*

The decoration of the floor, and any levels used on the floor, will do much to create the desired effect of the total design. In the design shown in Plate 145, for instance, the polished and sophisticated shape and appearance of the floor adds to the impression created by the chandelier and elaborately framed pictures on the back wall to establish a sense of class, elegance and richness in an otherwise rather

Plate 148. *THRUST-STAGE SETTING USING WOODEN ELEMENTS AS A UNIFYING FEATURE: The period flavor of this setting for* Henry IV parts I & II *is achieved primarily through careful choice and arrangement of wooden planking and the wooden framing of the stairs, platforms and second level units. Produced at The Guthrie Theatre, Minneapolis, MN, with scenery designed by Douglas Stein. (Photo by Michal Daniel)*

simple setting. The setting for *Henry IV*, shown in Plate 148, on the other hand, utilizes coarse planking to unify the floor with the multi-level back wall and suggest a rough-hewn early Renaissance tavern. (Note, also, the use of the trap door entrance to the stage—a very effective device where the architecture of the stage allows for openings in the floor.) Planking is also a key element in the setting for *Uncle Vanya* shown in Plate 149. Here the floor harmonizes with the simplified architectural struc-

ture used to suggest the exterior of the late 19th century Russian dwelling at the rear of the stage. A wide variety of elements—planking, stones, weeds, wire, etc.—constitute the floor treatment shown in Plate 147 and provides perhaps the strongest design statement in this particular setting. Other effective floor treatments may involve the use of carpet and rugs, sawdust, grass mats, flagstone (painted or dimensional), and many other textural and painted effects. Since it frequently constitutes the largest single area that can be used for design purposes, the floor may be the most dominant element in a thrust-stage design and it should be given extremely strong consideration throughout the entire design process.

Other significant elements on the extended stage area are furniture, properties, levels, low scenic units, and costumes. Proper selection and execution of furniture and set properties play an extremely

the first few rows. Plate 144 provides a good illustration of the use of levels on the main stage area. The settings shown in Plates 145 and 146 also use levels, but these do not protrude to far into the extended stage area, allowing more open floor space. Any furniture, properties, or set pieces in this area must be so arranged as to allow the actors to play to as large a portion of the audience as possible. No one

Plate 149. *THRUST-STAGE SETTING USING SIMPLIFIED ARCHITECTURAL FORMS: Decorative architectural details have been virtually eliminated in this setting for* Uncle Vanya, *allowing the plain wooden flooring to harmonize with the simplified wall units at the rear. Note the use of projected leaf patterns to complete the sense of outdoors. Designed by Douglas Stein for The Guthrie Theatre, Minneapolis, MN. (Photo by Michal Daniel)*

important role in the effectiveness of the design, since these are the primary three-dimensional elements that may be used. As always, selectivity is the keynote. A single furniture item that is totally specific about the place or period of the play is far better than a carload of furniture of indeterminate age or origin. Note, for instance, the effective use of furniture and properties in the settings in Plates 145 and 149. Levels and set pieces may be used for some productions although, as mentioned earlier, these must be kept low enough not to interfere with the sightlines of the audience members that are seated in

portion of the audience area should be favored over another in either the design or the staging of the production, and proper arrangement of furniture and set pieces will facilitate blocking the play to provide interest and action for each section of the auditorium.

Multiple-setting productions may very well run into difficulty on a thrust stage. It is far less easy to shift settings on this type of stage than on a proscenium stage, or even an open stage. The portions of the setting used upstage may frequently be changed with facility—depending, of course, on the space and equipment in that area. The thrust portion of the stage, however, presents more difficulties. Items in use here must be either carried or rolled on and off or, better yet, shifted about or altered in form in some way that will change the appearance of the area. The difficulties of effecting rapid changes here with no curtain to conceal the change and deaden the sound have led to the extensive use of permanent settings and unit settings for thrust stage productions—limiting the movement of scenery on- and offstage to simple furniture and small set pieces. In many ways, designing a multisetting show for the thrust stage can be one of the biggest challenges facing a designer, for here he is able to rely upon few of the standard scenic techniques and must therefore rely on his own ingenuity to create settings that can change in appearance quickly and easily without any great movement of scenery on- and offstage. Keeping in mind the necessity for three-dimensional scenic units, the designer must then proceed to develop as many units as possible that can open up, fold out, turn over, reverse, expand, contract, or change in any other conceivable manner. Here, again, *simplicity* is the keynote —in concept and form, if not necessarily in the manner in which the units are decorated.

In essence, settings for thrust stages must be simple in concept and sculptural. Realistic depiction of place is difficult and undesirable. Great reliance is placed on the upstage scenic area and on the decoration of the floor, with carefully selected furniture and properties adding the finishing details. Although restrictive to the scenic designer in many ways, the thrust stage may also offer him exciting possibilities and challenges. In many ways it incorporates the best qualities of both the proscenium theatre and the arena theatre.

### The Arena Theatre

*Theatre Characteristics.* Arena theatre is a term used to refer to any theatre so arranged that the stage is completely surrounded by the audience with a 360° stage view (see Plate 150); however, the exact form of the theatre varies widely —from the intimate 100-seat theatre in a converted meeting room to the huge 1,000- to 2,000-seat musical tent theatre. The stage area itself varies just as greatly in size and shape, although square, round, and oval are the most popular shapes, and the average size is approximately 24' by 24'. Ideally, the audience should be seated in areas of equal size surrounding the stage, and each row of seats should be raised one or two steps above the row ahead so that each member of the audience will have a clear view of the stage.

Actors' access to the stage is provided by a minimum of four aisles spaced at equal intervals around the area. These may be the same aisles used by the audience members, they may be vomitories leading up from a lower room, or a combination of both may be used. These entrances are used not only by the actors but by the crews shifting the settings, so they must be large enough to accommodate furniture, properties, and scenic units.

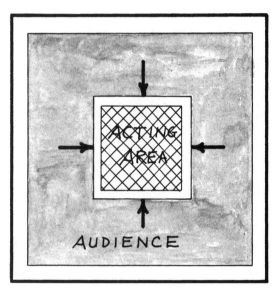

Plate 150. *ARENA THEATRE STAGE-AUDIENCE RELATIONSHIP*

Lighting instruments are, for the most part, situated directly over the stage and the first few rows of the audience. These may be partly concealed by one or more masking teasers surrounding the stage, or they may be recessed into a masking gridwork of wood or metal.

Usually there is little more to an arena stage than has just been described. Basically, it is an acting area surrounded by an audience seating area. Offstage in this type of theatre means being completely out of the theatre area, hence there is usually no easily accessible offstage storage space for scenery. There is usually little or no fly space available—only enough to conceal small units in or above the lighting instrument area. The vast majority of scenic units and properties used must come in and out through the aisles leading to the stage. This, plus the fact that the audience completely surrounds the stage, puts severe limitations on the scenic designer.

*Designing for the Arena Theatre.* No scenic unit may be used that blocks the view of the stage from any seat in the auditorium; this virtually eliminates the use of any standard flat units. As a matter of fact, only five basic types of device may be used by the designer: *the floor; furniture and properties; scenic units* that do not block the view of the audience; *space above the stage,* including primarily the lighting instrument masking surface; and miscellaneous *special scenic areas,* which will vary from show to show and from theatre to theatre.

scene is indoors, then rugs of the proper period, richness, and age may be set about the stage, actual or simulated flooring may be installed, vinyl or wood, planking or parquet. For the setting in Plate 151 commercial vinyl tiles add reality to the kitchen. If the play occurs outdoors, then grass, rocks, or earth may be simulated. The effectiveness of the setting in Plate 152 is a direct result of the realistic deck and dimensional flagstone treatment of the floor. Because of the proximity of the audience, painted floor treatments will suffice only if the setting is somewhat stylized. The simulated tile and terrazzo designs that are employed in the setting illustrated in Plate 153 enhance the decorative qual-

Plate 151. *ARENA SETTING FOR A REALISTIC INTERIOR KITCHEN: Real kitchen cabinets and appliances, an actual vinyl tile floor, and furniture from a furniture store create a very believable kitchen setting for* The Island *produced by the Georgia Repertory Theatre, Athens, GA. Scene design by the author.*

THE FLOOR: As with the thrust stage, this is a major scenic device. Almost every member of the audience will have a view of some portion of the stage floor and, in the absence of framed scenery, this provides the largest surface to be decorated. The choice of a design, for the floor, can do much to convey the desired environment of the setting. If the

ity created by the ornate furniture and suspended lanterns.

The floor also may serve as a reflecting surface. Projected patterns may suggest light streaming through leaves or various types of windows or doors. A projected decorative arched doorway or a barred window image will quite effectively suggest

Plate 152. *ARENA SETTING FOR A REALISTIC EXTERIOR PATIO: Actual planked deck, three-dimensional flagstone and fieldstone pool combine with live plants to create a strong sense of reality in this setting for* In This Day and Age *produced by the Georgia Repertory Theatre, Athens, GA with scenery by Crawford C. Pratt. The lower photo shows a detail of the setting, including the pool ornament with actual running water (there were even goldfish in the pool!).*

an elegant room or a jail cell, particularly when combined with appropriate furniture and property items. Note the contribution the leaf patterns make in creating an outdoor feeling in Plate 152.

The floor may also serve as a reflecting surface upon which patterns of light may be projected. Leaf patterns, patterns of doors and windows, or even abstract patterns may be projected onto the floor to create a very definite impression of locale. A projected image of a stained glass window or of a barred window will quite effectively suggest a cathedral or a jail cell, particularly when combined with appropriate furniture and property items.

FURNITURE AND PROPERTIES: Because the arena setting depends to a great extent upon its furniture and properties for the suggestion of the desired locale, great care must be taken in selecting and arranging these items. Those chosen should be particularly indicative of the period and locale of the

commercially made cabinets for *The Island*, shown in Plate 151, reinforced the reality of the kitchen setting, and the shop-built units, such as the suspended light fixture, were carefully crafted to add to the realism. In the same way, the practical fountain shown in Plate 152 coupled with the dimensional rocks and the real plants scattered around created a real sense of an outdoor patio.

From the practical point of view, all of the furniture chosen should be low backed. Sofas and chairs ordinarily should have backs no higher than the shoulder height of a seated person, and even lower backs are preferable. China cupboards, upright pianos, and other tall pieces should be avoided wherever possible. Backless seats and seats that face in two or more directions simultaneously are extremely useful and versatile (see Plates 153 and 155). As a general rule, more provision for seating must be made in an arena setting than in a corre-

Plate 153. *ARENA SETTING USING SIMPLIFIED SCENIC UNITS: Both real and fabricated cast-iron furniture, suspended Japanese lanterns, a simplified painted floor treatment, and a flower-covered trellis archway are used to suggest an elegant outdoor patio. A setting for* Ring 'Round the Moon *produced at the University of Georgia with scenery by Matt Bond.*

play and, wherever possible, the actual furniture items should be used. Mock-up furniture is not usually credible in an arena theatre because the audience is seated so close to the stage. The use of

sponding proscenium setting, since the director will want to move his actors around a great deal so as not to favor one side of the auditorium above another.

In positioning the furniture, the seating units

should be arranged so as to face as large a portion of the audience as possible. However, a completely circular arrangement is not usually desirable. The seating should be arranged in such a way as to provide a number of conversation areas throughout the stage area. At the same time, entrances and exits should be kept clear, and there should be open paths from entrance to entrance. A large unit placed in the center of the stage should have free passage around

stage as possible. Whenever ornamental frames of this sort are used, they should be as decorative as possible in keeping with the desired locale. Use of detailed cutouts or three-dimensional decor will greatly add to the effectiveness of these types of unit. Reliance on painted detail should be avoided whenever possible since the audience is too close for this sort of decor to be truly effective. An effective use of simplified scenic units is shown in

Plate 154. *ARENA SETTING ILLUSTRATING GOOD SELECTION AND ARRANGEMENT OF FURNITURE AND PROPERTIES: Furniture which is well crafted and unified in style is arranged to provide a good variety of movement patterns and seating arrangements in this setting for* The Circle *produced at the University of Georgia with scenery by Paul A. Camp. (Photo by Gates Studio)*

it. Study carefully the particularly good arrangements of furniture detailed in Plates 151 and 154.

SCENIC UNITS: Moderate use may be made of scenic units so long as they are designed not to block the audience view. Low walls, railings, bushes or hedges may be placed in or around the acting area to aid in defining the scenic environment. Skeletal frames may be used to suggest architectural units – doors, windows, walls, porches, roofs, etc. The tops and bottoms of the units can and should be fairly elaborate, but the central portion, which is in line with the audience view of the stage, should be kept simple and small in order to block as little of the

Plates 154 and 155. Note the decorative archway in the right foreground in both designs. Scenic units when placed at the actors' entrances, as is this one, are particularly usable since in this position they will block less of the audience than they would in any other location. One point to remember about such units, however, is that if they are used for multi-set productions, they should be as light as possible since they will probably have to be brought in by hand. Also, the size of the entrance aisles should be taken into account so that the units will not be too large to move easily in and out.

SPACE ABOVE THE STAGE: Here, again, is a very

usable area, since items placed here will not block the audience view of the stage. Chandeliers, suggestions of ceilings, roofs, building tops, foliage, and other such scenic elements may be placed above the stage and will greatly aid in localizing the action of the play (see Plates 151 and 153). The – an important entrance area is emphasized by the use of levels and a special scenic unit. In the setting shown in Plate 152, no actual audience space was taken over, but the floor treatment was extended into the audience entryways, expanding the setting beyond the actual stage area. The fountain, in close

Plate 155. *ARENA SETTING EMPLOYING STYLIZED FORMS AND A SPECIAL ENTRANCE AL-COVE: The foliage pieces in this setting for* Man and Superman *are an obviously stylized treatment of hedges and bushes and match well the simplified architectural forms in the entrance area. Produced by the University of Georgia, scenery by Paul A. Camp.*

masking teaser surrounding the lights will also provide a useful location for scenic devices, although care should be taken to avoid overelaboration, which might distract attention from the stage itself. One other point to remember in placing items above the stage is that you must be careful not to block the beam of any of the lighting instruments. Occasionally it may be possible to arrange this area so that small scenic units may be flown in and out to aid in changing settings.

SPECIAL SCENIC AREAS: A variety of other sorts of area may be used at various times in various theatres to aid the scenic environment. Sometimes a few rows of seats may be eliminated to provide space for an alcove or entrance space that may include larger scenic devices than may be used within the actual stage area. An example of this is seen in Plate 155 proximity to the audience, reinforced this implied expansion.

In some theatres, the wall area surrounding the audience may be used for small scenes or, barring that, may be decorated in a manner that will serve to suggest the locale of the play. Skylines, forests, buildings, or simply decorative devices may be used here and will provide a strong reinforcement of the environment suggested by the scenic elements used onstage. Weather effects, such as rain and snow, which would be extremely difficult—if not impossible—to achieve onstage may be suggested through lighting on this surrounding area. Various theatres may have other nooks and crannies to serve as locations for scenic devices to supplement those onstage. Be on the lookout for such areas in your own theatre.

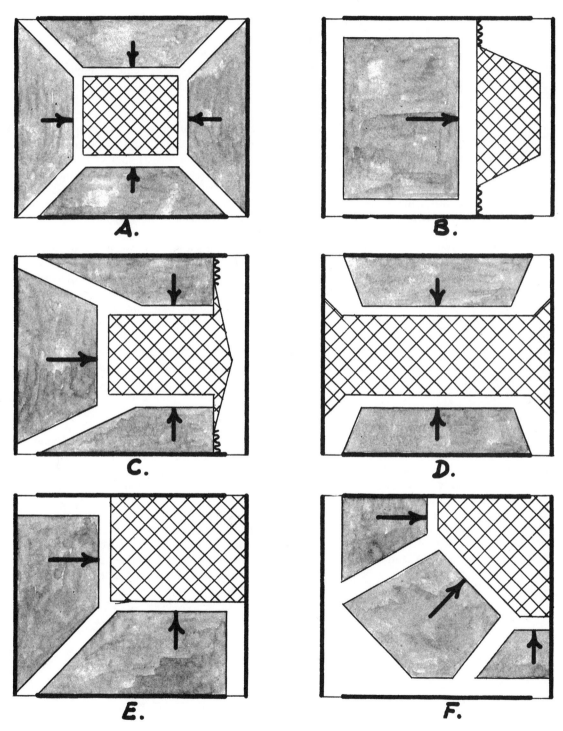

Plate 156. *THE FLEXIBLE OR "BLACK BOX" THEATRE:  One room capable of a variety of stage-audience configurations:  (a) arena; (b) proscenium; (c) thrust; (d) opposite side, or "alley" seating; (e) L-shaped; (f) corner stage.*

In concluding this section on designing for the arena, it might be well to emphasize that the types of scenic elements that may be used are extremely limited and therefore should be selected and executed with great care. The closeness of the audience to the stage also requires that careful attention be paid to the construction of all scenic elements. Carelessness and sloppy work that might be passable on a proscenium stage become distressingly obvious on an arena stage.

*The Flexible Theatre, or "Black Box"*

The flexible theatre is a form that has become increasingly popular—particularly for experimental and educational theatre. As with other types of theatres, the variety of sizes and shapes of flexible theatres is wide, but the basic form remains the same. In general, this consists of a large bare room, preferably square. Frequently it is converted from some other use such as a ballroom, meeting room, or large classroom. Within this bare space, through the use of movable platforms and seats, the seating and stage space is arranged and rearranged as desired for each production. One production may be set up in the conventional proscenium or open-stage arrangement, another may be presented in a thrust or ¾-round form, still another may be produced in a full arena, and any other arrangement may be used that is thought to be of particular advantage to the play in production—L-shaped, corner stage, or opposite-side seating (see Plate 156). Although this type of theatre is usually not suitable for any large permanent structure, many directors and designers feel that the flexibility offered is particularly desirable for experimental productions, studio productions, or educational theatre. In this type of theatre the persons involved have an opportunity to learn the benefits and drawbacks of particular types of staging, and often find that plays can take on new and deeper meanings when produced in a variety of forms of staging. There is opportunity for experimentation here not usually found in theatres designed for one particular type of staging.

Along the same lines, many new theatres are being designed in such a way as to provide for various types of staging. Some of the most extreme of these provide automated movable seating that can convert from a proscenium arrangement into an arena at virtually the flick of a switch. Less extreme examples use hydraulic lifts to convert the orchestra pit in a proscenium, or modified proscenium, theatre into a forestage playing area, thereby providing a semi-thrust or open-stage arrangement. The danger in this sort of theatre is that in attempting to provide a theatre that will function in a variety of ways, the architects or designers produce a theatre that will not function very adequately in any one particular form. For instance, several new theatres have been built in such a way as to incorporate both a thrust-stage and a standard proscenium arrangement. Unfortunately, the seating requirements for the two types of stage are entirely different and, consequently, the resultant theatre will usually function well for only one of the two setups or, even worse, will not function adequately for either. Combination theatres of this sort are not impossible, but they do require very careful planning if they are to function properly.

This chapter has presented only a cursory glance at some of the basic types of theatre arrangement. If you should be involved in planning a new theatre, it would be a wise idea to consider very carefully all the advantages and disadvantages of each type of theatre arrangement before making any final decisions. Visit examples of the various theatres if you can and study closely the advantages of each. Consult with experienced theatre practitioners or professional theatre consultants, and seek their advice on your own special requirements and the ways in which they can best be met. You cannot be too careful during the planning stages of a theatre; once the construction has begun it is obviously too late to make any drastic changes.

# chapter IX

# SPECIAL SCENIC DEVICES

It is extremely difficult to be specific about the process of designing settings. So many factors must be taken into consideration when planning a design that there can be no step-by-step instructions for achieving the desired goal. Size and shape of theatre, elaborateness of technical facilities, interpretation, availability of materials, skill of technicians, and – usually the largest factor of all – budget, all affect the design of any play. No two settings are ever alike – nor should they be. This makes very rocky the way of an author of a book on scenery. Usually the best that can be done is to describe theories and techniques that have worked well in the past and might be adapted for future use.

So far I have been dealing with what might be called the more standard techniques of design and stagecraft, applying these to the more common types of setting. I have attempted to compile this collection of information and suggestions into an organized presentation that might be useful to a novice designer. However, a number of items should be mentioned that would not fit into any of the foregoing chapters. This miscellany of information is to be pre-sented in this chapter, in no particular order other than a general sort of classification.

## SIMPLIFIED SETTINGS

As was pointed out in Chapter IV in connection with *Lawyer Lincoln*, there are occasions when, because of time, budget, or other considerations, it is not desirable to mount a complete setting for a play. At the same time, it is not desirable to eliminate the scenic environment entirely. Fortunately, several types of setting might serve in such instances. These are termed *simplified settings*, or "minimal scenery," and consist of two basic types: *cut-down or fragmentary settings*, and *spot settings*. Both depend upon a neutral backing of some sort— preferably a set of black draperies or a sky cyc. Other colors are usable, but they limit the setting

design, since the color of the setting should not clash with the color of the surround. Black does not present this problem and, moreover, its use creates a background that virtually disappears, isolating the setting in infinite space. This centers the attention on the setting and the action occurring within its boundaries. Variety and added visual interest can be obtained when these settings are backed up with projected images. A discussion of that technique concludes this chapter.

### Cut-down or Fragmentary Setting

The cut-down setting is just what the name implies – a setting whose top has been cut off, leaving only the bottom portion plus window and door frames. The line of the walls is indicated by a 2' to 3' high portion of the wall – frequently a bottom portion of paneling. Door and window units are high enough to provide full-size openings, but they are usually not continued much above the top of the window or door. Tall units of furniture and special architectural units such as fireplaces and bookcases may be set in raised portions of the wall.

The fragmentary setting is similar in form, except that the scenic units are not necessarily connected by low wall panels. Here architectural elements such as doors or windows, ceiling pieces, decorative elements such as pictures and draperies, or natural elements such as tree trunks and foliage pieces, are placed around the stage to form the visual composition. Low platforms and step units, balustrades, or moulding pieces may be used to visually connect these individual elements together. Here, again, as with the cut-down setting, these scenic elements are seen against some form of neutral background, such as black draperies.

Planning these types of settings is similar to planning any other – the floor plan, for instance, is identical. However, certain factors should be kept in mind. First of all, the doors, windows and special units receive a strong focus of attention since they are the tallest portions of the setting. The principal means of visually balancing the setting, then, is through achieving a balance of these elements. Furniture plays only a relatively minor role in bal-

It is usually a wise idea to vary the heights of the tall portions of the settings. Although the windows and doors themselves are usually the same height, the decorative treatment surmounting the units can

Plate 157. *A THREE-DIMENSIONAL FRAGMENTARY/SPOT SETTING: A wall and roof unit combined with a suspended window frame and a bench unit form this fragmentary/spot setting for* The Crucible. *Produced by Richmond Professional Institute with scenery by the author.*

ancing this type of setting.

Another point to keep in mind is that the visual interest and unity of the setting must be achieved by the use of fewer scenic elements than in a full-size setting. Here again, the tall units become the major devices to be used in achieving this unity and variety. For the sake of visual interest, the tops of these units usually must be more decorative than they might otherwise be, since strictly rectangular shapes can quickly become visually monotonous. It does not require much detail, however, to create a more interesting shape. In Plate 158, for instance, the tops of the door and window units are made more interesting through the addition of relatively simple cut-out profiles, while the somewhat more elaborate profile on the central fireplace unit provides a visual focus to the center of the setting. This is a good example of a simple but well-designed cut-down setting.

be varied to achieve a difference in height. An example of this may be seen in Plate 159. Another interesting element of this same set is the suggestion of a ceiling achieved with a two-dimensional, false-perspective cutout suspended above the setting. Such a device is an excellent way of adding interest and providing an added dimension to the design. This type of suggested ceiling is not, of course, limited to use with cut-down scenery.

Usually in the cut-down setting there is no attempt to provide backings for the doors or windows. Actors entering and exiting may be seen above the low walls of the setting. An interesting variation on this may be observed in the setting, shown in Plate 159, in which, in addition to the conventional cut-down interior, a portion of the exterior is suggested by the use of a few bush silhouettes and a bit of stone wall. Here, although the actors may still be observed entering and exiting, there is some sense of place, as opposed to the complete void of black ordinarily used. Such a device is not necessary but can provide an interesting sideline to the setting. However, if such suggested backings are used, they should be kept simple to harmonize with the simplified nature of the main setting.

The treatment of the cut-down setting may be as realistic as desired. The walls may be given a three-dimensional aspect, as has been done in the setting

mean a saving in time or money. You still must plan carefully to use stock elements wherever possible. For instance, narrow flats may be turned on their sides to provide portions of the low walls. Door and window frames may be used and embellished with decorative profile tops Even though there is less scenery required than in a standard box setting, unless stock units are planned into the setting, the time and money spent in constructing the irregularly shaped and unusual size units may be equal to, or

Plate 158. *CUT-DOWN SCENERY WITH A PROFILE CEILING: An interesting variety of contours on the window and door units is reinforced by the decorated floor and a cut-out ceiling unit with chandeliers. A setting for* The Misanthrope *produced by the University of Iowa with scenery by Max Wiese.*

in Plate 159, or they may be presented in a more two-dimensional form, as in Plate 158. This is determined by the choice of style for the setting. Although the cut-down setting is a stylized setting of sorts, it does not preclude the use of very realistic scenic elements and properties. As a matter of fact, in spite of the conventionalized nature of the basic setting, a very realistic atmosphere can be achieved by using the proper scenic elements and proper lighting.

One further comment on cut-down settings. The use of this type of setting does not automatically

even greater than that spent putting together a standard box setting from stock units. However, with careful planning and the use of stock units wherever possible, the cut-down setting can be a quicker and more economical manner of providing the scenic environment for a play.

*Spot Settings*

The spot setting is first cousin to the cut-down setting. Here again, the setting is composed of scenic units isolated against a neutral background—most often drapery (preferably black) or a cyc.

Plate 159. *CUT-DOWN SCENERY WITH A THREE-DIMENSIONAL QUALITY: Thickness pieces on door and window frames, plus three-dimensional moldings on the wall panels bring an added level of interest to this setting for* The Miser. *Note, also, how the low exterior walls carry the setting offstage. Designed by A.S. Gillette for the University of Iowa.*

These scenic units are not connected to one another, but are spaced around the stage in such a way as to create an impression of the area enclosed by the imaginary setting. For example, simple cut out windows might be used together with silhouetted trees and landscape to visually supplement an otherwise relatively simple arrangement of platforms and stairs. Since this form of platforming may

Plate 160. *A PORCH-INSPIRED SPOT SETTING: With motifs derived from middle-America front porches, this setting for* The Fantasticks *is isolated against a large expanse of neutral background. Produced by Richmond Professional Institute, designed by the author.*

often be accomplished with stock platform units, the available time and money may be spent on creating cut-out elements which are visually interesting and will fill the space above and around the platform

Frequently, spot setting units may be fleshed out by decorative backgrounds. The units used to suggest a portion of the Brooklyn Bridge, shown in Plate 161, are reinforced both dramatically and

Plate 161. *SPOT SETTING FOR THE BROOKLYN BRIDGE: A lamppost, balustrade, and portions of a bridge support structure isolated against a lighted city skyline, serve to suggest a New York bridge in this setting for* Luv *produced at the University of Georgia. Scenery by the author.*

units. This is an extremely economical use of materials, yet the quality of the setting would not be diminished. Fewer scenic elements are used in the setting shown in Plate 157; however, the elements used are more three-dimensional and arranged to visually encompass the entire stage space. The suspended window unit and the stool placed stage left fill what would otherwise be vacant stage space. It is also worth noting that the masking flats have been painted to suggest vertical planking, which also serves to flesh out this very fragmentary setting. In the setting shown in Plate 160 an even smaller spot setting is isolated against a large expanse of neutral background. Here the focus is pulled to the central unit by the varied profile offered by the multiple levels and the vertical trellises. Additional interest is created by the different forms of trellis treatments found in the platform facings and the upright units.

aesthetically by the suggestion of a lighted city skyline in the background. Yet the means to achieve this effect were simple—holes cut into a solid surface and covered with gel and then lighted from behind with small floodlights. The remainder of the background consisted of black draperies. In the setting shown in Plate 163, a simple low-cost shadow projector has been used to create the map image which is used to visually fill a stage which otherwise would be very sparse with only a throne unit and a table platform onstage.

At this point I think it bears repeating that whenever you use only a few scenic units in a setting, each unit must be more decorative and visually interesting than would be the case in a full-stage setting. This elaboration of decoration, of course, should be appropriate to the style of the production and the locale and period of the play. Note, for instance, the decorative quality of the units used in the settings shown in Plates 158, 159, and 162. Simpler elements are used in the spot settings shown in Plates 160 and 161; however, these elements have been arranged in a striking and effective visual composition. In any of these types of setting, the arrange

Plate 162. *A FRAGMENTARY SETTING USING SIMPLE FLAT FORMS: Rectangular flat forms enlivened with decorative painting are supplemented with columns and platforms to create a simple yet interesting setting for* Love for Love *at the University of Iowa. Scenery by Vincent Gagliardi.)*

ment and juxtaposition of units play a prime role in the visual interest of the final product. Interesting and decorative units will not necessarily combine into an interesting composition unless careful thought is given to their relationship. The design principles of rhythm, balance, center of interest and unity with variety must not be forgotten when planning these types of setting. The very fact that the scenic units are limited in number means that each must play an important role in creating a pleasing composition. They are not selected and arranged at random, but are carefully coordinated to create the total composition of the setting. Only in this way can an interesting and effective simplified setting be achieved.

## FOR THE POVERTY–STRICKEN

I have mentioned, wherever possible, methods for economizing in design and construction. The types of setting mentioned above, for instance, are useful for the economy-minded. There are times, however, when simple economy is not sufficient; when the setting must be put together from "toothpicks, string and spit." At such times standard stagecraft techniques must be dispensed with and inexpensive substitutes found. For that reason, this section will include possible low-cost substitute materials as well as sources for such materials.

First of all, however, I should like to encourage designers always to be on the lookout for usable materials. They may be found in the unlikeliest places and at the unlikeliest times. Frequently, when such opportunities are passed up, they do not occur again. For instance, some modern packing materials are extremely useful for various stage purposes. Air-filled plastics and light foam pebbles are frequently substituted for the more common newspaper and excelsior, and these materials can be used in many ways. I have found them useful for window coverings, simulated pebbles, and a number of other things. Many products are delivered to and construction—makers of fabrics, plastic sheeting and materials, carpeting, foam and particleboard panels, and other materials. Frequently roll ends, "seconds", and excess materials may be obtained from these sources for little or no cost — especially to educational or community-based organizations.

Plate 163. *SPOT SETTING WITH PROJECTED BACKGROUND: The projected map background in this setting fills out a stage which contains only a large throne unit and a few other set pieces. Scenery by Irene Corey for* Henry V *at Centenary College.*

market in materials which may be usable onstage. Foreign-made motorcycles, for example, are shipped in cases made of beadfoam. We once constructed an entire rough-stone setting from such discarded motorcycle packing materials (there was some cost for structural lumber, glue, and paint, but the bulk of the setting was free for the asking). With some moderate detective work, other such supply sources may be found. Of course, the most attractive feature of these materials is that they don't cost anything, since they may be obtained from regular shipped goods.

It always pays to investigate sources close to home. Many communities house manufacturers whose products may be useful for scenery design Frequently, educational institutions have access to government surplus storehouses and, where this source is available, many excellent items can be found at very nominal costs. Although the materials must be secured on a catch-as-catch-can basis, you may often find such items as tents, canvas goods, parachute nylon, netting of various types, and, occasionally, items of lumber, wire, and rope. When the fabrics are found in bolts they are particularly useful, but even the ready-made items can be helpful at times. The dominant element in the setting shown in Plate 165 is an army surplus tent found at just such a source. The remaining portions of the setting were made up of stock furniture, stock lighting instruments, plus the muslin and poles used for the side masking posters and banner—total cost, approximately $60. In another example, extensive use was made of camouflage netting from government surplus for the setting seen in Plate 122.

On rare occasions, the materials commonly used for decorations at school dances can be adapted to scenery. Boxboard (corrugated cardboard) and kraft paper can be used to form surfaces for painting—with the addition of lumber for support framing. The

nic materials used sparingly. The setting shown in Plate 164 consists primarily of large swags constructed from inexpensive muslin, strings of standard Christmas tree lights, stock standard window shades, a couple of sawhorses and planks, and a few cases and drawer units constructed to hold the props for the show. It is the arrangement of these relatively simple items that creates a visually interesting but low-cost setting.

Another helpful source may be salvage compa-

Plate 164. *CLOTH SWAGS AND CHRISTMAS TREE LIGHTS ARE PRINCIPAL ELEMENTS IN LOW-BUDGET SETTING: In addition to the above items, the remaining set pieces for this production of* Godspell *are a few constructed drawer and shelf units for properties, plus sawhorses and planks. Produced by the University of Georgia with scenery by the author.*

danger here is that these materials are considerably more flammable than traditional scenery materials and must be handled with extreme caution. There is no way to adequately flameproof these materials, so where fire regulations are strictly enforced, they may not be usable at all. On those occasions when budget (or lack thereof) forces consideration of cardboard and paper as scenic materials, extra precautions must be taken to keep them away from heat of any sort.

Low budget shows may be created from carefully planned combinations of "found" and standard sce-

nies. Useful architectural items such as fireplaces, stair bannisters and newel posts, architectural trim, and even lumber may be found in houses being razed. Although some salvage companies have begun to look upon themselves as sources of valuable antiques and have priced their goods accordingly, it is still possible in many instances to find very useful items at reasonable prices.

Simple but effective settings may often be composed primarily of what I call "found" objects – items readily available around the building or in the neighborhood. These may be used as is or may be temporarily altered for use in the play. The setting shown in Plate 166 was created almost entirely from items found in scenery and property storage and adapted for the production. The only new elements were the framed paintings scattered around the stage. Other items which may be useful for various productions include three-fold screens, free-standing blackboards and bulletin boards. The surfaces of these may be covered with either framed or unframed cloth and painted or decorated to fit the production. In a pinch, boxboard may serve the same purpose, but, for

conceal the fact that they are theatrical events – frequently with the actors talking directly to the audience. Although the most familiar of these plays is *Our Town*, others of the same variety include *Under Milkwood, Spoon River Anthology, The Rimers of Eldridge*, and, in the musical line, *The Fantasticks*. Settings for these types of productions can be as simple as the budget requires, making no attempt to conceal theatrical devices and equipment, and providing only such scenic items as are necessary to the action of the play – often merely a simple

Plate 165. *ARMY SURPLUS ITEMS PROVIDE DOMINANT SCENIC ELEMENT FOR A LOW-BUDGET SETTING: An army surplus tent forms the bulk of this setting for* He Who Gets Slapped *, together with a few furniture items and cloth posters. Designed by the author for Richmond Professional Institute.*

reasons cited above, this is not recommended as a standard practice. Useful items might be salvaged from dance decorations, and I have even heard of instances in which productions utilized "jungle gyms." Often a wealth of scenic possibilities is ready at hand if the designer is ready to recognize them as such.

Although the final decision is usually not in the designer's province, the selection of a play can often reduce the necessary scenic expenditure. A number of plays of recent vintage require very little in the way of scenery. They are written in an episodic, presentational manner, not making any attempt to

arrangement of levels. The danger here is of overlooking the necessity for providing visual interest and pleasing composition in even such a utilitarian setting. The arrangement of the levels and the addition of any other scenic elements – whether they be practical theatrical equipment or not – should be so designed as to create an interesting stage picture.

### NEW AND DIFFERENT

Modern technological innovations coupled with designers' dissatisfaction with conventional forms of stagecraft have brought about many experiments, suggestions and new trends in forms and styles of scenery. Although these are too numerous to discuss in any detail, several new forms of design and a be used in settings (other than the traditional lumber and canvas) are metal sheets, wire, metal tubing, wrought iron, glass panels and glass brick, mirrors, plastic sheeting, extruded plastic and plastic tubing,

Plate 166. *A LOW-BUDGET "PROP ROOM" SETTING: Aside from a few framed and ripped paintings, the principal elements in this setting were fashioned from items found in scenery and property storage. A production of* The Cuttlefish *at the University of Georgia, designed by the author.*

number of new materials do bear mentioning.

Realistic depiction of scenic environment has decreased significantly in the latter part of the century—particularly in European theatres. Designers are producing striking settings that project strong dramatic and atmospheric effects with only a suggestion of locale. Great emphasis is placed on three-dimensionality and texture, coupled with dramatic lighting effects. Materials are used for their structural qualities and their emotional impact—their strength, flexibility, lightness, roughness, gloss, transparency, and the way in which they reflect, absorb, or transmit light. Frequently the materials are used per se, and the emotional and aesthetic impact of the setting is determined by the inherent qualities of the chosen materials and the manner in which the materials are combined. Plate 167 shows a setting designed with this approach. Among the materials to

artificial resins, an astonishing variety of foam materials, latex, Formica, Plexiglas, cork, leather, straw, artificial fabrics, and various types of paper and cardboard.

Metals have proved very useful for settings, although frequent use requires special tools and skills for cutting, bending, welding, etc. The strength and rigidity of the material makes it particularly useful for such things as platforming and delicate tracery silhouettes. Extremely airy structures, which are at the same time very strong and rigid, can be formed from metals – something which is difficult to accomplish with lumber. Aluminum is available in very strong yet amazingly light piping and rods that may be worked into very light but stable structures. Several touring and repertory companies have used aluminum to construct unit-type platform structures that can be fastened together in a variety of ways to provide a permanent or semi-permanent setting for plays in repertory. There are even available on the market quick-attachment fittings for joining aluminum pipes without welding or threading, allowing for quick and easy assembling of frames with no special tools. Theatres without the means for

be telescoped and secured at one-inch intervals with bolts through the perforations—particularly useful for creating varied height legs on stock platforms. *Slotted steel* is "L"-angled steel lengths perforated with holes and slots, which allows for bolting two lengths together through matching holes. *Slip-on*

Plate 167. *A "JUNKYARD" SETTING: Industrial steel girders together with real textures and a variety of objects which might be found in a local junkyard provide a grittily realistic environment in this setting for* On the Open Road *produced by The Goodman Theatre, Chicago, with scenery by George Tsypin. (Photo by Liz Lauren)*

actually working in metal may make use of these types of metal products or may take advantage of readymade metal frames such as may be found in scaffolding.

There are a variety of ready-to-assemble metal products available for the shop unequipped for welding and fitting. *Unistrut* (a trade name) is a steel channel grooved to accept spring-held nuts which allow it to be bolted to other elements. Special corner angles, flanges, and other hardware allow the channels to be assembled into numerous shapes and forms. The Unistrut Corporation also produces *Telespar* which is perforated square steel tubing available in graduated sizes so that each size fits within the next larger size. This permits sections to

*pipe fittings* in a variety of configurations are designed to slip onto and secure easily to standard sizes of pipe for the quick and easy creation of both two-dimensional and three-dimensional pipe constructions.

Decorative effects may be achieved with metal wire, netting, perforated sheets in a wide variety of designs, and thin-wall steel or plastic conduit pipe. The latter has become very popular because it is lightweight, inexpensive, and easy to bend.

For many years, three-dimensional shapes and forms were created primarily through the use of papier mache or cut and carved wooden forms. Beginning approximately in the 1960's, however, a wide variety of new materials has come on the

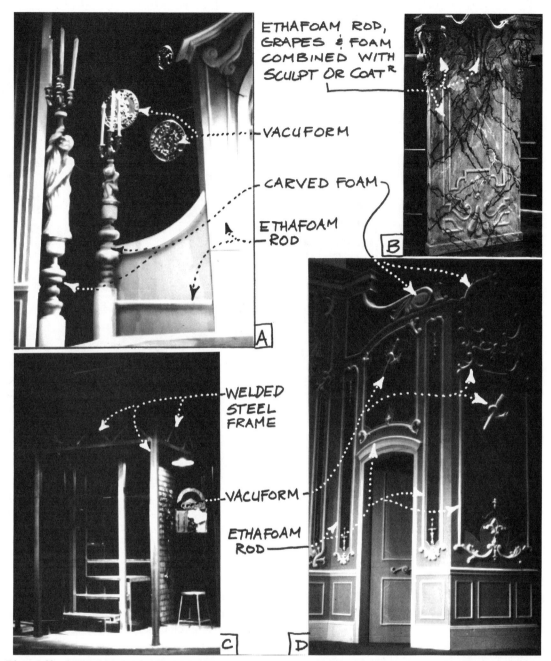

Plate 168. *MODERN SCENERY CONSTRUCTION MATERIALS: Scenic units in "A", "C", and "D" are from productions designed by the author. Scenic unit "C" is from* Tartuffe *designed by Eric Olson for Samford University—see also* Plate 7. *(Photo by Eric Olson)*

market and been adapted for stage use. One of the earlier materials was *Celastic*, a cloth impregnated with cellulose nitrate and a fire retardant which softened when dipped in acetone and could be shaped or molded over or into three-dimensional forms. No longer manufactured, Celastic has been partially replaced by *Solvoset*, muslin and canvas impregnated with plastic, also softened with acetone. Although it sticks better to itself, this material takes much longer to dry than did Celastic and may even need to be force air dried before finishing and painting. It is important that it be thoroughly dry before applying any surface coating. A word of warning: acetone is a toxic and flammable liquid which should be handled with great care—working with acetone should be done only in a well-ventilated space while wearing gloves and a respirator.

Far less dangerous to use, but somewhat more expensive, are a variety of *thermo-plastic* products designed to be soaked in hot water (160-180' F), at which point the material softens and may be shaped into three-dimensional forms. When cooled the material retains that shape. Available from craft stores under the tradename Friendly Plastic, this type of material (under such names as Vara-Form, Protoplast, Fabric-Form, and Adapt-It Pellets) may be purchased from several theatrical suppliers as light- and heavy-weight mesh sheets, solid or perforated sheets in thicknesses up to 3/16", as pellets which melt down to become solids, and as thermoplastic-covered fabric. Most useful for smaller props and decorative details on settings, some of these materials may be reused by soaking again in hot water and shaping into a new form. *Fiberglass* is another material that has been used with good results in the fabrication of three-dimensional forms. A positive or negative mold is first coated with a releasing agent and then covered with pieces of fiberglass cloth that are sealed together by being saturated in a solution of fabricating resin and hardener. Varying the proportions of the hardener and resin in the solution will provide varying degrees of hardness in the final form. The fiberglass cloth is available in many types and weights — some of which are quite translucent. Fiberglass is also an excellent transmitter of light and, when combined with lighting instruments, can produce exciting and unusual effects. Another word of warning, however: many chemicals in the fiberglass process are very hazardous and the fiberglass cloth itself is made up of fibers of actual glass. Appropriate ventilation and the wearing of protective garments is essential when working with this material.

A slight variation on fiberglass is *casting resin*—essentially the same resin used to harden and solidify the fiberglass, but available in small quantities in hobby shops along with several other types of resin. These are useful for casting small properties, jewels and simulated glass objects. Molds made of ceramic, silicone rubber or polypropylene are used, or a parting agent such as silicone is used to keep the resin from adhering to the mold. As with fiberglass, a catalyst hardener is mixed with the resin. Curing of the cast item may take as long as 12 or more hours.

Also useful for small three-dimensional objects is *laminated felt*. Strips of felt coated with polyvinyl glue are built up over a form that has first been covered with aluminum foil. A hard surface is achieved by applying several coats of a glaze of thinned shellac or clear acrylic paint. Flexibility in the felt objects can be kept by using a flexible polyvinyl glue.

Pre-shaped architectural forms and textures are available from several manufacturers in lightweight vacuum-formed plastic. The detail in these forms is excellent but they are not very sturdy and will not stand much abuse – they serve better for appearance than for use. The sheets may be decorated with casein, latex, acrylic, or enamel paints. They may be joined or secured in place with masking tape, staples, tacks, polyvinyl glue or contact cement. A fairly wide variety of scenic, costume and property shapes are currently available, and new ones are constantly being developed.

It is also possible to construct a vacuum-form machine for use in your own shop. Following instructions which can be found in Nicholas Bryson's book, *Thermoplastic Scenery for the Theatre* or in various articles in *Theatre Design and Technology*, the process is relatively inexpensive and not particularly difficult. The machine consists of two parts: an oven to heat plastic sheets until they soften, and a vacuum table where the softened plastic is pulled down over a three-dimensional mold. For many shops a machine large enough to form sheets 24" x 36" in size would be sufficient. A number of firms offer architectural details (mouldings, carvings, swags, rosettes, etc.) in reinforced plaster or cement. While these are meant to be purchased in bulk and applied to building interiors or exteriors, they may be purchased individually and used as molds for vacuum-forming whereby inexpensive and lightweight copies may be produced for application to settings.

Large-sized three-dimensional solids which are also very lightweight may be constructed from several varieties of foam materials. *Polystyrene*, commonly called *Styrofoam*, comes in the very familiar "beadboard"—a favorite packing material for electronic devices but which may also be used for rough-cut 3-D shapes. Denser polystyrene, usually light blue or pink in color, is more fine-grained and is useful for carving and shaping objects requiring finer detail. Both rigid and flexible *polyurethane* foams are also available for creating three-dimensional objects. Both polystyrene and polyurethane foams are available in sheets of varying thicknesses which may also be glued together to create thicker buildups. Polyvinyl glue and a number of other adhesives especially formulated for foam work may be used for gluing sheets together and also for adhering foam to the surfaces of flats or other objects. Both foams may be carved with knives, saws, and other cutters; hot-wire cutters may be used on polystyrene but should never be used on polyurethane. Care should be taken when working with any foam. Foam dust and chips can get into the eyes and nose, and potentially toxic vapors are emitted during carving—especially carving with hot-wire cutters. Work should be done in a well-ventilated area and appropriate protective gear should be worn.

Chemicals are available on the market that may be used for foam casting in the scenic shop. A hollow mold is made of the object to be cast, the surface of the mold is sealed with shellac, than a coating of wax or paraffin is applied to serve as a parting agent. Quasi-prepolymer and resin-catalyst chemicals are mixed with a high-speed mixer for approximately forty seconds in a disposable container and then poured into the mold where they will convert to a rigid polyurethane foam. Additional chemicals can increase the density of the foam to between 2 and 12 pounds per cubic foot. The 12-pound density is sufficiently strong to withstand a hammer blow.

Carved or cast foam objects usually must receive an outer coating to provide a surface which will accept scene paint and, frequently, protect the foam from being broken or chipped when located near stage action. Glue-soaked cheesecloth can serve this purpose, but there are also several liquids and pastes available which can provide protective outer coatings. Some of these are available in large quantities from commercial foam suppliers. A recent addition to the inventory of theatre-related materials is *Sculpt Or Coat*™—a thick creamy paste which may be used as a surface coating for foam (and many other materials) but which may also be carved and shaped for additional texture or dimensional detailing. *Sculpt Or Coat*™ may also be used as a weave filler on plastic mesh or net fabrics to construct larger scenic units, armor, masks, and

other property items.

Both synthetic rubber and plastic-based *Weave Fillers* are manufactured by Haussmann of Germany. These are flexible materials which may either be painted onto fabric mesh or applied through cake-decorator syringes for built-up ornamental designs. Haussmann also manufactures *Hatamold* which is a pourable mold material which allows casting in plaster molds at normal room temperatures. The resulting elastic object is unbreakable, nailable, and will accept adhesives. As with other casting materials, this is useful for creating emblems, medallions, reliefs, balusters, capitals, and other three-dimensional decorative items.

A wide variety of plastics and acrylics are available – far too many to mention in any great detail. From these materials can be obtained a variety of transparent, translucent and glossy surfaces that are usually resistant to breakage and, frequently, may be easily shaped through the application of heat. The reflection, refraction, absorption and transmission of light by plastics vary widely, and many exciting effects may be achieved through the combination of plastics and lighting. For instance, extruded acrylic rods are available that will conduct a beam of light from one end, through any turns or curves into which the rod is bent, and out the other end with little loss of intensity, providing the means for bending a ray of light around a corner or even turning it back upon itself. A translucent version of the same acrylic rod will glow like a neon tube when light is placed at one end. Such effects as these are only a few of the seemingly endless range of possibilities.

*Projections*

The combined use of lighting effects and unusual materials seems to be a predominant feature of modern stagecraft. More and more, the lighting, scenery, and directing of a production are becoming inextricably intertwined. Scenery has become more than just a background – or even an environment for the action. Lighting has, in many cases, supplemented or even replaced scenery. Projected effects form scenic vistas and effects in place of the painted backdrops once used. Projected effects in the form of slides and movies have even become an integral part of the action of plays, commenting on and supplementing the live action of the actors.

Projections are a unique combination of lighting design and scenery design. Without delving too deeply into the lighting design and equipment aspects, it would be remiss of me not to mention some of the scenic considerations and possibilities of projected images. Considerations that fall into the area of scenery design include the purpose the projections will serve (whether scenic or dramatic), the type of projection surface to be employed, and provisions for placement of the projector. Leaving a discussion of the purpose served by the projections for later, let us look at screen and projector placement considerations.

For projections which will strike the front of a

unwanted shadows or undesirably distorted images onto the surface.

Rear projection—where projector is on the side of the surface away from the audience—makes additional demands on a screen material. It must not only convey the image to the audience side of the screen, but, ideally, it will diffuse and conceal the light from the projector lamp. Rear projection (RP) screen material is available commercially from Rosco Laboratories and Gerriets, Inc. for moderate cost and comes in black, grey, translucent, and white with differing transmission characteristics for each.

Plate 169. *REAR PROJECTION FROM A SHADOW PROJECTOR: Forming the only scenic element in this setting, the bold and brightly colored projection was created with a direct-beam projector—a form of shadow projector. A production of* Shenandoah *at Oak Ridge Playhouse, designed by Paul Ebert.*

projection surface—where the projector is located on the same side of the surface as the audience, almost any type of material may be used. Both hard surfaced and cloth-covered flats, plain muslin or scrim drops, even moderate to heavily textured surfaces can serve to reflect a projected image, so long as the color of the surface is not too dark. The only difficulty here is making sure there is a position available for the projector where it will be out of the audience sightlines and will not cast

Plain muslin material makes a more-than-adequate screen, but it does not conceal the bright spot from the projector lamp, so some means must be provided to hide the projector from the view of the audience—behind a ground row or some other scenic unit, for example. *Pellon*, a nonwoven fabric long used in costume construction, makes a good rear projection screen, but only comes in relatively narrow widths. A variety of other plastic materials have been found to serve adequately as rear projection

Plate 170. *MULTIPLE PROJECTIONS FROM LENSED PROJECTORS: In this design from the master of projected images, multiple images were projected from front and back onto both scrim and screen surfaces to create an effect which is both realistic and impressionistic. A design by Josef Svoboda for* A Sunday in August *at the Tyl Theatre in Prague, Czechoslovakia.*

Plate 171. *PROJECTIONS USED FOR DRAMATIC IMPACT: During the song "Tomorrow Belongs to Me" in this production of* Cabaret, *projected images of Hitler and Nazi Germany served as counterpoint to the lyrics. Designed by the author for the University of Georgia.*

Plate 172. *PROJECTIONS USED FOR DIDACTIC PURPOSES: Projected images supplement information provided onstage for enhanced dramatic impact in this docu-drama.* In White America *produced by
the University of Hawaii. Designed by Richard Mason. (Photo by Frank Chong)*

Plate 173. *MULTIPLE PROJECTIONS TELL THE STORY: A scene from* Rosalie Pritchett *in which
multiple slide projections were used to supplement and expand the action and information presented
onstage. Produced by Morehouse-Spelman Players, designed by Luis Maza.*

Plate 174. *INTERACTIVE PROJECTIONS: In this production by the acknowledged master of projections, onstage characters interact with their filmed images projected on the large upstage screen.* The Last Ones, *scenography by Josef Svoboda for the Tyl Theatre, Prague, Czechoslovakia. (Photo by Jaromir Svoboda)*

screens—sometimes sprayed with translucent paints or dyes to help mask the projector lamp. With some experimentation, it is possible to find alternative materials for rear projection screens, depending on the required size and use.

Projection images may be created from a variety of devices and equipment. The simplest use of projections is to cast the silhouette of an object or person and for this any light source will work. There are several hundred commercially made gobos for use with ellipsoidal reflector lighting instruments to cast a variety of shadow images. Examples of this type of projected image can be seen in Plates 75 and 152. The Linnebach lantern (shadow-box projector) is a type of projector without a lens and casts a fuzzy image over a wide area. This can be used for abstract or stylized images such as those seen in Plates 163 and 169. For clearer images, it is often possible to use standard slide projectors, opaque projectors, overhead projectors, movie projectors and video projectors, which are usually available from school audio-visual departments. Achieving bright projected images larger than about 8' x 12' will require the use of projection equipment especially designed for theatrical use. There are several different types of equipment manufactured for this purpose, but all fall into the expensive to very expensive price category. Most of these are available on a rental basis, however, when need and budget allow. The background images seen in Plates 76, 89, and 169 were achieved with this type of scenic projector. The smaller images on the suspended screens in Plates 76 and 9 came from standard carousel slide projectors.

There are a variety of functions which projected images may serve in a production. The most obvious use is scenic enhancement—most often employing projections in place of painted backdrops (see Plates 76, 89, 163, 169 and 170). When the necessary equipment is available, this can be a most efficient and effective means of changing scenic backgrounds. (If the equipment is not readily available, however, it can be very expensive and time-consuming.) But projections may contribute much more than mere scenery to a production. Slides, movies, videotape, and even closed circuit television may be used to increase both the *breadth* and *density* of a theatrical production. The projected images may be used to broaden the nature of the onstage action by expanding the visual communication beyond that being presented live onstage. For example, during a production of *Mother Courage*, the projection of images showing historic wars from the Trojan War to Vietnam expanded and universalized the specific action onstage. Images of concentration camps, crematory ovens, and bodies of concentration camp victims used during the song "Cabaret" in the musical of the same name not only broaden the scene beyond the confines of the nightclub, but also serve as a grisly contradiction to the lyrics "Life is a cabaret, old chum." (See Plate 171.) In a production of *In White America*, images from racial conflicts in the South during the 1960's supplemented the live onstage action, as may be seen in Plate 172. Projected images of scenes and characters relevant to the plot and theme of the production may be superimposed over scenes being enacted live to reinforce that action, to contradict the onstage communication, to provide images with which the actors might even interact, or to create a total montage of information and dramatic communication. Images of the actors themselves seen in circumstances not depicted onstage presented to the audience the thoughts and memories of the main characters and also contradicted onstage communication in the production of *Rosalee Pritchett* shown in Plate 173. More direct communication between projected images and actors was seen in the production of *The Last Ones* seen in Plate 174. Josef Svoboda, an international leader in design for many years, fostered the use of interactive projections in theatrical productions, and this production, where the actors actually speak to and interact with their projected images, is an excellent example of his work.

As indicated above, the use of projected images is not a cure-all for budget ailments. In fact, unless equipment is already available it can be considerably more expensive and time-consuming. In addition many other problems have to be solved before any kind of projection will be satisfactory. There is a very real danger that the stage acting area lights will wash out the projected image. The placement of the projector must be carefully planned in relation to the size and location of the screen so that actors will not walk in the path of the light and cast a shadow on the screen. Unless the projector is directly in front of or behind the screen, there will be a distortion in the projected image that must be corrected in the slide. If a rear projection is used, space must be allowed behind the screen for the placement of the projector at the proper distance and, unless a very high-quality screen is used, the projector must be masked in some way so that the light source is not visible from the audience. Obviously, these problems can be overcome, but frequently compromises must be made in the lighting and scenery if the projection is to be fully effective. The materials and techniques mentioned in this section are but a few of those available to a designer. Modern technology adds new materials to the repertoire almost daily, and many of these remain unknown or unnoticed far too long. One reason for this, perhaps, is that the newer materials are frequently too expensive for the lower-budget educational and community theatres to use. Hopefully, as the use of the products increases, the price will decrease to the point where they may be of greater availability at a reasonable price.

## EPILOGUE

Although I have, in this book, dealt principally with the more commonly accepted practices of scene design and stagecraft, I think it is important to emphasize that the designer's work is judged by its effectiveness at the public presentation of a single production rather than for the use of standard materials or methods in the design or construction of the setting. In the final analysis, it matters little that the designer has followed each and every rule and precept of design and stagecraft if the setting is not helpful and appropriate to the production for which it was designed. It is probably true that theatre stagecraft is the most old-fashioned and outdated craft in the present world. Theatre is notoriously the last to adopt modern technology – particularly theatre as presented in educational- and community-theatre situations. A designer should, I believe, be constantly searching for new and better ways to meet the scenic requirements of plays – to better express the thematic, emotional or atmospheric qualities of plays. Always be on the lookout for materials and techniques that may be used onstage. Keep an interest in and awareness of current happenings in politics, business, science, industry, and the arts, for these will be the inspiration for settings aimed at modern audiences. It is much too easy to become settled into comfortable (and antiquated) methods of producing and designing plays, with a corresponding hesitancy to try anything new. Perhaps the key to successful and contemporary designing is the courage, insight and innovative spirit necessary to strike out in a new direction to find a better way of expressing the spirit and meaning of a play.

This, then, is the challenge I issue to you – create your designs to project the essential meaning of the play as seen by you and the director, and do not be hesitant to discard conventional methods or techniques if they are inappropriate. If the materials and techniques described in the book are helpful to you, then I am glad; but if you find they do not suggest meaningful ways of creating an appropriate environment and atmosphere for a play, then simply discard the book and work in the ways and means that will best suit the play. I would if I were in your place.

# appendices

# A GLOSSARY OF STAGE TERMINOLOGY

ACT CURTAIN (Main Curtain): A curtain directly behind the proscenium. It is raised and lowered to signal the beginning and end of acts or scenes.

ACTING AREA: The area on stage in which the action of the play occurs.

APRON: That portion of the stage between the Act Curtain and the footlights.

ARBOR (Carriage): A metal frame used to hold counterweights in the counterweight system of flying.

BACKDROP (Drop): A plain or painted curtain at the rear of the stage serving as a background for the acting area.

BACKING: A scenic unit placed behind openings in the set to conceal the offstage area.

BACK PAINTING: Painting the rear of flats to make them opaque or to take out any wrinkles or pock marks in the fabric.

BACKSTAGE: The area of a theatre behind the Act Curtain, including all areas pertaining to the production of the play. Also, that area of the stage that is out of sight of the audience.

BATTEN: Any long length of pipe or lumber used for attaching or stiffening scenery, or supported from the lines of a flying system.

BLACKS: A set of black drapery legs, borders, and curtains, often provided as standard equipment for a stage.

BLOCK: A pulley, or pulleys, with the accompanying frame.

BOOK FLAT: Two flats hinged together to fold like a book. Also called a Two-Fold.

BORDER: A narrow strip of any type of cloth hung above the stage to hide that portion of the stage from the view of the audience.

BOX SETTING: An interior setting, usually composed of three walls and, possibly, a ceiling.

CYCLORAMA (Cyc): A backdrop used to simulate the sky. May be straight, curved, or dome-shaped.

DOWNSTAGE: That portion of the stage nearest the audience.

DRESS REHEARSAL: The last rehearsal(s) of the play before opening, in which all technical elements are used—scenery, lighting, costumes, makeup, properties, and sound.

DRESSING (Set): Pictures, drapery, rugs, furniture, scenic properties, and decorative items added to a set for "believability."

DUTCHMAN: A narrow strip of cloth used to cover cracks between flats and make them appear as a solid wall.

ELEVATIONS: Scaled mechanical drawings showing flattened-out front or rear views of scenic units.

ESCAPE: Offstage steps or stairs providing means of access to platforms and levels.

FACING: Flats or cut-out pieces of board applied to the sides or edges of stairs and platforms to conceal the construction.

FLAT: Canvas- or hard surface-covered wooden frame--the principal scenic unit.

FLIPPER: Any narrow flat (2' or under) hinged to another flat—usually at a 90° angle.

FLOOR PLAN: A scaled mechanical drawing of the exact layout of the setting in relationship to the stage, shown from directly above the stage.

FLY: To raise and lower scenery by means of pulleys and rope or cable.

FLY GALLERY (Fly Floor): An elevated platform along one side of the stage to which the pin rail is attached, and used for the operation of flying scenery.

FLY LOFT: The area above the stage used for storage of flown scenery.

FOOTLIGHTS: A strip of lights recessed into the front edge of the stage floor.

FORESTAGE: Any portion of the stage extending beyond the footlights into the audience.

GRIDIRON (Grid): A structural framework near the top of the stage house, used to support equipment for flying.

GROUND CLOTH (Floor Cloth): A covering (usually canvas) for the floor of the acting area, often painted as part of the setting design.

GROUND ROW: A low silhouette or painted cut-out representing skylines, hills, bushes, etc., placed at the rear of the stage and used to mask lights placed along the bottom of backdrops and cycs.

HEADER: A small flat or scenic unit placed between two standard flats to form the top of a door, archway, or window.

HOUSE: The seating portion of a theatre.

JOG: A narrow flat inserted into a setting wall to form an offset or niche.

KILL: To remove from a scene or setting, *e.g.*, to *kill*

a prop.

LASHING: Joining two flats by means of a cord looped around alternating cleats and tied off at the bottom.

LEGS: Narrow drapery or scenery located at the sides of the acting area, used to mask the wings of the stage.

LEVEL: A platform, or any raised portion of the stage, is often called a level.

LINE: A rope or cable used for flying scenery.

MASKING: Scenic units or drapery used to conceal portions of the stage not in use.

OFFSTAGE: That portion of the stage out of the view of the audience.

ONSTAGE: That area of the stage seen by the audience.

PARALLEL: A type of folding platform.

PIN RAIL: A metal railing attached to the fly gallery, containing pins onto which lines used for flying scenery are tied off.

PLUG: A small flat used to fill an opening in or between flats for the purpose of closing off or reshaping the opening.

PORTAL. A false inner proscenium, usually designed and constructed for a particular show, often from flat-framed teasers and tormentors.

PRACTICAL: Said of any property or piece of scenery capable of being used, *e.g.*, windows that open are *practical*.

PROPERTIES (Props): All items used in a production other than scenery, costumes, lighting, and sound--set furniture, decoration, small hand props carried by the actors, etc.

PROSCENIUM: The wall separating the stage from the auditorium, containing the *proscenium arch*, which outlines the *proscenium opening*, through which the audience views the play.

RAKE: To set at either a horizontal or vertical angle — a "raked stage" or "raked rear wall."

RETURN: A flat, usually black, running offstage parallel to the footlights from the downstage end of a setting, finishing off the setting and serving masking purposes.

REVEAL: A board, or any stiff material, attached around an opening in a setting to give the illusion of thickness to the wall.

RIGGING: Equipment and operations related to the flying system.

SCRIM: A loosely woven cloth resembling cheesecloth, used onstage for window glass, to suggest distance, and for "disappearing wall" effects.

SET: Short term for setting or scenery; also used to mean to place into position onstage, *e.g.*, to *set* a chair for the scene.

SHUTTER: The actual door within a door frame.

SIGHTLINES: Lines of vision from the seats in the most extreme positions in the auditorium.

SILL IRON: A narrow strip of metal placed across the bottom of the opening in a door or fireplace flat to ensure rigidity and accurate measurements.

SIZE: A mixture of glue and water, used to shrink canvas on flats, and mixed with dry pigment to form scene paint.

SPIKE: To mark on the stage floor the position of any piece of scenery or furniture.

STIFFENER: A batten secured at right angles to one or more flats or a piece of scenery to ensure rigidity.

STRAIGHTEDGE: Straight strip of wood or metal, 4 to 6 feet long, with beveled edges, used for painting straight lines.

STRIKE: To remove from the stage area any piece of scenery or properties.

SWEEP: Board cut to form the curved portion of an arch.

TEASER: Drapery or scenery placed behind the top of the proscenium arch, used to alter the height of the proscenium opening.

TECHNICAL DIRECTOR: In non-Broadway theatres, the Technical Director is responsible for all technical aspects of the production, including purchasing and supply, set construction and rigging, lighting and sound, set-up, shifting, run of production, striking, and scenery disposal.

TECHNICAL REHEARSAL: First rehearsal in which scenery shifting, lighting, properties, and sound are incorporated into the production—it may or may not involve the actors.

THICKNESS PIECE: Same as *Reveal*.

TORMENTOR: Scenery or drapery placed behind the sides of the proscenium arch, used to alter the width of the proscenium opening.

TRAP: Removable portion of the stage floor.

TRAVELER: A track used for hanging and operating draw curtains; also the curtain or backdrop operated on such a track.

TRIM: To adjust flown scenery so that it is parallel with the stage floor.

TRIPPING: Methods of rigging scenery to fly when the fly loft area is less than normal height.

TUMBLER: Lumber, 1" x 3", hinged between the second and third flats of a three-fold, serving as a spacer to allow the third flat to fold over the other two.

TURNTABLE: A revolving disc set into or on the stage floor for the purpose of shifting scenery.

UPSTAGE: That portion of the stage area furthest from the audience.

WAGON: Rolling platform used for shifting scenery.

WINGS: Offstage areas on either side of the stage between the edge of the proscenium arch and the stage wall; also, scenery or drapery set parallel to the footlights in rows along the sides of the stage to conceal that offstage area.

# appendix B

# U.S. INSTITUTE FOR THEATRE TECHNOLOGY (USITT) SCENIC DESIGN AND TECHNICAL PRODUCTION GRAPHIC STANDARD

This standard is intended to be used by both scenery designers and scenic technicians. It is important that drafters provide useful information to the end user (e.g., shop drawings need to show the breakdown of subassemblies, while design drawings typically convey information regarding profile and finish). In either instance, the information provided must be specific, accurate, comprehensive, and tailored to the needs of the end user.

Drafters must determine for themselves which elements of this standard apply to the specific use for which the drawing is being prepared. The determination of which elements are appropriate will be dependent on whether the drawing is being prepared for a rigging crew, stage manager, director, prop master, or one of the other many specialty areas of the performing arts which communicate through the use of graphics. Whatever choices are made, however, such choices must be in the form of communication that is clear, consistent and efficient for both drafter and reader.

**LINES** (Plate 175)

*Line Weights*

The recommendation is a modified ANSI standard as follows:

> Pen: Thin: .010" to .0125" width
> (ANSI standard = .016")
> Thick: .20" to .025" width.
> (ANSI standard = .032")
> Pencil: Thin: 0.3mm
> Thick: 0.5mm

*Line Types*

BORDER AND DRAWING DIVISION:

2.2.1.1  BORDER.
A thick single or double line. See fig. 2.2.1.

2.2.1.2  TITLE BLOCK.
A thick single or double line.

2.2.1.3  DRAWING DIVISION.
A single thick solid line.

2.2.2  VISIBLE LINE EDGE.
A single thick solid line. See fig. 2.2.2.

2.2.3  HIDDEN EDGE LINE.
A thin, uniformly dotted line. See fig. 2.2.3.

2.2.4  "CEILING LINE."
A thin, uniformly dashed line. See fig. 2.2.4. A local note, "CEILING LINE," is recommended.

2.2.5  PLASTER LINE.
A thin, uniformly dashed line. See fig. 2.2.5. A local note "PL" or "PLASTER LINE" may be required for clarity.

2.2.6  SET LINE.
A thin solid line with short breaks separating it from tormentors or other coplanar features. See fig. 2.2.6. A local note "SL" or "SET LINE" may be required for clarity.

CENTER LINES:

2.2.7.1  CENTER LINES IN GENERAL APPLICATIONS.
A thin line of the form long-short-long. See fig. 2.2.7.

2.2.7.2  SPECIAL FORM FOR MAJOR ARCHITECTURAL FEATURES (e.g., STAGE CENTER LINES).
A thin line of the form long-short-long with a local note as "CL" appended near the lower edge of the view for emphasis. See fig. 2.2.7.

LEADERS:

2.2.8.1  LINEAR LEADERS.
A thin solid line which is inclined relative to the major horizontal and vertical axes and having an arrow pointing toward the feature referenced. See fig. 2.2.8.

2.2.8.2  SERPENTINE LEADERS.
A thin solid irregularly curved line with an arrow pointing toward the feature referenced. See fig. 2.2.8.

2.2.8.3  LEADERS TO AN OUTLINE.
A linear or serpentine form leader terminated by an arrow pointing to the referenced outline.

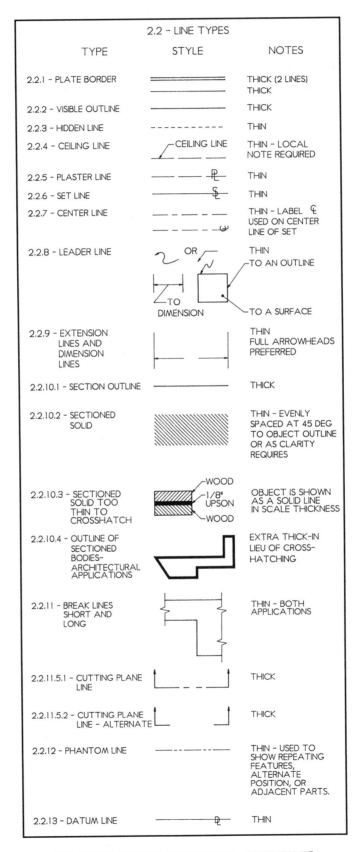

**Plate 175.** *USITT GRAPHIC STANDARD: LINE TYPES*

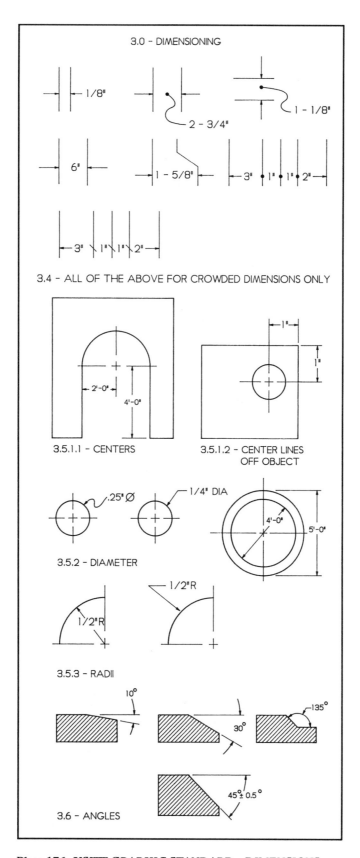

Plate 176. *USITT GRAPHIC STANDARD: DIMENSIONS*

**2.2.8.4  LEADERS TO A SURFACE.**
A linear or serpentine form leader terminated by a dot on the referenced surface. See fig. 2.2.8.

**2.2.9  EXTENSION AND DIMENSION LINES.**
Thin lines of the form shown in fig. 2.2.9.

## LINES RELATED TO SECTION VIEWS:

**2.2.10.1  SECTION OUTLINES.**
A thick solid line equivalent to a VISIBLE EDGE LINE. See fig. 2.2.10.1.

**2.2.10.2  SECTION LINES - USUAL FORM.**
Section lining—i.e., "cross-hatch"— consists of thin uniformly spaced di-agonal lines. See fig. 2.2.10.2. Other standard section lining patterns may be used to differentiate material as required. If used atypically these should be identified in the Legend or by local note.

**2.2.10.3  SECTION VIEW OF ITEMS TOO THIN FOR SECTION LINING (i.e., CROSS-HATCH)**
When a surface is too small to cross-hatch it may be depicted by a solid line of proper scale thickness. See fig. 2.2.10.3. (Variations from true scale are acceptable if required for clarity.)

**2.2.10.4  OUTLINE OF SECTIONED BODY - ARCHITECTURAL.**
The outline of section views of large architetural solids may be described by an extra thick line in lieu of section lining (cross-hatching). See fig.2.2.10.4.

**2.2.10.5.1  CUTTING PLANE LINE.**
A thick dashed line of the form long-short-short-long. Arrows at the ends of the cutting plane line indicate the direction of view. See fig. 2.2.10.5.1.

**2.2.10.5.2  CUTTING PLANE LINE – ALTERNATE FORM.**
Short thick lines at the terminations of the cutting plane. Arrows at the ends of the cutting plane line indicate the direction of view. See fig. 2.2.10.5.2.

**2.2.11  BREAK LINE.**
A thin line of the form shown in fig. 2.2.11. The line extends slightly beyond the edges of the object and is appropriate for both short and long break applications.

**2.2.12  PHANTOM LINE.**
A thin dashed line of the form long-short-short-long for use in adjacent part, alternate position or repeated feature applications. See fig. 2.2.12.

**2.2.13  DATUM LINE.**
A thin, solid line with a local note as "DL", which may be used in situations where clearly definable reference planes are not available, i.e., "Plaster Lines" in ground plans. See Section 4.1.3 (Refer ence Points and Planes). See fig. 2.2.13.

**LINES NOT SPECIFIED IN THESE RECOMMEN-DATIONS:** Any special lines not described in these recommendations should be noted in the legend of each sheet.

## DIMENSIONING (Plate 176)

**CRITERIA:**  Dimensions must be clear, consistent and easily understood.

**UNITS:**
*Metric:*  Dimensions less than one meter are to be noted as a zero, decimal point, and portion of meter in numerals. All measurements one meter and greater shall be given as a whole meter number, decimal point, and portion of meter:  0.1m, 0.52m, 1.5m, 2.35m.

*English:*  Dimensions less than 1'-0" are given in inches without a foot notation, such as 6", 9 1/2", etc. Dimensions 1'-0" and greater include the whole feet with a single apostrophe followed by a dash and then inches followed by a double apostrophe: 7'-1/2", 18'-5 1/4", 1'-3".

**GENERAL FORM:**
*Line Weight:*  See Section 2.2.9 (Lines: Extension & dimensions) & fig. 2.2.9.

*Orientation:*  Dimensions should be oriented to read from the bottom and/or righthand side of the drawing.

*Dimension/Extension Lines on Object:*  Dimension and extension lines may be placed on a drawn object provided object lines are clearly differentiated from dimension and extension lines by contrasting line weight.  See Section 2.2.2 (Lines: Visible Edge), Section 2.2.9 (Lines: Extension and Dimension) and fig. 3.5.1.1. ("Centers"). Extension lines typically begin approximately 1/16" away from the referenced features.

**3.4  CROWDED DIMENSIONS.**
Recommended methods include any of the configurations shown in fig. 3.4.  Note that dots or slashes may be substituted when arrows are too big for the available space.

**3.5  DIMENSIONING ARCS AND CIR-CLES.**
Recommended methods include any of the configurations shown in figs. 3.5.1.1, 3.5.1.2, 3.5.2, or 3.5.3.

**3.5.1.1  LOCATING CENTERS OF ARCS AND**

CIRCLES.
Arcs and circles are located by crossed center lines of the form shown in figs. 3.5.1.1, 3.5.1.2, or 3.5.3.

3.5.1.2 CENTER LINES ON AND OFF ROUND OBJECT.
For purpose of dimensioning, a center line may be extended beyond the boundaries of the circle to which it applies, in which case it becomes a thin solid extension line. See fig. 3.5.1.2.

3.5.2 SPECIFYING SIZE OF CIRCLES.
The size of circles are normally specified by the diameter. See fig. 3.5.2.

3.5.2.1 LARGE OBJECT EXCEPTION TO STANDARD METHOD FOR DIMENSIONING ROUND OBJECTS.
Very large round objects such as revolves may be dimensioned by their radii if required for clarity or convenience of fabrication.

3.5.3 SIZE OF ARCS SPECIFIED BY RADII.
The size of arcs are normally specified by their radii. See fig. 3.5.3.

3.6 DIMENSIONING ANGLES.
See fig. 3.6.

**SCENERY SYMBOLS IN PLAN** (Plate 177)

TERMINOLOGY: The terms "Ground Plan" and "Floor Plan" are considered to be synonymous and are equally acceptable.

DEFINITION: "A ground or floor plan is a horizontal section with the cutting plane passing at whatever level (normally 4'-0" above the stage floor) required to produce the most descriptive view. This cutting plane may be locally offset as required for clarity."

REFERENCE POINTS AND PLANES: Dimensions on Ground Plans and Sections are to be referenced from the stage floor (or ground level), Center Line, and Plaster Line. In the case of "found spaces" or other stage types where a clearly established Center Line and/or Plaster Line is not available, all dimensions are to be taken from easily established points or plane(s) of reference. The points or plane(s) of reference should be clearly labeled and noted both on the Ground Plan or Section, and in the Key (or Legend).

**FLAT SCENERY IN GROUND PLAN:**

4.2.1 SINGLE FLAT.
A flat is shown on a stage ground plan by a solid line of proper scale thickness. See Section 2.2.10.3 (Section Views of Items Too Thin for Section Lining). See fig. 4.2.1.

4.2.1.1 TWO OR MORE FLATS IN CONTACT.
When it is necessary to show how flats butt together in assembly, the method shown in fig. 4.2.1.1 is recommended. Note that the open line figure above is presented only to show the derivation of the plan view representation.

**STANDARD OPENINGS IN FLAT SCENERY:**

4.2.2.1 ARCHWAY.
See fig. 4.2.2.1.

4.2.2.2 DOORWAY.
See fig. 4.2.2.2. The shutter is normally drawn standing partially open to show      how it will be hung. Note the swing line is a thin solid line swung from the door hinge center. The swing line may extend to the limit of travel if required.

4.2.2.3 WINDOW.
See Fig. 4.2.2.3. Show muntins and mullions of windows as designed.

4.2.2.4 SLIDING DOOR.
See fig. 4.2.2.4.

4.2.2.5 DOUBLE ACTING DOOR.
See fig. 4.2.2.5. Note the swing line is a thin solid line swung from the door hinge center. The swing line may extend to the limit of travel, if required.

4.2.2.6 CASEMENT WINDOW.
See fig. 4.2.2.6. Show muntins and mullions of windows as designed. Note the swing line is a thin solid line swung from the window hinge center. The swing line may extend to the limit of travel, if required.

4.2.3 SHOWING CASINGS AROUND OPENINGS.
Casings may be shown in stage ground plans where their inclusion would significantly clarify information required for design, fabrication, or assembly.

**SCENERY SYMBOLS IN PLAN (continued)** (Plate 178)
**PLATFORMS, STEPS, AND RAMPS IN GROUD PLANS:**

4.3.1 PLATFORM BOUNDARIES:
The edges of platforms are shown by standard visible, i.e., thick, lines. See fig. 4.3.1.

4.3.2. CONFIRMING LEVEL STATUS OF PLATFORMS:
Platforms which are level are so indicated by thin crossed lines. See figs. 4.3.1 and 4.3.3.

4.3.3 PLATFORMS OF THE SAME  HEIGHT IN

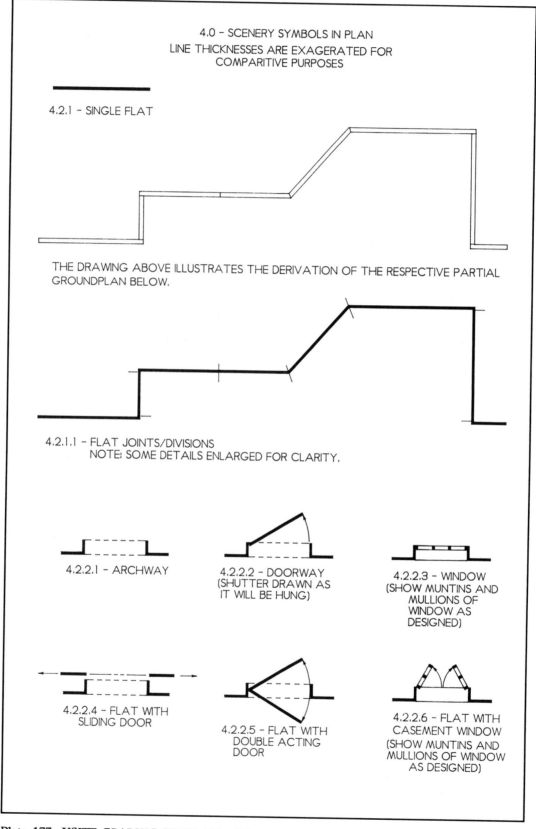

Plate 177. *USITT GRAPHIC STANDARD: SCENERY SYMBOLS IN PLAN (Line thicknesses are exaggerated for comparative purposes)*

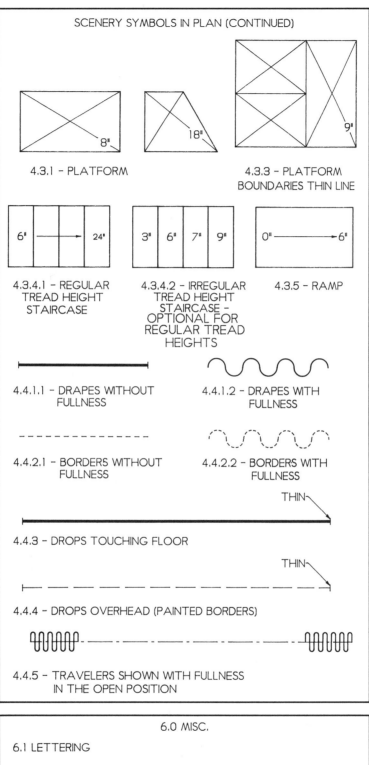

SCENERY SYMBOLS IN PLAN (CONTINUED)

4.3.1 - PLATFORM

4.3.3 - PLATFORM
BOUNDARIES THIN LINE

4.3.4.1 - REGULAR
TREAD HEIGHT
STAIRCASE

4.3.4.2 - IRREGULAR
TREAD HEIGHT
STAIRCASE -
OPTIONAL FOR
REGULAR TREAD
HEIGHTS

4.3.5 - RAMP

4.4.1.1 - DRAPES WITHOUT
FULLNESS

4.4.1.2 - DRAPES WITH
FULLNESS

4.4.2.1 - BORDERS WITHOUT
FULLNESS

4.4.2.2 - BORDERS WITH
FULLNESS

4.4.3 - DROPS TOUCHING FLOOR

4.4.4 - DROPS OVERHEAD (PAINTED BORDERS)

4.4.5 - TRAVELERS SHOWN WITH FULLNESS
IN THE OPEN POSITION

6.0 MISC.

6.1 LETTERING

ABCDEFGHIJKLMNO
PQRSTUVWXYZ
0123456789

Plate 178. *USITT GRAPHIC STANDARD: SCENERY SYMBOLS IN PLAN (Continued)*

CONTACT:
When necessary to show platforms of the same height in contact, the respective boundaries may be delineated by a thin solid line. See fig. 4.3.3.

4.3.4 PLATFORM AND STEP HEIGHT.
Platform and step height are indicated by the height in inches above or below the stage floor. Heights below the stage floor are shown by applying a negative sign to the figure. Heights without a negative sign are assumed to be positive.

4.3.4.1 INDICATING STEP HEIGHTS - REGULAR TREADS.
See fig. 4.3.4.1. Note that an arrow points away from the principal level - typically the stage floor.

4.3.4.2 INDICATING STEP HEIGHTS - IRREGULAR TREADS.
See fig. 4.3.4.2. This method may also be used for steps having regular tread heights, if desired.

4.3.5 RAMPS.
Note that an arrow points away from the principal level - typically the stage floor. See fig. 4.3.5.

**SOFT GOODS IN GROUND PLANS:**
*Drapes (Legs) Touching or Nearly Touching the Floor:*

4.4.1.1 DRAPES FLAT HUNG.
Flat hung drapes are indicated by a solid line of 1/2" scale thickness and by being terminated on each end by a short thin perpendicular tic mark. See fig. 4.4.1.1.

4.4.1.2 DRAPES HUNG WITH FULLNESS.
Drapery hung in fullness may be indicated by a wavy line approximating a sine wave having a peak to peak amplitude of 3" to 6" in the scale of the drawing. See fig. 4.4.1.2.

4.4.1.3 DRAPES (LEGS) FLAT HUNG, BUT SHOWN WITH WAVY LINE.
An Alternative to Section 4.4.1.1. Flat hung drapery may be shown by a thin wavy line otherwise similar to 4.4.1.2, but having a local note as "LEGS - FLAT HUNG" or equivalent.

*Overhead Drapes (Borders):*

4.4.2.1 OVERHEAD DRAPES (BORDERS) FLAT HUNG.
Flat hung overhead drapes (borders) are shown by a thin uniformly dotted line. See fig. 4.4.2.1.

4.4.2.2 OVERHEAD DRAPES (BORDERS) HUNG WITH FULLNESS.
Overhead drapes (borders) hung in fullness are shown by a thin, wavy uniform dotted line approximating a sine wave having a peak-to -peak amplitude of 3" to 6" in the scale of the drawing. See fig.4.4.2.2.

4.4.2.3 OVERHEAD DRAPES (BORDERS) FLAT HUNG BUT SHOWN WITH WAVY LINE.
An alternative to 4.4.2.1. (Overhead drapes [Borders] Flat Hung). Flat hung overhead drapery (borders) may be shown by a thin, uniformly dotted, wavy line otherwise similar to 4.4.2.2 but having a local note as "BORDERS FLAT HUNG" or equivalent.

4.4.3 DROPS TOUCHING OR NEARLY TOUCHING THE FLOOR.
Drops are indicated by a solid line of 1/2" scale thickness and by being terminated on each end by a short, perpendicular tic mark. See fig. 4.4.3.

4.4.4 DROPS OVERHEAD.
Drapes overhead—e.g., painted borders—are indicated by a thin, uniformly dashed line equivalent to that used for OVERHEAD DRAPES (BORDERS) FLAT HUNG. See fig. 4.4.4.

4.4.5 TRAVELERS.
See fig. 4.4.5.

**HARDWARE SYMBOLS IN ELEVATION** (Plate 179)

HIDDEN LINES IN ELEVATIONS:
Hidden lines in elevations may be omitted for clarity.

5.1.1 CORNER BLOCKS AND KEYSTONES.
See fig. 5.1.1.

5.1.2 OMISSION OF CORNER BLOCKS AND KEYSTONES.
Corner blocks and keystones may be omitted from elevations at the discretion of the drafter, except as required for clarity. See fig. 5.1.2.

5.2.1 RIGID FOOT IRON.
See fig. 5.2.1.

5.2.2 FOLDING FOOT IRON.
See fig. 5.2.2.

5.3.1.1 TIGHT PIN HINGE.
See fig. 5.3.1.1.

5.3.1.2 TIGHT PIN HINGE ON OPPOSITE FACE.
See fig. 5.3.1.2.

5.3.2.1 LOOSE PIN HINGE.

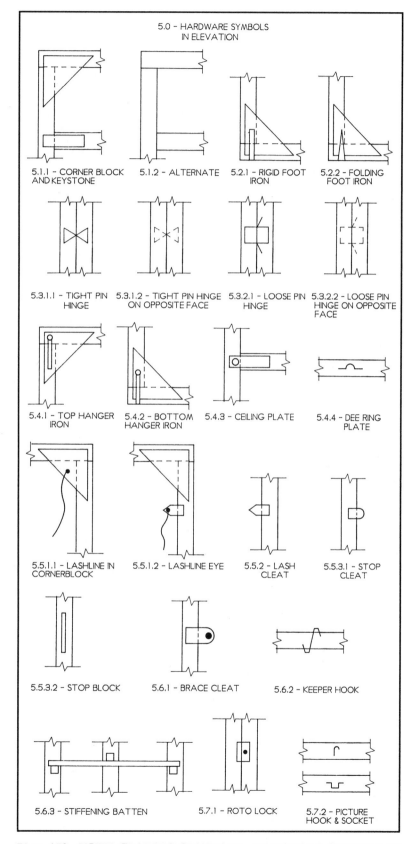

Plate 179. *USITT GRAPHIC STANDARD: HARDWARE SYMBOLS IN ELEVATION*

See fig. 5.3.2.1.

5.3.2.2 LOOSE PIN HINGE ON OPPOSITE FACE.
See fig. 5.3.2.2.

5.4.1 TOP HANGER IRON.
See fig. 5.4.1.

5.4.2 BOTTOM HANGER IRON.
See fig. 5.4.2.

5.4.3 CEILING PLATE.
See fig. 5.4.3.

5.4.4 DEE RING PLATE.
See fig. 5.4.4.

5.5.1.1 LASHLINE IN CORNER BLOCK.
See fig. 5.5.1.1.

5.5.1.2 LASHLINE EYE.
See fig. 5.5.1.2.

5.5.2 LASH CLEAT.
See fig. 5.5.2.

5.5.3.1 STOP CLEAT.
See fig. 5.5.3.1.

5.5.3.2 STOP BLOCK.
See fig. 5.5.3.2.

5.6.1 BRACE CLEAT.
See fig. 5.6.1.

5.6.2 KEEPER HOOK.
See fig. 5.6.2.

5.6.3 STIFFENING BATTEN.
See fig. 5.6.3.

5.7.1 ROTO LOCK.
See fig. 5.7.1.

5.7.2 PICTURE HOOK AND SOCKET.

See fig. 5.7.2.

**MISCELLANEOUS** (Plate 178)

6.1 LETTERING:
Lettering should be legible and the style should allow for easy and rapid execution. Characters which generally conform to the single stroke Gothic style meet these requirements. Only upper case letters should be used on drawings unless lower case letters are needed to conform with other established standards or nomenclature. Hand lettering should be generally similar to the mechanically generated characters of fig. 6.1, while acknowledging individual stylistic differences.

TITLE BLOCK:
*Location:* The title block should be in the same location on all drawings of a single project. The title block should be located in either the lower righthand corner of the drawing or in a strip along the bottom of the drawing.

*Format:* Internal title block division and placement of information is generally unique to the producing organization and is not specified as a part of these recommendations.

*Contents:* Regardless of form, the following information should be included:

1. Name of producing organization.
2. Name of production, act and scene, if appropriate.
3. Drawing title.
4. Drawing number.
5. Predominant scale of the drawing.
6. Date the drawing was drafted.
7. Designer of the production.
8. Drafter, if different from the designer.
9. Drawing approval, if applicable.

APPROVED BY
USITT BOARD OF DIRECTORS
DALLAS, TEXAS
21 NOVEMBER 1992

# TOOLS, HARDWARE, AND MATERIALS

In this section are listed those items most useful in the construction of scenery. It is not necessary, however, to possess every item mentioned in order to be able to construct scenery. Each of these has its own particular purpose, but only a few are completely indispensable. For this reason, I have provided at the end of this section a list of minimum tool requirements for a scenic shop. This is intended to serve as a guide for those who must equip a new shop under somewhat limited budgetary conditions – although no bulk purchase of tools is ever going to be cheap, nor should tools be selected with an eye to price alone.

## TOOLS

With a few exceptions, the tools listed are designed for woodworking operations. They are divided into categories according to their purpose and use.

*Measuring and Marking Tools (Plate 180)*

STEEL MEASURING TAPES: Tapes with a minimal length of 12' should be provided in quantity, as they are used for all general measuring. At least one 50' tape is desirable for use in laying out the stage floor and for measuring oversized units of scenery.

COMBINATION SQUARE: Used to check 45° and 90° angles – particularly when marking lumber preparatory to sawing.

FRAMING SQUARE: Used for checking 90° angles in the construction of flat frames, and particularly useful in laying out stair carriages.

BEVEL GAUGE: The blade may be set at any angle – very useful for checking unusual angles and for transferring angles from one unit to another.

SPIRIT LEVEL: Centering the bubble within the clear tubes of liquid will establish true horizontals or verticals.

TRAMMEL POINTS AND BAR: Used for scribing large arcs and circles.

PROTRACTOR: Essential for marking accurate angles –

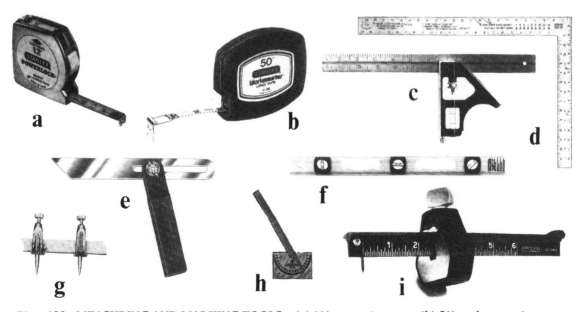

Plate 180. *MEASURING AND MARKING TOOLS: (a) 12' measuring tape, (b) 50' steel measuring tape, (c) combination square, (d) framing square, (e) bevel gauge, (f) spirit level, (g) trammel points and bar, (h) protractor, (i) marking gauge (tools by Stanley).*

Plate 181. *CUTTING TOOLS: (a) hand saw (Stanley), (b) rip saw teeth, (c) cross-cut teeth, (d) utility knife with retractable blade (Stanley), (e) trimming shears, (f) backsaw and miter box (Stanley), (g) table saw (Delta), (h) radial arm [pull-over] saw (Delta), (i) hand circular saw (DeWalt), (j) band saw (Delta), (k) hand jigsaw (DeWalt), (l) scroll saw (Delta), (m) cut awl.*

the type with an extension blade being the most useful.

MARKING GAUGE: A useful tool in measuring rip-cuts and dado cut depths.

## Cutting Tools (Plate 181)

### HAND

RIP SAW: Designed for cutting parallel with the grain of lumber (along the length of the lumber). It has wide set, chisel-pointed teeth– 6 to 8 teeth per inch – that chip out the lumber.

CROSSCUT SAW: Designed to cut across the grain of lumber. The teeth are sharply pointed to cut through the grain – 8 to 12 teeth per inch.

UTILITY KNIFE (Mat Knife): General purpose knife with replaceable blades—to trim excess canvas from flats, as well as for other general cutting purposes. The safest knives have retractable blades.

TRIMMING SHEARS (Scissors): A general purpose cutting tool, sharp and strong enough to cut canvas, if necessary.

BACKSAW AND MITER BOX: A fine-toothed crosscut saw with a stiffened back. The miter box guides the saw in cuts from 45° to 90° – useful in mitering moldings for cornices, picture frames or paneling.

### POWER (Straight Cut)

TABLE SAW: Designed for heavy-duty straight cutting: ripping, mitering, and crosscutting; also routing and shaping with special accessories.

RADIAL ARM SAW (Pullover Saw): The pullover action of the saw makes it extremely accurate and safe for crosscutting and mitering. It can also be used for ripping; and special accessories can convert it into a router, shaper, lathe, planer, sander, grinder, wood drill, polisher, or jigsaw. It is the most useful and versatile of the stationary power tools.

HAND CIRCULAR SAW: A portable saw designed for straight cutting.

### POWER (Irregular Cutting)

BANDSAW: The narrow blade of this tool makes it useful for cutting curves and for simple scroll cutting – limited, however, to outside cutting or to pieces no larger than the depth of its throat.

HAND JIGSAW: One of the most useful cutting tools in the shop—its narrow blade enables it to cut highly irregular shapes, but it may also be used for standard straight cuts. It replaces many older manual saws—keyhole saw, compass saw, coping saw, etc.

SCROLL SAW: The extremely narrow blade and the deep throat of this tool allow it to cut more delicate work in larger sizes. It is still somewhat limited, however, and the hand jigsaw and Cut-Awl have replaced it in many shops.

CUT-AWL: A portable saw designed for light, very detailed irregular cutting. The cutting head revolves 360° to allow for cutting extremely delicate and complicated designs. Although it can cut up to 3/4" plywood, it works best on composition board and 1/4" plywood. It requires a padded table or bench for best results.

## Shaping and Smoothing Tools (Plate 182)

### HAND

BLOCK PLANE: Designed for cutting across the grain of lumber – to pare down the ends of a board, for instance.

SMOOTHING PLANE: Larger and heavier than the block plane, this is used to pare off or smooth the edges and faces of lumber.

WOOD FILE: These come in a variety of shapes – circular, curved and flat – and are designed primarily for smoothing purposes.

WOOD RASP: The sharp teeth allow for cross-grain paring and shaping. It does, however, leave a rough surface that must be finished with a file or sandpaper.

WOOD CHISEL: Straight-shafted with a knife-like edge, it is tapped with a hammer to notch or shape lumber.

SANDPAPER: Not technically a tool, this is a final smoothing device available in a variety of textures from very coarse to very fine. *Medium* and *fine* sandpaper are most useful in a scenic shop.

### POWER

BENCH GRINDER: Designed to smooth and shape metal, this can also be used for wood shaping and for sharpening tools.

LATHE: For shaping round stock, such as that used for the legs of furniture.

ROUTER: Designed to notch for countersinking, groove and dado, it can also, with accessories, be used for cutting simple moldings.

BELT SANDER: Perhaps the most efficient hand power sander, it is available with sanding belts ranging from very coarse to very fine and can be used both to rough-shape and to final-finish wooden objects.

## Boring Tools (Plate 183)

### HAND

SCRATCH AWL: Designed for punching small holes in soft materials.

RATCHET BRACE: Designed for clamping and turning a wood bit, it is provided with a swivel handle, an offset handle for turning, and a ratchet head that allows the bit to be turned with a back and forth motion of the offset handle.

AUGER BIT: Designed for slow-speed wood cutting, it is usually operated by the brace.

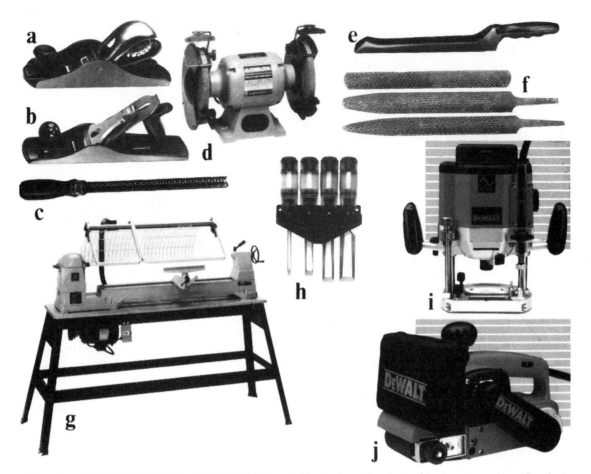

Plate 182. *SHAPING AND SMOOTHING TOOLS: (a) block plane (Stanley), (b) smoothing plane (Stanley), (c) round wood file (Stanley), (d) bench grinder (Delta), (e) wood rasp (Stanley), (f) wood files, (g) lathe (Delta), (h) wood chisels (Stanley), (i) router (DeWalt), (j) belt sander (DeWalt).*

EXPANSION BIT: Can be used to cut holes from 1" to 1-1/2" in diameter. Designed for use with hand drills, such as the ratchet brace.

HAND DRILL: Twist drills held in the jaws of this tool are turned by operation of the small, geared wheel. Although only small diameter bits may be used, it is designed to work on either metal or wood.

PUSH DRILL: Spring return spirals located in the shaft allow this tool to be operated with a pushing motion on the handle – useful only for light work.

### POWER

DRILL PRESS: Designed for drilling holes in wood and metal, it may also be converted into a planer, sander, router and shaper, with the proper accessories.

HAND ELECTRIC DRILL: This portable tool, when equipped with the proper bits, may be used for all types of drilling operations—wood, metal, concrete, etc.—and for driving screws. The battery-powered model, with attachments providing for the insertion and removal of screws, has become almost indis-pensable in many shops—replacing many operations formerly accomplished with nails. (Be sure to have extra batteries and a battery charger!)

TWIST DRILL: Designed for higher-speed drilling, this may be used with the hand drill or the power drills for either wood or metal cutting.

COUNTERSINK: Used to countersink flat-head screws.

SPADE BIT: For high-speed wood drilling and hole-cutting.

HOLE CUTTER: Designed to cut oversized holes at high speeds, it is limited in depth of cut. Available in a variety of diameters.

COMBINATION DRILL AND COUNTERSINK: Especially useful where many screws of the same diameter and length are to be inserted, this device both pre-drills the screw hole and provides a countersink for the screwhead.

REAMER: For enlarging previously drilled holes. (not pictured)

### Wood-Joining Tools (Plate 184)

HAMMER: Used for driving nails or staples. The

Plate 183. *BORING TOOLS: (a) scratch awl (Stanley), (b) ratchet brace (Stanley), (c) auger bit (Stanley), (d) expansion bit (Stanley), (e) hand drill (Stanley), (f) push drill (Stanley), (g) drill press (Delta), (h) battery-powered hand electric drill (DeWalt), (i) twist drill, (j) electric hand drill (DeWalt), (k) countersink (Stanley), (l) spade bit (Stanley), (m) hole cutter (Skil), (n) combination drill and countersink (Stanley).*

curved jaws of the *claw hammer* are designed for pulling nails, whereas the straighter jaws of the *rip hammer* are better used to pry apart joined lumber. The rounded head of the *ball-peen hammer* is designed for shaping metal.

MALLET: The rawhide, wood, or rubber head is designed for use when nonmarring blows are required – particularly useful with wood chisels.

SCREWDRIVER: A metal shaft with a wooden or plastic handle, the end of the shaft is shaped to fit the slot of a screw head. The most useful types are the slot-, Phillips-, and hex-tipped variations.

RATCHET SCREWDRIVER: The spring-return spiral shaft allows the insertion or removal of screws by pushing on the handle – much more quickly and easily than with a standard screwdriver.

PLIERS: For gripping, holding, clamping, bending, and working in places too small for fingers. The most useful varieties in the shop are the *slip-joint combination*, the *side-cutting*, and the *needle-nose* pliers.

GROMMET SETTING DIE: Necessary for the insertion of grommets in backdrops and drapery.

STAPLE GUN: Used for attaching paper, cloth and thin composition board – virtually replaces carpet tacks.

PNUEMATIC HAMMER NAILER: A compressed air tool, this is usable only where an air compressor is available. Obtainable in a variety of styles for inserting both nails and staples, it makes inserting fasteners up to 16d sizes very quick, easy, and feasible in situations not possible

with manual hammers. A word of warning, however—it nails hands as easily as wood.

RATCHET "SOCKET" WRENCH AND SOCKETS: Provided with removable sockets in a variety of sizes, this tool speeds up the insertion and removal of nuts and bolts.

CLAMPS: The *C-clamp*, the *hand-screw clamp*, and the *bar-clamp* are designed to hold various types of glued wood joints while the glue sets, but they can be used in many other ways in the shop and onstage.

LOCKING-GRIP PLIERS (Vise-Grips): The adjustable locking action allows this tool to clamp onto an object with immense pressure.

CLINCH PLATE: A flat metal plate inserted under scenery joints to be secured by clout nails—clinches the projecting points of the nails as they are driven in. (not pictured)

*Basic Metalworking Tools (Plate 185)*

The following are principally used in the fabrication of pipe devices. More sophisticated metal working, including various forms of welding, will require many more specialized tools.

HACK SAW: The blade is tempered to cut metal, but the depth of cut is limited. The hand jigsaw may also be fitted with a metal-cutting blade.

TIN SHEARS: Designed for cutting thin sheet metal and screen wire.

COLD CHISELS: The cutting edge is tempered to be used on metal – can cut small diameter metal rods and pipe.

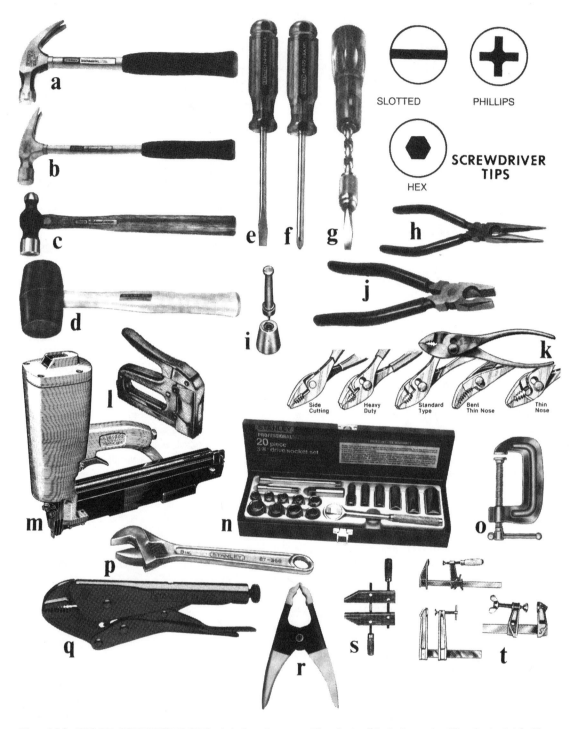

Plate 184. *WOOD JOINING TOOLS:* *(a) claw hammer (Stanley), (b) rip hammer (Stanley), (c) ball peen hammer (Stanley), (d) mallet (Stanley), (e) slot screwdriver (Stanley), (f) Phillips screwdriver (Stanley), (g) ratchet screwdriver (Stanley), (h) needle-nose pliers (Stanley), (i) grommet-setting die, (j) side-cutting pliers (Stanley), (k) slip-joint combination pliers [with variations] (Stanley), (l) staple gun (Swingline), (m) pneumatic hammer nailer (Paslode), (n) ratchet wrench and socket set (Stanley), (o) C-clamp (Stanley), (p) open-end adjustable "crescent" wrench (Stanley), (q) locking grip "vise-grip" pliers (Stanley), (r) spring clamp (Stanley), (s) hand-screw clamp (Jorgensen), (t) three varieties of bar clamp.*

PIPE VISE: Necessary for pipe cutting and threading operations.

PIPE CUTTER: Equipped with cutting wheels that, when rotated around the pipe, make a straight, clean cut.

PIPE WRENCH: Used in pairs to join or separate pipes and pipe fittings.

T-HANDLE TAP WRENCH AND TAPS: Used to thread the inside of pipes. Taps should be provided to thread the same diameter pipes listed below.

FILES: Metal files in all sizes and shapes – round, flat, and triangular – are used for shaping and smoothing metal.

PIPE THREADER: Equipped with interchangeable dies. A scene shop should have dies to thread pipes of 3/4", 1", 1-1/4" and 1-1/2" diameter.

PIPE BENDER: For the large-scale bending of heavy pipe. (not pictured)

*Miscellaneous Tools and Equipment (Plate 186)*

OIL AND OIL-CAN: Both *lubricating oil* and *cutting oil* for metal cutting and drilling.

WOODWORKER'S VISE: Used for holding wooden objects during cutting, shaping, or joining operations. Attached to the work bench, it is provided with wood-lined jaws to prevent marring the objects held.

MACHINIST'S VISE: A stronger vise than the woodworker's vise – intended for metal work.

SAWHORSE GRIPS: General-purpose sawhorse grips lock 2X4 lumber into the grips in these devices—a very quick and effective method for creating work stations as needed.

CORNER VISE: Useful for joining mitered corners with glue and nails—may be used for picture frames, wall-molding pieces, etc.

NAIL SET: For driving finish nails into or below the surface of wood so that they may be subsequently concealed by putty, etc.

CENTER PUNCH: For starting screws in the exact center of holes in hardware such as hinges, cleats, hanger-irons, etc.

SAFETY GOGGLES: Essential for the protection of eyes when working with power tools.

NAIL PULLER: Designed to pull nails whose heads have been hammered flush with a surface. The jaws are driven down around the nail head by pounding the metal handle against the built-in stops, then the long handle is used as a lever to pry loose the nails.

RESPIRATORS: There is a wide variety of respirators (face masks) available to meet the diverse needs of a scenery shop—masks to block out dust particles and paint as well as filtered respirators to block out heavy paint and chemical fumes. The current concern for safety makes the availability and use of such devices mandatory in any scenic shop.

GOGGLES, GLASSES, ETC.: Protection for the eyes is as essential as protection for the lungs. Some of the equipment available for this purpose is illustrated. Equipment designed for more specialized hazards (welding, etc.) may be found in hardware catalogues, or in local supply stores.

RUBBER GLOVES: Several types of gloves should be available in any scenic shop. Rubber gloves are effective in protecting against chemical hazards found in the use of acetone, aniline dyes, etc.

HEAR PROTECTION: When using power machinery (saws, drills, lathes, etc.) earmuffs should always be used to protect the worker's hearing.

GRAPHITE PENCILS: It is wise to lay in a large stock. Nothing seems to disappear quite so rapidly as a pencil in a shop. (not pictured)

GREASE PENCIL: Useful for marking on metal and glass. (not pictured)

PENCIL SHARPENER: Not essential, but a most handy item to have around. (not pictured)

CHALK AND CHARCOAL: Useful for marking and laying-out – particularly for patterning purposes. (not pictured)

OIL STONE: For sharpening cutting tools. (not pictured)

## HARDWARE

*Stage Hardware (Plate 187)*

LOOSE-PIN BACKFLAP HINGES: Used for temporary joining of scenic units, the pin may be easily removed to separate the flaps. Available in two sizes: 1-1/2"x3-1/2" and 2"x4-1/2". The "Sure" hinge has flaps which are identical and interchangeable and which are scored to be easily bent around the edges of flats or lumber.

TIGHT PIN BACKFLAP HINGES: Used for permanent joining of scenic units – often on folding flat units, where the hinges and joints are then covered with a dutchman. Available in the same sizes as the loose-pin hinges, and they can usually be purchased locally.

STRAP HINGES: Available locally in a variety of sizes, these are particularly useful in attaching doors, and for holding independent door and window frames in flats.

PICTURE HANGER AND SOCKET: Used to securely, but temporarily, fasten light- to medium-weight objects to scenery walls—not just pictures, but also panels, cornices, moldings, and similar objects.

BATTEN CLAMP: Designed to fit around the wooden batten at the top of a backdrop in order to secure it to a flying line.

LASH CLEATS: Attached to the inner edge of a stile, this device engages the lashline used when temporarily lashing two flats together. They are available in several different styles, two of which are pictured in Plate 182.

LASH EYE: Attached to the inner edge of a stile, this device engages the hooks of a standard stage brace used to hold scenery erect.

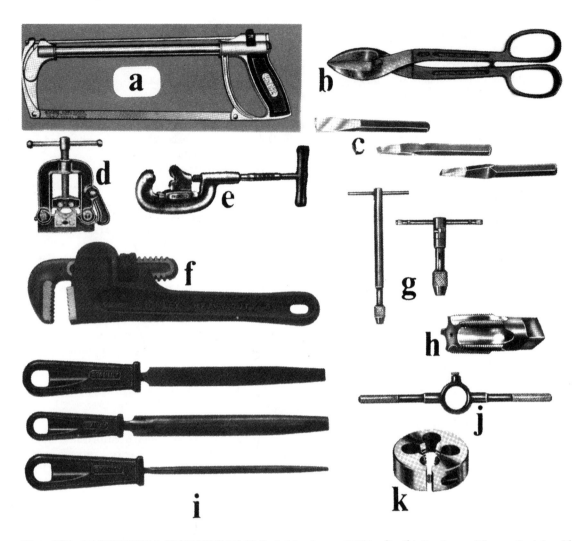

Plate 185. *BASIC METAL-WORKING TOOLS: (a) hack saw (Milford), (b) tin shears (Cresent), (c) cold chisels--straight cut, diamond point, round nose (Stanley), (d) pipe vise, (e) pipe cutter, (f) pipe wrench (Stanley), (g) T-handle tap wrenches, (h) pipe tap, (i) metal files--flat, semi-circular, triangular, (j) pipe threading die stock, (k) pipe threading die.*

STOP CLEAT: Fastened so that their ends project beyond the edges of the flat, these cleats prevent one flat from slipping past another when the two are lashed together.

BRACE CLEAT: Screwed to the inner edge of a stile, these are particularly useful in attaching doors, and for holding independent door and window frames in flats.

T-PLATE: A pre-drilled metal plate, this can be used as a substitute for a keystone.

MENDING PLATE: A pre-drilled metal plate, this is used to repair or reinforce cracks or breaks in 1" x 3" framing members.

CORNER PLATE: Pre-drilled metal plates, these are used as substitutes for corner blocks or to reinforce the joints of independent door and window frames.

THIMBLE: Secured into a cable loop to prevent sharp bends, flattening and wear on the cable.

KEEPER HOOK (S-Hook): Used to attach stiffening battens to the rear of a series of flats.

SNAP HOOKS (swivel-eye snap hooks): A safe and easy device for attaching a line to an eye or to another line.

FOOTIRON: Used to fasten scenery to the floor by means of a stage screw. The *flat footiron* is attached to the bottom edges of units, the *bent footiron* is attached to the rear of scenery, as is the *hinged footiron*, which may be used for scenery that does not stand perpendicular to the floor. The hinged footiron may be folded out of the way when scenery is being shifted or stored.

NON-SKID FLOOR-PLATE: Used to secure stage braces to floors where screws or other devices may not be driven into the floor.

CEILING PLATE: Used for securing flying lines to ceilings.

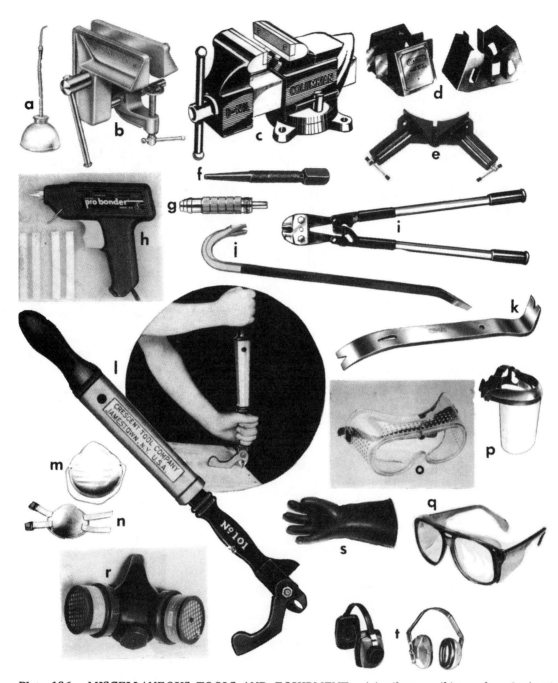

Plate 186. *MISCELLANEOUS TOOLS AND EQUIPMENT:* *(a) oil can,* *(b) wood-worker's vise,* *(c) machinist's vise (Columbian),* *(d) sawhorse grips (Stanley),* *(e) corner vise,* *(f) nail set,* *(g) center punch,* *(h) hot-glue gun (Dremel),* *(i) bolt cutters,* *(j) & (k) pry bars (Stanley),* *(l) nail puller (Crescent),* *(m) dust respirator,* *(n) paint and dust respirator,* *(o) safety goggles,* *(p) safety face mask,* *(q) safety glasses,* *(r) paints and fumes respirator,* *(s) rubber gloves,* *(t) hearing protectors.*

HANGER IRON: Attached to scenery to provide means of securing lines for flying. The hooked hanger iron is attached under the bottom edge of the scenic unit, whereas the straight hanger iron is attached to the top of the stile. For heavy units, both are used—the line being attached to the hooked hanger iron and then running up through a straight hanger iron placed directly above at the top of the unit.

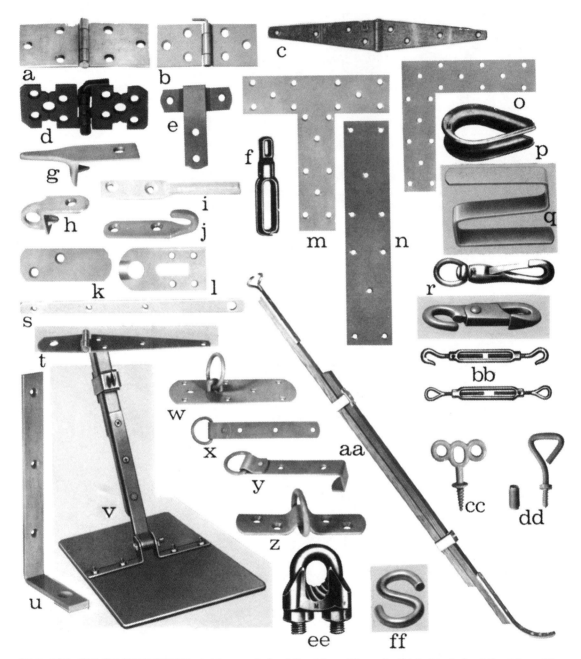

Plate 187. *STAGE HARDWARE: (a) loose-pin backflap hinge (Rosco), (b) tight-pin backflap hinge (Tru-Roll), (c) strap hinge (Mutual), (d) loose-pin "sure" hinge (Rosco), (e) picture hanger and socket (Tru-Roll), (f) batten clamp (Mutual), (g) lash cleat (Tru-Roll), (h) lash eye (Tru-Roll), (i) round lash cleat (Tru-Roll), (j) lash hook (Tru-Roll), (k) stop cleat (Tru-Roll), (l) brace cleat (Tru-Roll), (m) T-plate (Tru-Roll), (n) mending plate (Tru-Roll), (o) corner plate (Tru-Roll), (p) thimble (Mutual), (q) keeper hook (Clancy), (r) snap-hooks--swivel-eye and straight, (s) flat footiron (Tru-Roll), (t) hinged footiron (Clancy), (u) bent footiron (Tru-Roll), (v) non-skid floor plate (Clancy), (w) ceiling plate (Tru-Roll), (x) straight hanger iron (Tru-Roll), (y) hooked hanger iron (Tru-Roll), (z) floor plate (Tru-Roll), (aa) stage brace (Tru-Roll), (bb) turnbuckles (Mutual), (cc) stage screw (Tru-Roll), (dd) improved stage screw (Tru-Roll), (ee) cable clamp "Crosby" (Mutual), (ff) S-hook.*

FLOORPLATE: Used when lines or cables must be securely attached to the stage floor—not intended for used with stage braces. The plate is secured to the stage floor with lag bolts.

STAGE BRACE: A device for bracing a flat upright. The upper hooks are engaged in the brace cleat and the rocker heel at the bottom is secured to the floor with a stage screw.

TURNBUCKLE: Attached to the end of flying lines, these can be used as a means of trimming scenery, or they may be inserted into lengths of wire cable as a means of drawing the cable taut.

STAGE SCREW: A large, hand-operated screw used to secure stage braces and footirons to the floor. With the improved stage screw, the threaded plug is inserted into the floor at the desired point and provides a more secure anchor for the scenery.

CABLE CLAMP: Known by the trade name of "Crosby", these are used for attaching wire cables to battens or other scenic units.

S-HOOK: An all-purpose fastening device, these are frequently used to secure drapery to traveler tracks and similar purposes. Additionally, secure fastening may be obtained by squeezing the ends of the hook closed with pliers after they have been placed in position.

*Joining Hardware (Plate 188)*

NAILS

COMMON: This nail has a hefty shaft and a round, flat head. It is used for all general purpose wood construction. The most useful sizes are 4d, 6d, 8d, and 10d. Bulk quantities of 6d and 8d sizes should be purchased.

FINISHING: A thin-shafted nail with a narrow, round head, this is used for finishing work where the nail head should not be obvious. Most useful sizes are 6d and 8d.

DOUBLE-HEADED: Useful for semi-permanent joining of scenic units from which the nails must later be extracted, these have been replaced in many shops by TEK screws inserted and extracted by power drills with screwdriver attachments.

SCENERY: A 3/4" nail with a round head, these are used for attaching corner blocks and keystones, and are resincoated to provide greater grip. Extremely useful, but available only from Mutual Hardware.

CLOUT: A soft-metal nail with a rectangular shaft, this is designed to be driven through lumber with the protruding point being bent back over by means of a clinching plate. A traditional method of joining flats, it has largely been replaced by scenery nails or screws inserted and removed by power drills with screwdriver attachments. The most useful size is the 1 1/4" length.

When purchasing nails, plan to lay in large quantities of the 6d and 8d common nails, the scenery nails, and (possibly) clout nails and double-headed nails. Be aware, however, that TEK screws in a variety of sizes, coupled with power screwdrivers, have largely replaced the use of double-headed nails and clout nails. Other sizes and types of nails may be purchased as the need arises.

SCREWS: Flat-head, bright steel wood screws are used for attaching hardware and for more secure joining of lumber and scenic units. When using power screwdrivers, the Phillips head version works best. Available in different shaft diameters and lengths, the most useful sizes are, in the No. 8 diameter, 3/4" long, 1" long, and 1 1/4" long; and in the No. 10 diameter, 2" and 3" lengths. The largest amounts purchased should be of the 3/4" long No. 8's, since these are used most often.

Round head wood screws are occasionally used for attaching metal hardware to wooden frames when the hardware pieces are not supplied with countersunk holes. Useful sizes are the same as for the flat head screws.

The bugle-head drywall screws ("TEK" screws) are among the most useful items of joining hardware to come on the market in recent years. Used with power screwdrivers, these sharp pointed screws are self-tapping and self-countersinking and have taken over many of the tasks formerly accomplished with nails, ordinary screws, and bolts. They may be easily inserted and removed with little damage to the wood. Stocks should be maintained in sizes from 1" to 4".

Lag screws (also called "lag bolts") have a hexagonal head for driving with wrenches and are used for heavy joining, such as securing floor plates to stage floors.

Screw eyes and screw hooks (not pictured) are useful for attaching cords and other objects to, or hanging objects from, wooden elements. The gate hook and eye is useful for a variety of quick and easy connections of scenic units.

BOLTS: Used to provide secure joining of large, heavy units of scenery. Most useful are the 3/16" diameter stove bolts in 2" and 3" lengths, and the 3/8" diameter carriage bolts in 3", 4" and 6" lengths. Machine bolts, which require two wrenches to install and remove, are sometimes used in lieu of stove bolts for heavy-duty fastening. U-bolts are available in a variety of diameter openings and are useful for securing pipes, dowels, conduit, etc., to scenery. Flat washers should be available to match all sizes of bolts. Both external-tooth lock washers (for use with wood) and helical spring lock washers (for use with metal) should be supplied when extra secure fastening is required. Hexagonal nuts, shaped for securing with wrenches, should be supplied in all sizes. Wing nuts are useful for rapid hand-fastening of scenic units—during scene changes, for example.

STAPLES: Purchase to fit your staple gun in 3/8" and 1/2" lengths.

*Specialty Hardware (Plate 189)*

CASTERS: Casters for stage use should always be rubber tired, with the 4" tire diameter being the most used

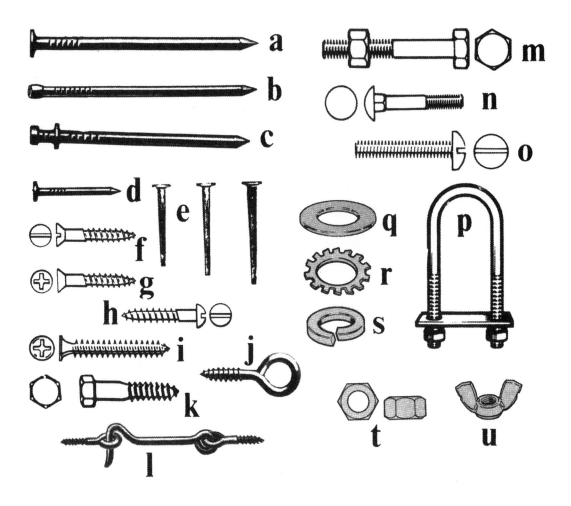

Plate 188. *JOINING HARDWARE: (a) common nail, (b) finishing nail, (c) double-headed nail, (d) scenery nail (Mutual), (e) clout nails (Mutual), (f) slot-head flat head wood screw, (g) Phillips-head flat head wood screw, (h) round head wood screw, (i) bugle head drywall "TEK" screw, (j) screw eye, (k) lag screw, (l) gate hook and eye, (m) machine bolt, (n) carriage bolt, (o) round head stove bolt, (p) U-bolt, (q) washer, (r) external tooth lock washer, (s) helical spring lock washer, (t) hexagonal nut, (u) wing nut.*

size (be sure to check on load ratings on casters before purchasing). The swivel caster allows for complete freedom of movement of the rolling scenic unit, while the rigid caster provides for more controlled movement—used for turntables, and one-directional wagon movement.

### WAGON SECURING DEVICES

DE-STA-CO CLAMP #608: One of the most effective devices for temporarily holding a wagon in place, this device provides a plunger action which extends a rod to the floor, raising the wagon off its casters (a minimum of two clamps is necessary for effective securing).

SPRING ACTION DOOR HOLDER: May be used to hold doors or rolling scenery in place. Foot pressure both sets and releases the holder; however, it is not very secure for wagons which have very active actor movement.

FLIP-DOWN DOOR HOLDER: One of the least effective holding devices—requires holders on every side of a wagon to provide security.

CANE BOLT: This bolt device can be extended down into pre-drilled holes in the stage floor to provide very secure holding of wagons in place.

### MISCELLANEOUS HARDWARE

CABINET LATCH: Designed for touring cabinets and cabinets which must withstand much abuse, this latch, with its wing-nut locking action can quickly and firmly

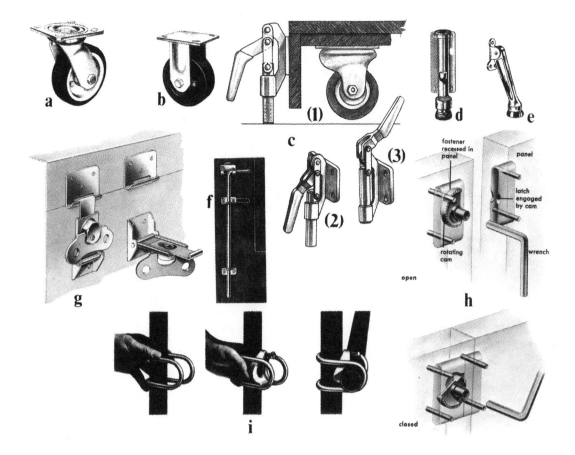

Plate 189. *SPECIALTY HARDWARE: (a) rubber-tired swivel caster, (b) rubber-tired rigid caster, (c) De-Sta-Co Platform Clamp #608 [1] clamp in operation, [2] clamp extended, [3] clamp retracted, (d) spring-action door holder, (e) flip-down door holder, (f) cane bolt, (g) cabinet latch, (h) coffin lock, (i) Roto-Lock.*

attach two scenic units together—especially useful for rapid scene changes.

COFFIN LOCK: Designed to be inserted into the thickness of plywood, or similar panels, this device is excellent for concealed joining of scenic units. It is especially useful for the temporary or semi-permanent joining of low-rise platforms, wagons, and turntables where it would be difficult, if not impossible, to get under the units for more traditional bolting or other means of fastening. In some productions, using coffin locks, actors have almost instantaneously joined units together onstage in full view of the audience.

ROTO-LOCK: This device is used to join pipes without bolting or threading. Available to fit most pipe diameters and in a variety of configurations, it allows for quick and easy—but secure—creation of scaffolding or other forms of pipe structures.

*General*

ROPE

BRAIDED COTTON ROPE: A soft, flexible rope used for lashline, lightweight rigging, and as draw lines on travelers. Most useful sizes are *1/8" awning cord, No. 8 sash cord,* and *No. 10 braided rope.*

MANILA ROPE: Three-strand manila rope is stronger and less flexible than cotton rope. The 1/2" and 3/8" manila ropes are used for lightweight rigging, breasting, and saddling, and 3/4" manila is used for heavy rigging—in the hemp flying system and as the purchase line in the counterweight system.

WIRE ROPE: Useful for supporting heavy units of scenery without being conspicuous—very strong for its size. *Aircraft cable,* which is extremely strong and nearly invisible at a distance, is the most useful—in 1/32", 1/16", and 1/8" sizes.

CHAIN: Primarily used as weight for stage draperies, although it is sometimes used for special rigging, or for visual purposes in hanging practical lamps. Most used sizes are *1/2"* and *3/4" jack chain.*

## MATERIALS

### LUMBER

This is the most used framing material in scenic construction. To meet the requirements of scenery, the lumber used must be light, strong, straight-grained, easily worked, and inexpensive. Several varieties of lumber meet all, or most, of these requirements.

WHITE PINE: The best all-around and most-used lumber for scenery. Supply, however, is limited in some areas of the country, and the price is accordingly higher.

PONDEROSA PINE (West Coast yellow pine): A good subsitute for white pine—light and easily workable, but is sometimes twisted and has a slight tendency to split.

REDWOOD: Light, strong, usually soft and straight, but with a slight tendency to split.

DOUGLAS FIR: Straight and strong, but splinters easily—good for weight-bearing supports.

Lumber is sold in grades according to its quality, which is determined by straightness of grain and freedom from knots. "Select" grades are designed for finished surfaces and are sold in letter grades—A, B, C, and D. C-select is the usual grade used for professional scenery. "Common" grades are listed 1, 2, 3, 4, and 5, and are not designed for finished work—the lumber having a higher percentage of knots and a greater tendency toward curvature. No. 2-common is the most often used grade for amateur scenery.

Lumber is available in a variety of sizes, the widths and thicknesses being specified in inches and sold in lengths that are divisible by two—thus a standard lumber size might be 1" x 3" x 4'. The widths and thicknesses listed are rough-cut sizes, however, and when the lumber is dressed (planed and smoothed on all sides) approximately 1/4" is lost in width and thickness. Standard 1" x 3" lumber, then, is actually closer to 3/4" x 2 3/4". Lengths, however, are full measure. This discrepancy in width and thickness must be taken into account when calculating cutting measurements for lumber used in construction.

Lumber is sold by the board foot (1" x 12" x 12") and all prices are calculated on this basis. All lumber sizes can be converted to board feet when estimating cost by determining the number of board feet contained in the desired running feet (actual footage of lumber desired). A 16' length of 1" x 3" lumber, for instance, contains 4 board feet. Lumber less than 1" thick is sold by the square foot.

The sizes of lumber most used in scenery construction are as follows:

1" x 2"— small framing units and diagonal braces.
1" x 3"—standard flat framing.
1" x 4"—battens, and framing on oversized units.
1" x 6", 8", 10", 12"—stair risers and treads, door and window frames and reveals.

2" x 4", 6", 8"—heavy weight-bearing supports and frames.

### Covering Materials (Plate 190)

### FABRIC

COTTON DUCK: In the 8-oz. weight, this is the most used material for flat covering—particularly in professional scenic construction. It is strong and takes paint well. With proper care, it will last indefinitely.

MUSLIN: Heavyweight (5-6 oz.) unbleached muslin is a popular lower-priced substitute for cotton duck. It requires care in handling because it is not as strong as duck and will tear and stretch easily. It is particularly useful for backdrops and for repairing and dutchmanning flats.

SCENERY CLOTH: This is a fabric produced by several manufacturers as a substitute for muslin and duck as a flat-covering material. It has a slightly looser weave than muslin, but is stronger and heavier—similar in many ways to cotton duck. Strangely enough, it costs less than muslin at the present time.

BURLAP: Used by some for flat covering, this coarse, loosely woven fabric does not work well for that purpose. It is, however, useful as a texturing material for covering three-dimensional objects such as trees and rocks, and also for providing a textured surface for flats or scenic units under special conditions.

SHARKSTOOTH SCRIM (Plate 190): A material loosely woven in a rectangular pattern, this is useful for "disappearing wall" effects and for helping to create a sense of distance in exterior scenes.

BOBBINETTE (Plate 190): A very lightweight, fragile netting with a hexagonal weave. This is used primarily to create a sense of haze or distance.

THEATRICAL GAUZE (Plate 190): Considerably less expensive than sharkstooth scrim and more coarsely woven, this netting may be used for some of the same type of effects—although the result will not be quite as effective as if the more expensive scrim had been employed.

SCENERY NETTING (Plate 190): With 1" square openings in the netting, this material is used to provide support for irregularly shaped and free-form areas of cut drops. Available in both natural and black colors, it is glued to the backside of the cut portions of drops and almost totally disappears into background decoration or sky cyc.

VELOUR: A very opaque material with a soft, deep pile, this is available in a variety of weights, qualities, and colors, and is the best material to use for stage draperies. It has a deep, rich appearance under lights.

DUVETYN: This is a velour substitute with a soft, woolly flat nap on one side, and is used for draperies when a tight pocketbook will not allow the purchase of the more expensive velour.

COTTON REP: This is an inexpensive ribbed material

that is strong, drapes well, and can be easily cleaned. It is often used for drapery where opacity and a rich surface are not the prime requisites.

SATEEN: An inexpensive lightweight material with a smooth, shiny surface on one side, this is useful for tableau curtains and brail curtains, where the heavy weight of velour or duvetyn is a hinderance.

In purchasing fabrics, it is usually less expensive to buy by the bolt—50 or 60 yards. Covering materials such as cotton duck, muslin, and scenery cloth should not be less than 72" wide. Sharkstooth scrim and bobbinette come in 30' widths and are usually sold by the yard. Velour, duvetyn, rep, and sateen are sold in widths up to 54" and can be purchased by the yard, although, here again, a bolt is usually less expensive in the long run.

### HARDBOARDS

Most of the types of composition board listed below are sold in sheets measuring 4' x 8', although oversized sheets such as 5' x 9', 4' x 10', or 4' x 12' may occasionally be stocked by dealers.

Plywood: A wood product formed by bonding together an uneven number of thin sheets (plys) of wood. The sheets are glued together with the grains going in alternate directions, thus imparting great strength to the finished product. Douglas fir plywood, good one side, is the variety most used in the shop, in the following thicknesses.

1/4"— for keystones and cornerblocks, facings, curved surfaces, and profile cutouts.
1/2"—for lightweight surfacing and construction, also for heavy-duty cutouts.
3/4"—for general purpose construction—most often used for platform flooring, stair treads and carriages, and extra heavy-duty cutouts.

LUAN: Available in 3/16" thicknesses, this is a relatively inexpensive panelboard which is often used for hard-surfaced flats, cut-out profiles where strength is not a factor, and for curved surfaces, such as the thickness pieces on arches. A natural wood product, it may also be stained and used to simulate thicker wood surfaces.

UPSOM BOARD: A laminated paper product in 1/8" and 3/16" thicknesses, often used for lightweight, delicate cutouts, facings, and curved surfaces, such as the insides of arches. Widely replaced by the less expensive Luan panels.

MASONITE: A compressed wood pulp product, this is also available in a variety of thicknesses, of which 3/16" is most useful in the shop. This is a very heavy board with a very hard surface. Tempered Masonite has an extremely hard, smooth surface and is sometimes used as flooring.

### PAINTS

For many reasons, including non-inflammability, ease of mixing, ease of cleaning (from clothes and brushes), lack of sheen when dry, and speed of drying, water-base paints are almost exclusively used for theatrical work. Two principal types of scenic paints are commercially available: dry pigment and pre-mixed.

*Dry Pigment:* The traditional form of scenic paint, dry pigments must be mixed with a glue binder and water in order to be used (as explained in Chapter IV). These are the least expensive paints and are available in the widest variety of colors (Gothic Color Company lists approximately 35 colors). Although possessing many advan-

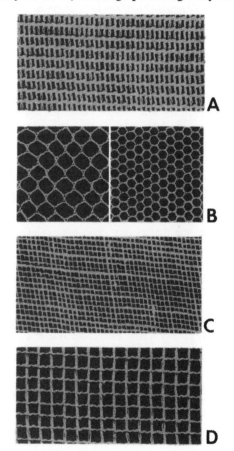

Plate 190. *THEATRICAL GAUZE: (a) sharkstooth scrim, (b) bobbinet, (c) theatrical gauze, (d) scenery netting.*

tages, there are also some difficulties in its use: the mixing procedure is time consuming and requires careful attention to proportions of glue + pigment + water; the paint does not always coat evenly; it sometimes changes color in the bucket overnight; and the pigment-glue mixture spoils after a short period of time, creating a particularly rank odor.

*Pre-Mixed Paints:* Although available in a narrower range of colors, there are several varieties of pre-mixed paints especially prepared for theatrical use:

PROTEIN BINDER paints including casein-base, such as *Gothic Casein Fresco Paints,* and soya-protein-base paints, such as *Iddings Deep Colors* and *Luminall Fresco Colors,* are available in concentrated form in quarts and gallons. The paint is thinned with water to a good working consistency (anywhere from two-to-one to six-to-one water to paint proportions), and will accept additives such as dry pigment, dye, bronzing powders, and other water-base paints. It works best on porous and semi-porous materials. When covered with a thin layer of water and kept in a tightly-closed container, the paint will last for long periods of time. Some colors, however, tend to spoil and turn rank after exposure to air.

VINYL (*Flo-Paint Scenic Decorator Colors*), **acrylic** (*Cal-Western Show and Display Colors*), and **vinyl-acrylic** (*Rosco Super Saturated Paint*) paints are permanent when dry and cover most porous and nonporous materials equally well. Not to be confused with latex or vinyl paints available at local paint stores, these colors are especially formulated for theatrical use, come in highly concentrated form, and are available in a range of saturated colors. Also available is a clear gloss medium which can provide a shiny surface to objects similar to oil paints or varnish. When kept in sealed containers, these paints will last indefinitely.

New on the market is a **resin** base paint (*Artist's Choice* from Sculptural Arts Coating, Inc.) which has promise of becoming a favorite among scenic artists. It is highly pigment saturated, has excellent covering qualities (a problem with some of the vinyl-acrylic colors), and can be extended by as many as 20 or more parts water without losing all color and binding capacity. Clear gloss and a truly flat water base varnish are available from the same source.

DYES

Dyes are especially bright and transparent colorants which become part of a fabric by chemical process—the opposite to paint, which is a coating applied to the surface. This staining action makes them particularly useful for such effects as stained-glass windows, translucent backdrops, and for backdrops that must be folded and stored in a small space. Dyes are prepared by boiling in water, with variations in hue achieved by adjusting the amount of water used. Dyes are extremely brilliant—a teaspoonful of dye frequently making several gallons of color. Sometimes binders such as gum arabic, dextrine, or clear vinyl must be added to prevent the dye from spreading or bleeding. A word of caution, however: dyes must be used carefully since most have toxic prop-

erties; true **aniline** dyes, derived from coal tar compounds, are too toxic for safe use.

COLOR PALETTE

Although colors vary somewhat from one type of paint to another and from one manufacturer to another, a basic supply of colors should include the following:

CHROME YELLOW: generally the closest to primary yellow.

RED: called variously Turkey Red Lake, Fire Red, or Spectrum Red, the closest to primary red.

ORANGE: also called French Orange, Mineral and Moly Orange, this is a bright, slightly reddish orange.

ULTRAMARINE BLUE: a bright blue with a slight red content—close to primary blue.

COBALT BLUE: also called Cerulean and Green-Shade Blue, this is a light, slightly green blue, better for mixing with greens than Ultramarine.

CHROME GREEN: a straight middle green.

YELLOW OCHRE: a tan or golden color; when not available, Raw Sienna is a close substitute.

BURNT SIENNA: a rich red-brown, or brick color.

RAW UMBER: a gray, slightly greenish, brown.

BURNT UMBER: a rich, deep walnut brown.

With the addition of black and white, this basic palette can provide most of the color mixes necessary for a production. Other useful accent colors that are available in some brands include: Purple Lake (a rich reddish violet); Prussian Blue (a deep blue-green, almost black); Emerald Green (a brilliant yellowish green); and Van Dyke Brown (a rich dark brown).

GLUES

*Gelatin* and *carpenter's* glues are the glues traditionally used as binders for dry pigment scenic paints. Available in flake form, they must be cooked and then used in proportions of approximately 1 part glue to 8 or 10 parts water. In addition to use as a binder for paint, this mixture may be combined with whiting and used to size flats.

*Polyvinyl* glue (the everpresent "white" glue) is available in liquid form in large containers. Used as binder for dry pigment in proportions of approximately 1 part glue to 5 parts water, it serves many other purposes in general scenery and property construction.

PAINTING SUPPLIES AND EQUIPMENT (*Plate 191*)

Brushes: Good paint brushes art indispensable for scene painting—the best for this purpose being 100 percent bristle. Must be kept in good condition—washed immediately after use, stored properly to avoid mussing the bristles, and kept out of any type of oil paint. Scene paint brushes fall into four categories: priming brushes, lay-in brushes, decorating brushes, and lining brushes.

*Priming brushes:* 6" to 8" wide, used for rapid application of paint—usually too heavy and unwieldy for the beginning painter.

*Lay-in brushes:* 3" to 5" wide, used for general base coating and covering of large areas, also for such techniques as blending, scumbling, spattering, and dry-brushing.

*Decorating brushes:* 2" to 3" wide, flat and round, used for more detailed painting, free-hand painting, and for painting small areas and objects.

*Lining brushes (fitches):* long-handled, special scenic brushes in sizes from 1/4" to 1 1/2" with a flat, chiseled edge – used for free-hand and straightedge detail painting.

*Sash brushes:* domestic painters' brushes, flat brushes 1" to 3" wide, the most useful being those with a diagonally cut bristle. (not pictured)

*Wood grain brushes:* specialty brushes available from theatrical and decorator painting suppliers, these brushes have individual, separated bristles for creating the effect of wood grain. Some of these brushes have bristles which are moveable, allowing for greater variety of graining effects.

It is usually a wise idea to keep a few smallsized, inexpensive brushes on hand for use in glue and oil paints. This saves wear and tear on the scenic brushes.

NATURAL SPONGES: Often difficult to locate and somewhat expensive, these are invaluable for a variety of textural effects. Every attempt should be made to have several on hand at all times.

MANUAL PAINT SPRAYERS: Hand compression sprayers often used for spraying insecticides, these are extremely useful for all sorts of painted effects.

SPRAY GUN WITH AIR COMPRESSOR: An electrically-driven, constant pressure sprayer with an assortment of nozzles to control the shape of the spray. The sprayer must be cleaned after every use, however, and the pain should be strained before spraying.

PAINT ROLLER WITH ACCESSORIES: Available locally, these allow for rapid application of flat coats of paint. Coarse-textured and specialty rollers may be used to apply textural effects to scenery.

PLUMB BOB: Attached to a string and suspended from above to establish true verticals on an upright scenic unit.

LARGE COMPASS: Designed to hold chalk or charcoal, this is used for marking out large circles.

POUNCE WHEEL (pattern tracing or tracing wheel): A marking instrument with a small, spur-like wheel, which, when rolled over a pattern drawn on paper, will punch a line of holes in the paper. The perforated paper is then placed over a surface and dusted with powdered charcoal, which sifts through the holes and marks the pattern onto the surface. This instrument is obtainable from costume supply houses where it is listed as a "pattern tracing or tracing wheel."

STRAIGHT EDGE: A piece of well-varnished straight wood 3" to 4" wide and 1/2" to 3/4" thick with beveled edges and a handle or drawer pull attached for easier use. The 6' length is standard, but it is useful to have on hand 18" and 36" lengths for cramped spaces. For painting on the floor, long pole-handles may be attached in place of the door handles.

BUCKETS AND CANS: It is essential to have on hand a large number of containers of various sizes for mixing and holding paint. Buckets in 14- and 16-quart sizes and No. 10 cans are the most generally useful containers, although a few smaller cans for lining and detail colors come in very handy. Plastic buckets and cans are usually more easily cleaned of water-based paints. Smaller cans with lids are useful for storing "touch-up paints" over long periods of time.

PLASTIC TRAYS: These are useful as painting "palettes" for combining ready-mixed colors into different colors when painting more elaborate scenic effects.

CHALK LINE: Cord rolled in a container filled with chalk or charcoal dust. When rolled out and stretched taut between two points, it can be snapped, depositing a straight line of chalk or charcoal between those two points. The cord should be at least 50' long.

DRAWING STICK: Light bamboo, 4' long, split at one end to hold chalk or charcoal and used for sketching out the scene to be painted. (not pictured)

YARDSTICK: For general measuring and laying-out. (not pictured)

LARGE PROTRACTOR: Useful for laying out designs which require precise angles, these are usually available from suppliers of teachers' equipment. (not pictured)

STOVE OR BURNER: a gas or electric burner or hot plate is necessary when using gelatine or carpenter's glue for any purpose – both for cooking the glue and for keeping the mixed paint warm to prevent the glue from congealing or mixing out. The *electric glue pot* is an improvement for cooking the glue, since it is impossible to burn the glue in one of these, but the electric or gas burner is still necessary for warming the paint. (not pictured)

MISCELLANEOUS PAINTING TOOLS: Various heavily textured fabrics and other materials such as thick-napped carpets, etc., are useful for the creation of painted texture effects. Sheets of 1/2" to 1" *foam rubber* may be attached to plywood and cut into patterns to create scenery "stamps" for rapidly adding repeated designs to a surface—leaves, flowers, wallpaper motifs, border motifs, etc. For painting on the floor (the continental method of scene painting), long-handled "wands" are essential to prevent backbreaking leaning or squatting to paint. There are long-handled scenic brushes available commercially, as well as fiberglass and aluminum wands to attach to or hold various fitches and decorating brushes. More economically, wands may be fashioned from bamboo

Plate 191. *PAINTING SUPPLIES AND EQUIPMENT: (a) priming and lay-in brushes (Mann Bros.), (b) decorating and lining brushes [fitches] (Rosco), (c) wood-graining brush, (d) natural sponges (Mann Bros.), (e) manual paint sprayers (Chapin), (f) air compressor, (g) spray gun, (h) paint roller and tray set (Mann Bros.), (i) textured paint rollers (Mann Bros.), (j) plumb bob (Stanley), (k) large compass (Macgregor), (l) pounce wheel (tracing wheel), (m) straight edge, (n) plastic bucket, (o) galvanized metal bucket (Mutual), (p) small plastic pails with lids, (q) plastic trays, (r) chalk line (Stanley).*

rods which are usually available locally and are both light-weight and easily adapted.

MISCELLANEOUS PAINT ROOM SUPPLIES

ROSCO TOUGH PRIME: As the name implies, a surface coating for hard-to-cover materials such as plastics, foams, metals, and other surfaces that do not readily accept water paints.

ALCOHOL: An aid in mixing dry-pigment colors that do not dissolve readily, and also aids in the mixing of dye colors.

ALUM: Mixed with size water to form alum-size, a sealer for flats that have dusting undercoats or are stained with glue or dye.

LIQUID WAX: For glazes—either as a final coat or mixed with the paint to provide a sheen. Clear gloss vinyl-acrylic or resin varnish may be used for the same purpose, but these are usually more expensive.

SAL AMMONIAC AND BORAX: For mixing a flameproofing compound—1 lb. sal ammoniac, 1 lb. borax to 3 qts. of water. Ready-mixed flameproofing compounds are also commercially available.

OIL OF WINTERGREEN/FORMALDEHYDE/ACETONE: Preservatives—added to glue-binder paints and protein-base paints to delay spoilage. Use only in well-ventilated areas with respirators.

BASIC TOOL LIST

The following list represents the tools I consider minimal to the efficient handling of all the operations involved in putting together a setting:

*Construction Hand Tools*

12' steel measuring tape 1 each worker
50' steel measuring tape 1
rip hammer 1 each 2 workers
claw hammer 1 each 2 workers
combination square 1 each 2 workers
framing square 1 each 4 workers
6" screwdriver 1 each 2 workers
slip-joint pliers 1 each 2 workers
crescent wrench 1 each 6 workers
trimming knife 1 each 2 workers
bevel gauge 1
rasp 1
files (wood and metal) 1 each
circular file 1
pinch bar 1
C-clamps 6 (assorted sizes)
backsaw and miter box 1

grommeting dies and sets
  for #2 grommets 1

*Power Tools*

SABER SAW: Purchase a good quality, heavy-duty saw (1/3 to 1/2 horsepower), preferably with variable speeds, plus a variety of blades.

HAND POWER DRILL: Here again, you should purchase a good quality heavy-duty (1/3 to 1/2 horsepower) tool—a multiple-speed drill with a 3/8" chuck is a good minimal choice, with a good selection of bits, of course.

In the case of both tools listed above, if budget will allow it would be advisable to purchase one of the many battery-powered models currently on the market. This is particularly true for the Power Drill which, with the appropriate bits, also may be used to insert and remove screws. Obviously, battery recharger units and spare batteries should be purchased as well. The increased portability of these units vastly increases their versatility, speeds up construction work, and thereby tends to offset the increased initial cost.

(A word to the wise: with the exception of perishable items such as measuring tapes, it is always preferable and cheaper in the long run to purchase good quality tools at the outset. Don't be fooled by "bargains." A tool so poor in quality that it must be replaced after only a few months' use is hardly a bargain when compared with a quality tool that will last for years. Buying by price alone is usually false economy.)

*Painting Equipment*

lining brushes: 1/4", 1/2 ",
  1", 1 1/2" 1 each
decorating brushes: 2", 3" 1 each
lay-in brushes 4" 1 each 2 workers
6' straightedge 1
yardstick 1 each 2 workers
14-quart buckets 9
No. 10 cans 6
stove or burner (if scene
  paint is used) 1
Chalk line 1

*Priorities for Adding Tools*
The following list indicates my priorities for adding power tools to the shop equipment. Additional quantities and varieties of hand tools, brushes, etc., should be added as money allows or as need dictates.

*Construction Tools*
1. RADIAL ARM SAW: The ease of use, flexible, and safety of this tool make it the obvious choice as the first permanently mounted piece of equipment to be purchased.

2. CUT-AWL: Addition of this tool gives a shop the capability of producing any degree of detail in wood cutting and profiling.

3. TABLE SAW: Addition of this tool for straight cutting and ripping frees the radial arm saw for other, more complicated operations.

4. BAND SAW: Takes the pressure off the saber saw and Cut-Awl by providing another tool for cutting curves and simple scrolls.

5. DRILL PRESS: Provides more accurate drilling in many instances than the hand drill, as well as being adaptable for many other purposes.

6. BENCH GRINDER: This and the following pieces of equipment are, in a sense, "luxury" tools, and their addition to the shop is principally determined by availability of funds, particular need, or personal preference.

7. POWER SANDER

8. ROUTER

9. PANEL SAW: A wonderful device for safely cutting large panels of plywood, masonite, luan, etc. It relieves many of the hazards of cutting these materials on the table saw.

*Painting Tools*

1. SPRAY TANK: An economy sprayer. If funds will allow purchase of the electric spray gun, there is no need to bother with this one.

2. ELECTRIC SPRAY GUN

A major addition to a scenic shop would be a large air compressor unit which would allow for the use of pneumatic tools. Hammers, staplers, drills, sprayers, and many other tools can be very efficiently powered by air, and can provide construction methods which are difficult to achieve by other means. Pneumatic hammers and staplers, for example, can insert fasteners with one stroke into flexible materials which otherwise are almost impossible to secure manually. Paint sprayers powered by air are much more controllable and efficient than tank sprayers.

These types of tools do present some hazards, however. Pneumatic hammers can just as easily insert nails into human flesh as into wood, unless care is taken in their use. Untrained personnel should not be turned loose with pneumatic tools unless careful supervision is provided.

SHOP LAYOUT

The size and shape of space available for a scenic shop varies so greatly from theatre to theatre that it would be senseless to try to present any form of ideal shop arrangement. I will, however, make a few general suggestions

and comments that might be of value in arranging more efficiently the space you do have.

1. The work of the shop is broadly divided into construction and painting. As much as possible, the areas for these two operations should be separated in the shop—at least in the storage and placement of tools and supplies.

2. In the construction area, storage must be provided for materials and tools. Lumber needs a long, narrow area so that it can be stored horizontally— laid straight and flat. Plywood and upsom are best stored horizontally, but can be stored upright if well supported on both sides to prevent bending and curving. You will also need some form of storage for all smaller lengths of lumber that accumulate during construction. Each hardware item (nails, screws, hinges, stage hardware, etc.) needs to have its own separate place of storage—well-organized wooden boxes, bins, or drawers. At the University of Georgia we acquired a secondhand rotary bin such as is found in hardware stores, and it has proved wonderfully efficient in the storage of such items. Hand tools and small power tools should be kept in locked cabinets. I like to have large, shallow cabinets in which each tool can be hung separately. If the silhouette of each tool is painted onto the cabinet, then it is extremely easy to see if any tools are missing before the cabinet is locked each day; and, furthermore, students seem to have more incentive to replace tools when they have finished work, if this idea is used.

3. As much as possible, all construction tools should be kept in one area of the shop, which can then be designated as the principal woodworking area. Large-stand power tools such as the band saw, the table saw, and the grinder should be mounted on casters so that they may be easily moved to the most convenient spot for usage, and when not in use may be moved out of the way.

4. Most of the construction processes of scenery require that the work be done horizontally. Since flat units are usually large, this necessitates a good deal of work area. Large work tables (4' to 6' wide and 12' to 20' in length) can obviate the necessity for working on the floor, and save many a sore stiff back. If these tables are mounted on casters, they may be rolled out of the way when not in use.

5. Within or adjacent to the painting area should be provided one or more large sinks with deep traps to catch paint residue. Storage cabinets which allow brushes to hang and dry out without disturbing the bristles, and shelves or cabinets for paint storage should also be provided. There should also be shelves for both unused and used paint buckets (which accumulate in surprising numbers at times). A good addition to this area is a rolling cart with shelves to carry mixed paint to the painting area(s), with a metal or ceramic "palette" on top for mixing additional colors "on-the-spot." If dry pig-

ment is in use, then provision should be made for the stove or burner to heat the glue and keep the size warm.

6. The painting itself may be done either horizontally or vertically. If horizontally, there must be provided a great deal of clear floor space—possibly the area formerly used for construction, if that is not in use. Vertical painting is usually accomplished by means of a paint frame—a large wooden frame on one wall of the shop. This frame may be permanently attached to the wall or it may be be rigged to raise and lower into a well in the floor. If it is permanently attached to the wall, then the painting may be facilitated by use of a boomerang—a rolling 2- or 3-tiered painting tower.

If the shop is adjacent to the stage area, it is often possible to use the stage itself for construction or painting purposes, if this does not interfere with rehearsals or other events. In any case, large floor area and efficiently arranged storage space are the two prime requisites for a shop. It is also important that the shop be well lighted and ventilated, and equipped with sufficient electrical outlets for efficient use of power tools.

One final note. Keep the shop clean. It is wise to set aside the final five or ten minutes of the work period for general cleanup and tool replacement. Left for even one or two days, the shop area can become virtually a disaster area through the accumulation of sawdust, scrap lumber, dirty buckets, and general clutter. It is also a quick way to lose tools. Keep brooms, dustpans, and garbage cans available and use the last of the shop period to return the place to order.

# INTERNATIONAL SUPPLIERS OF STAGE MATERIALS

*General Theatrical Suppliers*

**ARGENTINA**

Vari-Lite Argentina, Agustin Alvarez 1844, Vincente Lopez, Buenos Aires 1602 Argentina, Phone: 54-1-795-6445

**AUSTRALIA**

Bytecraft Pty. Ltd., 23-27 Fonceca St., Mordialloc, VIC 3195 Australia, Phone: 61-39-587-2555; and Unit 5, 31 Bridge Rd., Stanmore, NSW 2048 Australia, Phone: 61-2-550-3955; and 30 Jeays Street, Bowen Hills, QLD 4001 Australia, Phone: 61-7-3252 5988

Coemar de Sisti Australia Pty. Ltd., 36A Clements Ave., Bundoora, Melbourne, VIC 3083 Australia, Phone 61-39-467-8666

Lightmoves Technologies (NSW) Pty. Ltd., 631 Parramatta Rd., Leichhardt, NSW 2040 Australia, Phone 61-2-560-0000

LSC Electronics Pty. Ltd., 7 University Pl., Clayton, VIC 3168 Australia, Phone 61-39-561-5255

Psycholites, 141 Strangways TCE, North Adelaide, SA 5006 Australia, Phone: 61-8-267-3719

**CANADA**

Alberta Stage Lighting Ltd., 11210 143 St., Edmonton, AB TSM 1V5, Canada, (403) 452-5483

Canadian Staging Projects Ltd., 571 Adelaide St., East, Toronto, ON MSA 1NB Canada, (416) 947-9400

Distribution Megaphoton, Inc., 150 SE Rue, Quebec, PQ G1L 2R4 Canada, (418) 529-8982

Far-Go Paint & Chemicals Inc., 5513 3rd St., SE, Calgary, AB T2H 1K1 Canada, (403) 255-2936 and (403) 255-2937

Farquhar International Ltd., 937 Dillingham Rd., Pickering, ON L1W 1Z7 Canada, (905) 420-3232

Jack A. Frost Ltd., 3245 Wharton Way, Mississauga, ON L4X 2R9 Canada, (800) 263-7678 and (905) 624-5344

Hiretech Systems Ltd., 29 Manitou Dr., Unit 1E, Kichener, ON N2C 1K9 Canada, (716) 748-2770

Ivan and Co. Lighting Inc., 837 Boul Decarie, St. Laurent, Montreal, PQ H4L 3L8 Canada, (514) 747-8487

Les Eclairages Projec, Inc., 150, 5E Rue, Limoilou, Quebec, PQ G1L 2R4 Canada, (418) 529-8982

Lighting by Monty Ltd., 12504 128th St., Edmonton, AB T5L 1C8 Canada, (800) 667-7969 and (403) 454-7969; and 480 C 36 Ave. SE, Calgary, AB T2G 1W4 Canada, (403) 287-2444

Lumitrol Ltd., 89 Research Rd., Ste. 2000 Toronto, ON M4G 2G8 Canada, (416) 424-4284

Neotech Resources, Inc., 390E Provencher Blvd., Winnipeg, MB R2H OH1 Canada, (800) 463-8324 and (204) 237-8324

Performance Solutions/Sapphire Staging, 29 Basin St., Toronto, ON M4M 1A1 Canada, (416) 461-9600

Scenework, 74 Liverpool St., Guelph, ON N1H 2L1 Canada, (800) 668-3431 and (519) 837-0583

**CROATIA**

Light Shop, CMP Savica-Sanci 133, Zagreb 10000 Croatia, Phone: 385-1-239-9012

**GERMANY**

Amptown Lighttechnik GMBH, Wandsbeker Str. 26, Hamburg 71 D-22179 Germany, Phone: 49-40-64600440

BBB, Am Forst 17, Postfach 1129, Weiden D-92636 Germany, Phone: 49-961-300929

Zilz International GMBH, Venloer Str. 703, Cologne D-50827 Germany, Phone: 49-221-58-30-31

**HONG KONG**

Vari-Lite Hong Kong, 6th Fl., Blk. 2 , Tien Chu Ctr., 1E Mok Cheong St., Tokawawan, Kowloon, Hong Kong, (852) 715-7878

**ITALY**

Coemar SPA, via Inghilterra, Castelgoffredo, (MN) 4604 Italy, Phone: 39-376-379-3364

Spotlight SRL, Via Sismondi 50, Milan 1-20133 Italy, Phone: 39-2-7611008139

**JAPAN**

RDS Corp., 7-2, 4-Chome, Shimbashi, Minato-Ku, Tokyo 105 Japan, Phone: 81-3-5470-1405

Technical Supply Japan Co., Ltd., 2-13-3, Takaban,

Meguro-ku, Tokyo 152 Japan, Phone: 81-3-3791-7501

## NETHERLANDS
W. Beyne & ZN. B.V., P.O. Box 76, Busson 1400 Netherlands, Phone: 31-35-6938692

## NEW ZEALAND
John Herber Ltd., P.O. Box 5172, Christchurch 5 New Zealand, Phone: 64-3-3524-588

Selecon New Zealand Ltd., 26 Putiki St., Grey Lynn, Auckland 2 New Zealand, Phone 64-9-3601718

## SINGAPORE
Hawko Trading Co., Pte Ltd., 605 Macpherson Rd., No. 01-15 Citimac Ind. Complex, 368239 Singapore, Phone: 65-287-0011

## SPAIN
Fresnel, S.A., C/. Providencia, 109-111, Barcelona 08024 Spain, Phone: 34-3-210-7351 and 34-3-219-9460; and Calle Lanuza, 25, Madrid 28028 Spain, Phone: 34-1-356-7035; and Calle Joaquin Bustamante, 14 (Local 44), Santander 39011 Spain, Phone: 34-42-34.71.94

## SWITZERLAND
Delux Theatre Lighting, Hardturmstr. 5, Zurish CH-8005 Switzerland, Phone: 41-1-272-7989

Power Light Production Co., Fabrikmattenweg 8, Arlesheim, Basel CH-4144 Switzerland, Phone: 41-61-701-8228

## TAIWAN ROC
Telestar Disco Lighting, No. 333, Cheng Kung 3rd Rd., Nankang Ind. Park, Nantou sien, Taiwan ROC, Phone: 886-49-255 933

## UNITED KINGDOM
AJS Theatre Lighting & Supplies Ltd., Hightown Ind. Est., Crow Arch Ln., Ringwood, Hampshire BH24 IND United Kingdom, Phone: 44-142-547-0888

Arri (GB) Ltd., 1-3 Airlinks, Spifire Way, Heston, Middlesex TW5 9NR United Kingdom, Phone: 44-181-213-5200

Brilliant Stages, Ltd., 20-22 Fairway Dr., Greenford, Middlesex UB6 8PW United Kingdom, Phone: 44-181-575-8888

British Harlequin PLC., Kent House, High St., Farmingham, Kent DA4 0DT United Kingdom, Phone 44-132-286-5288; and 33, Blvd. Grand-Duchesse Charlotte, Luxembourg L-1331 United Kingdom, Phone: 44-35-225-2929

Cerebrum Lighting Ltd. Units 4 & 5, Shannon Comm. Ctr. Beverley Way, New Maiden, Surrey KT3 4PT

United Kingdom, Phone: 44-181-949-3171

Donmar Ltd., 54 Cavell St., Whitechapel, London E1 2HP United Kingdom, Phone: 44-171-790-1166

Philip L. Edwards (Theatre Lighting), S. Highwood Close, Glossip, Derbyshire SK13 9PH United Kingdom, Phone: 44-145-786-2811

Doughty Engineering Ltd., Crow Arch Ln., Ringwood, Hants BH24 1NZ United Kingdom, Phone: 44-142-547-8961

Flint Hire & Supply Ltd., Queens Row, London SE17 2PX United Kingdom, Phone: 44-171-703-9786

Glantre Engineering Ltd., 20 Richfield Ave., Reading Berkshire RG1 8EQ United Kingdom, Phone: 44-173-464-0000

Northern Light, 39/41 Assembly St., Leith, Edinburgh EH6 7RG United Kingdom, Phone: 44-131-553-2383

Tele-stage Associates (UK) Ltd., Unit 14, Bunting Rd., Moreton Hall Ind. Est., Bury St. Edmunds, Suffolk IP32 7BX United Kingdom, Phone: 44-128-475-5512

Unusual Rigging, The Wharf BugBrooke, Northants, Middlesex NN7 3QD United Kingdom, Phone: 44-160-483-0083

## UNITED STATES
Alcone Co., Inc., 5-49 49th Avenue, Long Island City, NY 11101, (718) 361-8373

BMI Supply, 28 Logan Ave., Glens Falls, NY 12801, (518) 793-6706

Bay Theatrical, 455 Reservation Rd., Ste. H, Marina, CA 93933, (408) 384-6977

California Stage and Lighting, 3609 W. MacArthur Blvd., #801, Santa Ana, CA 92704, (714) 966-1852

DesignLab Chicago, 806 N. Peoria St., Chicago, IL 60622-5438, (800) 43-DESLB

Holzmueller Productions, 1275 Minnesota St., San Francisco, CA 94107, (415) 826-8383

Indianapolis Stage Sales & Rentals, Inc., 905 Massachusetts Ave., Indianapolis, IN 46202, (317) 635-9430

Limelight Productions, Inc., RR1 Box 288A, Rt. 102, Lee, MA 01238, (800) 243-4950

The Magnum Companies, Ltd., 170-A Ottley Dr., NE, Atlanta, GA 30324, (404) 872-0553

Mainstage Theatrical Supply, Inc., 129 W. Pittsburgh Ave., Milwaukee, WI 53204, (800) 236-0878

McManus Enterprises, 111 Union Ave., Bala Cynwyd, PA 19004, (800) 523-0348

Miami Stagecraft Inc., 2855 E. 11th Ave., Hialeah, FL 33013, (305) 836-9356

Mikan Theatricals, 86 Tide Mull Rd., Hampton, NH 03842, (800) BUY-MIKAN

Musson Theatrical, Inc., 890 Walsh Ave., Santa Clara, CA 95050, (800) 843-2837

Norcostco Inc., 3203 N. Highway #100, Minneapolis, MN 5422-2789, (612) 533-2791; and 373 Rte. #46 West, Fairfield, NJ 07006, (201) 575-3503; and 2089 Monroe Dr., NE, Atlanta, GA 30324-4891, (404) 874-7511; and 500 N. Michigan Ave., Ste. 1920, Chicago, IL 60611-3703, (312) 440-1417; and 2607 Ross Ave., Dallas, TX 75201-2520, (214) 953-1255; and 5867 Lankershim Blvd., N. Hollywood, CA 91601-1035, (818) 760-2911

Northwest Theatrical, Inc., 63350 N. Hwy 97, Bldg "C", Bend, OR 97701, (800) 368-6667

Olesen, 1535 Ivar Ave., Hollywood, CA 90028, (800) 821-1656

Rosco Laboratories, Inc., 36 Bush Ave., Port Chester, NY 10573, (800) ROSCONY

SECT Theatrical Supply, Inc., 406 E. 18th St., Kansas City, MO 64108, (800) 279-5726

Stage Equipment & Lighting, Inc., 2231 N.E. 13th Ct., Miami, FL 33161, (305) 891-2010

Television/Theatre Production Service, Inc., 3514 Chamblee Dunwoody Rd., Atlanta, GA 30341, (800) 241-8700; and P. O. Box 210347, Nashville, TN 37221, (615) 646-6700

Theatrical Services and Supplies, Inc., 170 Oval Dr., Central Islip, NY 11722, (516) 348-0262

*Fabrics and Specialty Scenic Materials*

Advanced Technology, Inc., 311 Regional Rd. South, Greensboro, NC 27409, (919) 668-0488—*Mirroflex.*

Artifex Corp., 4007 W. Segerstrom Ave., Santa Ana, CA 92704-6326, (714) 549-0440—*Liquid Crystal, Fiber Optics, etc.*

Bamboo & Rattan Works, Inc., 470 Oberlin Ave., South, Lakewood, NJ 08701, (908) 370-0220 – *bamboo, rattan, matting, etc.*

Chicago Canvas & Supply Co., 3719 W. Lawrence Ave., Chicago, IL 60625, (312) 4778-5700—*canvas, muslin, etc.*

Chicago Latex Products, Inc., 1030 Morse Ave., Schaumburg, IL 60193, (708) 893-2880—*liquid latex, flexible-mold rubber, etc.*

Dazian Inc., 423 W. 55th St., New York, NY 10019, (212) 307-7800, and 132 Gardenia Ave., Ponte Vera Beach, FL 32082, (904) 285-0041, and 1758 N. Newcastle Ave., Chicago, IL 60635, (312) 622-1888, and 2014 Commerce St., Dallas, TX 75201, (214) 748-3450, and 165 S. Robertson Blvd., Beverly Hills, CA 90211, (213) 657-8900—*scenery, costume, drapery, and specialty fabrics*

Fomebords Co., 2211 N. Elston Ave., Chicago, IL 60614, (800) 362-6267—*Fome-Cor, Foam-X, Gatorfoam, etc.*

Fox-Rich Textiles, Inc., 54 Danbury Rd., Ste 228, Ridgefield, CT 06877, (914) 533-2445—*muslin,*

*duck, canvas, duvetyne, etc.*

Gerriets International, RD #1, 950 Hutchinson Rd., Allentown, NJ 08501, (609) 758-9121; and 8132 Andasol Ave., Northridge, CA 91325, (818) 705-1037—*projection screens, seamless muslin and gauze, velours, etc.*

Gladstone Fabrics, P.O. Box 566, Orchard Hill Rd., Harriman, NY 10926, (800) 724-0168—*display and specialty fabrics*

Chas. Harmon & Co., Inc., P.O. Box 787, Highlands, NC 28741, (800) 662-0466—*scenery canvas and muslin*

Hexacomb Corp., 75 Tri-State, Lincolnshire, IL 60069-4459, (847) 317-1991

Insta-Foam Products, Inc., 1500 Cedarwood Dr., Joliet, IL 60435, (815) 741-680

International Paper Co., P.O. Box 1839, Taylorsville Rd., Statesville, NC 28687-1839, (800) 438-1701—*Gatorfoam boards*

Rose Brand Textile Fabrics, 517 W. 35th St., New York, NY 10001, (800) 223-1624—*theatrical fabrics—muslin, canvas, scrim, velours, etc.*

Sculptural Arts Coating, Inc., P.O. Box 13113, Greensboro, NC 27415, (800) 743-0379—*SCULPT OR COAT$^R$ plastic cream for scenery, props, etc.*

Unnatural Resources Inc., 14 Forest Ave., Caldwell, NJ 07006, (800) 992-5540—*thermoplastics formable in hot water, Protoplast, Fabric-Form, etc.*

Urethane Products Co., Inc., 1750 Plaza Ave., New Hyde Park, Box 308, Long Island, NY 11040, (718) 343-3400—*polyurethane foam and associated supplies*

*Paints and Related Supplies*

Cal Western Paint, 11748 Slauson Ave., Sante Fe Springs, CA 90670, (310) 693-0872

Gothic Ltd., P.O. Box 189, 1 Continental Hill, Glen Cove, NY 11542, (516) 676-6600

Haussmann International USA Inc., 132 Ninth St., San Francisco, CA 94103-2603, (415) 431-1336—*also, suppliers of filling, texturing and casting materials*

Mann Brothers, 757 North La Brea Ave., Hollywood, CA 90038, (800) 245-6266

Rosco Laboratories, 36 Bush Ave., Port Chester, NY 10573, (800) ROSCONY

Shannon Luminous Materials, Inc., 304A N. Townsend St., Santa Ana, CA 92703, (714) 550-9931

*Rigging and Hardware*

Peter Albrecht Corp., 6250 Industrial Ct., Greendale, WI 53129-2432, (414) 421-6630

Automatic Devices Co., 2121 S. 12th St., Allentown, PA 18103, (215) 797-6000

J.R. Clancy, Inc., 7041 Interstate Island Rd., Syracuse,

NY 13209, (800) 836-1885

The Crosby Group, Inc., P.O. Box 3128, Tulsa, OK 74101, (918) 834-4611

ECTS Scenic Technology, Box 335 Shore Rd., Cornwall-On-Hudson, NY 12520, (914) 534-3558

Feller Precision, Inc., 377 Western Hwy., Tappan, NY 10983, (914) 359-9431

Grosh Scenic Studios, 4114 Sunset Blvd., Hollywood, CA 90029, (213) 662-1134

H & H Specialties, P.O. Box 9327, South El Monte, CA 91733, (213) 283-3562

Jeamar Winches Inc., 1051 Clinton St., Buffalo, NY 14206, (716) 854-3211

Mutual Hardware Corp., 5-45 49th Ave., Long Island City, NY 11101, (718) 861-2480

Sapsis Rigging, Inc., 233 Lansdowne Ave., Lansdowne, PA 19050, (800) SAPSIS-1

SECOA, 2731 Nevada Ave., North, Minneapolis, MN 55427, (800) 328-5519

Tiffin Scenic Studios, Inc., P.O. Box 39, 146 Riverside Dr., Tiffin, OH 44883, (419) 447-1546

(The above is a selected listing of manufacturers and suppliers. This list is current at time of print; check local directories for changes. For a complete listing, see the annual *INDUSTRY RESOURCES GUIDE* published by *TCI.*)

# BIBLIOGRAPHY

### HISTORY AND AESTHETICS OF SCENERY

Albright, Halstead and Mitchell, *The Principles of Theatre Art.* 2nd edition. Boston: Houghton Mifflin Company, 1968.

Appia, Adolphe, *Music and the Art of the Theatre.* trans. by Robert W. Corrigan and Mary Douglas Dirks, ed. by Bernard Hewitt. Miami: University of Miami Press, 1962.

Aronson, Arnold, *American Set Design.* New York: Theatre Communications Group, 1985.

Bablet, Deni, *Revolution in Stage Design of the 20th Century.* Paris: Leon Amiel Publisher, 1977.

Brockett, Oscar G., *History of the Theatre.* Boston: Allyn and Bacon, Inc., — .

Burdick, Elizabeth R., Peggy C. Hansen, and Brenda Zanger, eds., *Contemporary Stage Design U S A.* Middletown, CT: Wesleyan University Press, 1974.

Burian, Jarka, *The Scenography of Josef Svoboda.* Middletown, CT: Wesleyan University Press, 1971.

Clarke, Mary, and Clement Crisp, *Design for Ballet.* New York: Hawthorn Books, Inc., 1978.

Clay, James H., and Daniel Krempel, *The Theatrical Image.* New York: McGraw-Hill Book Company, Inc., 1967

Craig, Edward Gordon, *On the Art of theTheatre.* New York: Theatre Arts Books, 1956.

Elder, Eldon, *Designs for the Theatre.* New York: Drama Book Specialists, 1978.

Fuerst, Walter Rene, and Samuel J. Hume, *Twentieth Century Stage Decoration.* Vol. 1, text; Vol. 2, ill., New York: Dover Publications, 1968.

Gassner, John, *Form and Idea in the Modern Theatre.* New York: Holt, Rinehart & Winston, Inc., 1956.

Goodwin, John, ed., *British Theatre Design: The Modern Age.* New York: St. Martin's Press, 1989.

Gorelik, Mordecai, *New Theatres for Old.* New York: Samuel French, 1940.

Hainaux, Rene, ed., *Stage Design Throughout the World Since 1935.* New York: Theatre Arts Books, 1956.

——, *Stage Design Throughout the World Since 1950.* New York: Theatre Arts Books, 1964.

——, *Stage Design Throughout the World Since 1960.* New York: Theatre Arts Books, 1972.

——, *Stage Design Throughout the World Since 1970-75.* New York: Theatre Arts Books, 1976.

Hartmann, Rudolf, ed., *Opera,* trans. by Arnold J.

Pomerans. Secaucus, NJ: Chartwell Books, 1976.

Henderson, Mary C., *Theatre in America: 200 Years of Plays, Players, and Productions.* New York: Harry N. Abrams, Inc., 1986.

Jones, Robert Edmond, *The Dramatic Imagination.* Theatre Arts Books, 1965.

——, *Drawings for the Theatre.* New York: Theatre Arts Books, 1978.

Komisarjevsky, Theodore, and Lee Simonson, *Settings and Costumes for the Modern Stage.* New York: Benjamin Blom, 1966.

Larson, Orville K., *Scene Design in the American Theatre from 1915 to 1960.* Fayetteville, AK: The University of Arkansas Press, 1989.

Levy, Julien, ed., *Eugene Berman.* Freeport, NY: Books for Libraries Press, 1971.

MacGowan, Kenneth, and Robert Edmond Jones, *Continental Stagecraft.* New York: Benjamin Blom, Inc., 1964.

Mielziner, Jo, *Designing for the Theatre.* New York: Atheneum, 1965.

——, *The Shapes of Our Theatre,* New York: Clarkson N. Potter, Inc., 1970.

Molinari, Cesare, *Theatre Through the Ages,* trans. by Colin Hamer. New York: McGraw-Hill Book Company, 1975.

Oenslager, Donald M., *Scenery Then and Now.* New York: Russell and Russell, 1966.

——, *Stage Design: Four Centuries of Scenic Invention.* New York: Viking, 1975.

——, *The Theatre of Donald Oenslager.* Middletown, CT: Wesleyan University Press, 1978.

Rich, Frank, and Lisa Aronson, *The Theatre Art of Boris Aronson.* New York: Alfred A. Knopf, 1987.

Rischbieter, Henning, *Art and the Stage in the Twentieth Century: Painters and Sculptors' Work in the Theatre.* Greenwich, CT: —, 1970.

Roose-Evans, James, *Experimental Theatre: From Stanislavsky to Today.* New York: Avon Books, 1970.

Simonson, Lee, *The Art of Scenic Design.* New York: Harper & Brothers, 1950.

——, *Part of a Lifetime.* New York: Duell, Sloan and Pearce, 1943.

——, *The Stage is Set.* New York: Theatre Arts Books, 1964.

Smith, Ronn, *American Set Design 2.* New York: Theatre Communications Group, 1991.

Spencer, Charles, *Erte*. New York: Clarkson N. Potter, Inc., 1970.

Sporre, Dennis, *The Creative Impulse*. Englewood Cliffs, NJ: Prentice-Hall, Inc., 1987.

Svoboda, Josef, *The Secret of Theatrical Space,* ed. and trans. by J..M. Burian. New York: Applause Books, 1993.

## SCENIC DESIGN

Bay, Howard, *Stage Design*. New York: Drama Book Specialists, 1974.

Dorn, Dennis and Shanda, Mark, *Drafting for the Theatre*. Carbondale, IL: Southern University Press, 1992.

Gillette, A. S., *An Introduction to Scene Design*. New York: Harper & Row, 1967.

Payne, Darwin Reid, *Design for the Stage: First Steps*. Carbondale, IL: Southern Illinois University Press, 1974.

Pecktal, Lynn, *Designing and Painting for the Theatre*. New York: Holt, Reinhart and Winston, 1975.

_____ , *Designing and Drawing for the Theatre*. New York: McGraw-Hill, 1995.

Reid, Francis, *Designing for the Theatre*. New York: Theatre Arts Books/Routledge, 1989.

Rose, Rich, *Drafting Scenery for Theatre, Film and Television*. Cincinnati, OH: Betterway Books, 1994, distributed by Empire Publishing Service, Studio City, CA

Rowell, Kenneth, *Stage Design*. London: Studio Vista, 1968.

Sporre, Dennis J., and Robert C. Burroughs, *Scene Design in the Theatre*. Englewood Cliffs, NJ: Prentice Hall, 1990.

## ART, ARCHITECTURE, AND DECOR

Aronson, Joseph, *The New Encyclopedia of Furniture*. New York: Crown Publishers, 1967.

Ball, Victoria Kloss, *Architecture and Interior Design: Europe and America from the Colonial Era to Today*. New York: John Wiley & Sons, 1980.

Ching, Frank, *Architectural Graphics*. New York: Van Nostrand, Reinhold Company, 1975.

Clark, Arthur Bridgman, *Perspective*. Stanford, CA: Stanford University Press, 1944.

Edwards, Betty, *Drawing on the Right Side of the Brain*. Los Angeles: J. P. Tarcher, Inc., 1979.

Evans, Ralph M., *An Introduction to Color*. New York: John Wiley & Sons, Inc., 1948.

Feduchi, Luis, *A History of World Furniture*. Barcelona: Editorial Blume, 1975.

Fletcher, Banister, *A History of Architecture on the Comparative Method*. London: Charles Scribner's Sons, 1938 (this book is regularly updated).

Hornung, Clarence P., *Hornung's Handbook of Designs and Devices*. New York: Dover Publications, 1959.

Graves, Maitland, *The Art of Color and Design*. York, PA: The Maple Press Company, 1941.

Guptill, Arthur L., *Drawing in Pen and Ink*. New York: Reinhold Publishing corporation, 1961.

Jansen, H.W., *History of Art*. New York: Harry N. Abrams, Inc., 1978.

Jones, Owen, *The Grammar of Ornament*. London: Studio Editions, 1986.

Kornerup, A., and J. H. Wanscher, *Reinhold Color Atlas*. New York: Reinhold, 1962.

Meyer, Franz Sales, *Handbook of Ornament*. New York: Dover Publications, 1957.

Molesworth, H.D., and John Kenworthy Browne, *Three Centuries of Furniture in Color*. New York: The Viking Press, 1972.

Musgrove, John, ed., *A History of Architecture*. London: Butterworth Group, 1987.

Nuttgens, Patrick, *The Pocket Guide to Architecture*. New York: Simon & Schuster, 1980.

Praz, Mario, *An Illustrated History of Furnishings*. New York: George Braziller, Inc., 1964.

Reid, Richard, *The Book of Buildings*. Chicago: Rand, McNally & Co., 1980.

Sargent, Walter, *The Enjoyment and Use of Color*. New York: Dover Publications, 1964.

Sparke, Penny, Felice Hodges, Emma Dent Coad, and Anne Stone, *Design Source Book*. New Jersey: Chartwell Books, Inc., 1986. Speltz, Alexander, *The History of Ornament: Design in the Decorative Arts*. New York: Portland House, 1988.

—— , *The Styles of Ornament*. New York: Dover Publications, 1959.

Trachtenberg and Hyman, *Architecture from Prehistory to Post Modernism*. New York: Harry N. Abrams, 1986.

Whiton, Sherrill, *Interior Design and Decoration* (4th ed.). New York: J.B. Lippincott Company, 1974.

Yarwood, Doreen, *Encyclopedia of Architecture*. New York: Facts on File Publications, 1986.

## STAGE TECHNOLOGY AND CRAFT SKILLS

Arnold, Richard L., *Scene Technology* (3rd ed.). Englewood Cliffs, NJ: Prentice-Hall, 1994.

Bowman, Ned, *Handbook of Technical Practices for the Performing Arts*. New York: Scenographic Media, 1975.

Bryson, Nicholas L., *Thermoplastic Scenery for the Theatre, Vol 1: Vacuum Forming*. New York: Drama Book Specialists, 1972.

Burris-Meyer, Harold, and Edward C. Cole, *Scenery for*

*the Theatre* (Rev. ed.). Boston: Little, Brown, 1971.

——— , *Theatres and Auditoriums* (2nd ed.). New York: Reinhold, 1975.

Carter, Conrad, *Backstage Handbook*. New York: Broadway Press, 1988.

Collins, John, *The Art of Scene Painting*. London: Harrup Ltd., 1985.

Dorn, Dennis, and Mark Shanda, *Drafting for the Theatre*. Carbondale, IL: Southern Illinois University Press, 1992.

Gillette, A. S. and J. Michael Gillette, *Stage Scenery: Its Construction and Rigging* (3rd ed.). New York: Harper and Row, 1981.

Glerum, Jay O., *Stage Rigging Handbook*. Carbondale, IL: Southern Illinois University Press, 1987.

James, Thurston, *The Theatre Props Handbook: A Comprehensive Guide to Theatre Properties, Materials, and Construction*. White Hall, VA: Betterway Publications, Inc., 1987, distributed by Empire Publishing Service, Studio City, CA.

Kenton, Warren, *Stage Properties and How to Make Them*. New York: Drama Book Specialists, 1974.

Morgan, Harry, *Perspective Drawing for the Theatre*. New York: Drama Book Specialists, 1979.

Motley, *Theatre Props*. London: Studio Vista, 1975.

Payne, Darwin Reid, *Theory and Craft of the Scenographic Model* (Rev. ed.). Carbondale, IL: Southern Illinois Press, 1985.

Pinnell, William H., *Theatrical Scene Painting*. Carbondale, IL: Southern Illinois University Press, 1987.

Sweet, Harvey, and Deborah M. Dryden, *Graphics for the Performing Arts*. Boston: Allyn and Bacon, 1985.

Taylor, Douglas C., *Metalworking for the Designer and Technician*. New York: Drama Book Specialists, 1979.

Veaner, Daniel, *Scene Painting: Tools and Techniques*. Englewood Cliffs, NJ: Prentice-Hall, Inc., 1984.

Wedwick, Darryl, Briant Hamor Lee, and William-Alan Landes, *Corrugated Cardboard Scenery*. Studio City, CA: Players Press, Inc., 1994.

Wolfe, Welby B., *Materials of the Scene*. New York: Harper and Row, Inc., 1977.

### GENERAL

Bellman, Willard F., *Scene Design, Stage Lighting, Sound, Costume and Makeup* (Rev. ed.). New York: Harper and Row, 1983.

Fried, Larry K., and Theresa May, *Greening Up Our Houses: A Guide to a More Ecologically Sound Theatre*. New York: Drama Book Publishers, 1994.

Gillette, J. Michael, *Theatrical Design and Production: An Introduction to Scene Design and Construction, Lighting, Sound, Costume, and Makeup*. Palo Alto, CA: Mayfield Publishing Company, 1987.

Lounsbury, Warren C., and Norman C. Boulanger, *Theatre Backstage from A to Z* (3rd. ed.). Seattle: University of Washington Press, 1993.

Parker, W. Oren, and R. Craig Wolf, *Scene Design and Stage Lighting* (6th ed.). New York: Holt, Rinehart, and Winston, 1990.

### PERIODICALS

*TCI*

*Theatre Design and Technology*

# THEATRE BOOKS from PLAYERS PRESS

## THE THEATRE PROPS HANDBOOK   by Thurston James

A step by step guide to the design and construction of theater properties. This practical, profusely illustrated handbook explains the use of materials essential to the props builder and demonstrates the techniques involved in the construction of more than one hundred specific property items. Emphasis is placed on safety of construction and use of props, particularly those which use electricity or simulated fire.  An updated, detailed appendix lists sources for all the materials referenced in this book.                                    **272 pgs.   PB   8.5x11   0-88734-934-X**

## STAGECRAFTERS HANDBOOK     by I. E. Clark

A clear concise handbook detailing the responsibilities of each member of a Theatre Technical crew.  Not a How-to but a What to do!               **96 pgs.   PB   5.5x8.5   0-88734-649-9**

## CORRUGATED CARDBOARD SCENERY  by B.H. Lee and D.M. Wedwick

A comprehensive, profusely illustrated and detailed workbook on how to use cardboard for theatrical design and construction.  Written in a comfortable, easy to read style so that anyone involved in the design of props, sets, costumes and even puppets will be able to easily use this as a step-by-step guide.                         **192 pgs.   PB   8.5x11   0-88734-628-6**

## 101 Theatre Games   by Mila Johansen

A critically acclaimed workbook.  This popular hands-on theatre game book covers Warm-Up Games, Storytelling, Mime, Exercises, and much more.  It is explicit enough for beginners and in-depth enough for the advanced thespian.        **160 pgs.   PB   8.5 x 11   0-88734-911-0**

## ASSIGNMENTS IN MUSICAL THEATRE    by Haller Laughlin and Jacque Wheeler

Techniques for pre-performance analysis for musical theatre performers and directors.  Provides invaluable assistance in establishing a strong musical performance technique and more, A great source for novice and professional, student and teacher.     **192 pgs.   PB   8.5 x 11   0-88734-676-6**

## THE AMERICAN MUSICAL THEATRE   by Steven Porter

An indispensable guide for student and professional. It is a history, production blueprint, guide to criticism, and source of projects and assignments. It is an ideal workbook for student, writer or critic, actor or director, producer or teacher.  An important addition to any Musical Theatre Library.                                             **128 pgs.   PB   8.5X11   0-88734-686-3**

## LOOK, LISTEN AND TRUST   by Rawlins and Rich

Structural material/theatre games to enhance performance and social skills  This book is ideal for High School teachers and students.  It offers and excellent selection of new games and details the presentational techniques.                       **192 pgs.   PB   6x9   0-88734-618-9**

## PLAYING THE GAME   by Christine Poulter

100 step-by-step theatre games that can be used to develop acting, social and personal skills. This carefully divided book gives games in groups and quickly outlines the material.  This is a workbook that can be simply put to work.                 **160 pgs.   PB   5.5x8.5   0-88734-611-1**

## PRINCIPLES OF STAGE COMBAT HANDBOOK  by Claude D. Kezer

Punches, kicks and knock-outs...whips, swords, and knives... Learn it all, from your first fall to your first stabbing. Learn to behead, beat, and battle with the ease of a professional. A safety first guide. Don't get murdered without it!              **96 pgs.   PB   8.5x11   0-88734-650-2**

*Available at your Local Book Store or directly from:*

**PLAYERS PRESS**     **P.O. Box 1132, Studio City, CA  91614-0132  U.S.A.**
                           **20 Park Drive, Romford, Essex, RM1 4LH    U.K.**